FIVE YEARS IN TURKEY

FIVE YEARS IN TURKEY

BY
LIMAN VON SANDERS
General of Cavalry

WITH NUMEROUS TEXT ILLUSTRATIONS
AND THREE LARGE MAPS

The Naval & Military Press Ltd

Published by
The Naval & Military Press Ltd
Unit 10 Ridgewood Industrial Park,
Uckfield, East Sussex,
TN22 5QE England
Tel: +44 (0) 1825 749494
Fax: +44 (0) 1825 765701
www.naval-military-press.com

The Naval & Military
Press

MILITARY HISTORY AT YOUR
FINGERTIPS

… a unique and expanding series of reference works

Working in collaboration with the foremost
regiments and institutions, as well as acknowledged
experts in their field, N&MP have assembled a
formidable array of titles including technologically
advanced CD-ROMs and facsimile reprints of
impossible-to-find rarities.

INTRODUCTION

In presenting the first English translation of General von Sanders' *Five Years in Turkey* to the reading public, the Naval Institute believes that it is rendering service to those who may be interested in the events of the World War. The broad outlines of the war in Turkey are already well known, but the "frictions of war" with which leaders have to contend are not so well known.

The war in Turkey formed an interesting and important part of the World War. Its relative importance as a theater of operations has been the subject of much controversy. This account will add much information to the student and assist in forming the correct opinion of the relative merits of the so called "easterners" and "westerners."

The book gives the author's reactions from day to day as the various situations confronted him. For this reason the book is more valuable to students of war than books written after the war, in the light of knowledge which the commander did not have. The reader will be constantly reminded of the lack of information possessed by generals in the field, and of the difficulty of adjusting plans of battle to the resources available.

It throws light on the miserable condition of the Turkish lines of communication. It reveals the character of the Turkish officers and men, and while it points out their defects, it emphasizes their endurance and heroism. It frankly discloses the errors of officers in high places in Constantinople, and as bravely discloses the mistakes of the author himself.

The author prepared the notes for this book in Malta immediately after the Armistice, and the simplicity and frankness of the narrative attest the sincerity of the author, who has not failed to record his appreciation of his opponents in this great struggle.

Appreciation to the author is acknowledged for permission to translate and publish his book.

It is always difficult to give the correct Anglicized spelling of Turkish and Arabic words, particularly the latter; this is not made easier when they have been translated from a third tongue. Great care has been taken with the chapters dealing with the Dardanelles Campaign to give two or more spellings of the word so that readers of other books will have no difficulty in identifying names. For example there are: Kabatepe (Gaba Tepe), Saros (Xeros), Kodjadere (Koja Dere), Eltschitepe (Altchy Tepe) (Achi Baba), Tschanake-Kale (Chanak), Seddulbar (Sedd el Bahr), Besica (Bashika), Sigindere (Zighin Dere), etc. Marmara has been employed instead of Marmora.

In the chapters dealing with the operations in Palestine there is more difficulty but the reader should experience no trouble in the proper identification of places, although there are in several instances two spellings of the same word, sometimes three. Like the publishers of the *Revolt in the Desert* we agree with Lawrence and say "Why not?"

Thus the reader will find: Tul Keram, Tulkern; Besan, Beisan; Kilkilije, Kalkilji, Kal Kiliyas; Jenin, Djenin; Affuleh, Affule; Ed Damje, ed Damije; Scherif, Sherif; Kratranch, Kratraneh, Kratrane; Audja, Auja; Samach, Samakh, Semakh; Er Remte, Er Remtheh; El Kunetra, El Kuneitra, etc.

The translation and proof reading have been done by Colonel Carl Reichmann, U. S. Army (Retired), and in addition to him thanks for proof reading are due to Captain W. D. Puleston, U. S. Navy, Professor Allan F. Westcott, U. S. Naval Academy, and Mr. Meyer Cox, the latter two of the Institute staff.

U. S. Naval Institute.

Annapolis, Maryland, U. S. A.
June 15, 1927.

L. v. S.

Wahlspruch.

Führen ist Kunst,
Siegen ist Gottesgunst.

Liman von Sanders.

The above motto was sent to the Naval Institute for use in the English translation of General von Sanders' book. Translated it reads:

Leadership is an Art,
Victory is a favor of God.

FOREWORD

The following notes were made during my involuntary stay at Malta. On returning home I supplemented them from my records.

The five years of my service in Turkey were years of struggle, not only against the World War enemies, but against those who never ceased in their efforts to minimize the influence of the German military mission.

I hereby express my thanks to my German and Turkish comrades who faithfully stood by me in those trying days.

LIMAN VON SANDERS.

November, 1919.

CONTENTS

Chapter 1

How I came to be in Turkey.................................... 1

Chapter 2

Admiral Limpus and General Baumann; The diplomatic corps in
Constantinople... 13

Chapter 3

The military mission up to the beginning of the World War.......... 19

Chapter 4

During the neutrality of Turkey in the World War.................... 22

Chapter 5

Turkey's entry into the World War.............................. 31

Chapter 6

The first conflicts in the Caucasus and on the Suez Canal............ 37

Chapter 7

Before the beginning of the Dardanelles Campaign.................. 47

Chapter 8

First part of Dardanelles Campaign.............................. 57

Chapter 9

Second part of the Dardanelles Campaign.......................... 83

Chapter 10

Warlike events on other Turkish fronts during the Dardanelles
Campaign... 106

Chapter 11

Events in 1916 on the several fronts.............................. 112

Chapter 12

Events before the formation of Jilderim........................... 152

Chapter 13

Jilderim... 173

CHAPTER 14

The war in Turkey, outside of Jilderim........................... 187

CHAPTER 15

Events up to March 1, 1918....,............................. 193

CHAPTER 16

The month of March on the Palestine front....................... 198

CHAPTER 17

April.. 215

CHAPTER 18

May.. 221

CHAPTER 19

June... 238

CHAPTER 20

July.. 249

CHAPTER 21

August... 255

CHAPTER 22

September.. 268

CHAPTER 23

October.. 306

CHAPTER 24

Conclusion... 321

EPILOGUE... 326

CHAPTER 1

How I Came to be in Turkey

On June 15, 1913—the anniversary of the succession of H. M. the Emperor to the throne—I received a communication from the Military Cabinet, inquiring whether I was ready and willing to go to Turkey as Chief of a German military mission.

I was then one of the senior division commanders of the German Army and in command of the 22d Division in Cassel.

I had held many posts in the Prussian Army, had spent many years on the general staff, had travelled much in foreign parts, but had never visited Turkey or studied Turkish affairs.

Hence the inquiry was most unexpected. Enclosed with it was a telegram from the German Ambassador, Freiherr von Wangenheim, which set forth the purpose and scope of this new post as follows:

Convinced that German policy is sincere and friendly toward the consolidation of Asiatic Turkey, etc., etc., the Grand Vizir requests me to submit to His Majesty a request for a leading German general for the Turkish Army.

Details have not yet been worked out.

This position is meant to be one of far reaching powers in all military technical questions. The general must be a leader of all other German reformers and would be responsible for the uniform and purposeful reformation of the Turkish Army. His suggestions are to serve as the basis for the work of mobilization and for the operations in some future war.

For this position there is, of course, wanted a man of eminent military ability and one of wide experience in the work of the general staff with troops. Since the Turkish general officers and the general staff failed in the last war, one of the principal tasks will be to remedy these defects. It is desirable that the general selected should have conducted general staff journeys with conspicuous success as chief of staff of an army corps.

Furthermore, he should be a strong character who knows how to gain his point. Knowledge of the country and of the language is not absolutely essential since in the person of Major von. Strempel, etc., etc.

1

In my judgment the selection of a German general would silence all those who would make the German reformers responsible for the Turkish defeats. It also would check British influence seeking to have British administration reformers called to Turkey.

In case of refusal it is to be feared that the Sublime Porte may turn to other powers, since it is determined to break with the present, insufficient system of military reform.

Secrecy for the present urgently requested.

Sgd. Wangenheim.

Since the task promised to be one of honorable and wide activity, I accepted without hesitation.

After months of negotiations with the Turkish government the contract for the military mission was drawn up in Constantinople and submitted to the highest German authorities for examination. In November 1913 the contract was closed and I was authorized by H. M. the Emperor to sign it.

The activity of the military mission was to be strictly military. The wording of the contract plainly so stated. Many publications and newspapers asserted that the activity of the German military mission was to be extended to political matters, which is wholly incorrect.

That it did have a political effect toward the outside world is another matter. The decision to have a mission cannot but be considered a political decision because it was based on Turkish policies of long standing and might lead to feeding a flickering fire. That, however, has nothing whatever to do with the work of a military mission strictly limited to the reorganization of the Turkish Army.

The contract called for forty-two officers, the majority of them in the grades of major and captain.

At the end of November I was called before H. M. the Emperor who, after discussing some personal matters, spoke to me in the following terms:

It must be entirely immaterial to you whether the Young Turks are in power or the Old Turks. You are concerned with the army alone. Drive politics out of the corps of Turkish officers. Its greatest defect is its political activity.

In Constantinople you will meet Admiral Limpus, head of the British naval mission. Maintain good relations with each other. He works for the navy, you for the army. Each has his separate sphere.

His Majesty charged me with greetings to the Turkish crown prince and suggested that I invite him to military maneuvers in order to awaken in him an interest in the army and through it in his people. His Majesty was unaware that the crown prince, who was later to find such a tragic end, even then no longer had a mind of his own.

Shortly before our departure, December 9, the Emperor received me and the first contingent of officers detailed to the mission, at the new palace in Potsdam. He made a brief address, charging us to hold high the honor of the German name before the world and to confine ourselves to our military problems.

During the forenoon of December 14 we arrived in Constantinople. At the railway station of Sirkedji we were received by a crash of military music and by a company of the regiment of firemen as guard of honor, which regiment I found later in the Dardanelles Campaign to be an elite body of troops.

Numerous high Turkish officers headed by the excellent Minister of War, Izzet Pasha, were there and so were German officers who had been called to Turkey on prior occasions.

I knew Izzet Pasha very well; he had seen long service as an officer with the hussars in Cassel and afterward had been assigned to me personally for instruction in the duties of the general staff. I was then a general staff officer.

The German Embassy was not represented at this reception of the military mission, much to our surprise. We were soon to learn that the embassy was already beginning to keep aloof from the military mission though the origin of that mission must be ascribed entirely to the initiative of the embassy. The embassy believed that its position in Constantinople would be rendered more difficult by public association with the military mission which had caused so much excitement abroad. Hence it considered a certain reserve toward this new German creation expedient.

Since we were required to enter upon our service on the 14th—the first of the month in Turkey—we accompanied Izzet Pasha to the War Ministry. The service, however, began with a very quiet coffee *a la turka* served in the great reception room. In the next few days I was received by the Sultan. As he spoke Turkish only, of which I did not understand a word, Izzet Pasha acted as interpreter of the conversation which was limited to a few friendly words of greeting from the Sultan. Later I found in this ruler of the Turks a most kindly and liberal sponsor. Few foreigners knew that during the thirty years of his confinement to his palace and garden prior to his accession to the throne, this unassuming old gentleman had gathered much knowledge and wisdom and showed much greater independence of judgment than was generally assumed.

The Prime Minister of Turkey, Grand Vizir Prince Said Halim, combined the attitude of the Asiatic grand seignior with that of the modern diplomatist. Like all the other ministers he spoke French perfectly and had most engaging manners. This small and very lively gentleman showed himself later every inch a man and frequently and with consummate tact checked extravagant tendencies of the Young Turks until he had to relinquish his post in February 1917.

It is hard to understand why in the spring of 1919 the Entente included this highest Turkish dignitary among the personages sent into captivity to Mudros, though he was of moderate views and of absolutely irreproachable character. It was he who many times during the war extended a protecting hand to enemy aliens in Turkey.

Of the other ministers, Talaat, then the Minister of the Interior, stood out among all. No one could escape the charm of his sympathetic and attractive personality.

At the time in question Enver was a colonel and chief of staff of an army corps and lying ill in a hospital.

Djemal, the third of subsequent leaders in Turkey, I met within a week of my arrival when I took over from him the command of the First Army Corps in Constantinople. Though apparently somewhat of a Garibaldi, he unquestionably combined great intelligence with a very determined attitude. He always impressed me as unwilling to confide his ultimate thoughts and aims to another mortal.

The transfer of the command of the First Army Corps was one of the stipulations of the contract of the military mission. In October when this question was being considered, I had asked for it because it appeared to me helpful to show in the capital of the country an exemplification of military training from which the Turkish officers might learn.

I never thought that my assumption of this command would have political consequences, since not a single officer or man beyond those stipulated in the contract came to Turkey. I I had read the reports of former German reformers complaining of the difficulty of gaining radical influence in the Turkish Army and I had learned from other sources that in the training of the Turkish Army there had been an excess of theory and a lack of practical work. In making the decision I based myself entirely on German principles believing that the quickest way to progress was by exerting my personal influence on the training of troops.

After the contract had been drawn up and had been signed on the part of Turkey, the German Minister of Foreign Affairs, Herr von Jagow, repeatedly informed me that the Russian government was taking umbrage at it. He suggested that I take over the command of the Second Army Corps in Adrianople in addition to my duties as chief of the military mission, if I insisted on taking a practical part.

Such a change was impracticable, for the place of the chief of the military mission was in Constantinople until the ground could be prepared for further work, and Adrianople was twelve hours by train from Constantinople.

Nor was I willing to begin my activity with a change of the contract; it might have looked like giving way before Russian influence.

As I see it today, the reorganization of the army could have been effected without the command of the First Army Corps.

However, I held the command but a few weeks.

The Russian Ambassador, von Giers, together with the ambassadors from England and France, proceeded to take steps with the Grand Vizir. The ambassadors maintained that a German general could not be tolerated in possession of the highest military executive power in Constantinople. Prince Said Halim is said to have replied that the appointment of corps commanders was Turkey's own business.

But the sharp differences were not ameliorated. According to a conversation of Prince Lichnowsky with Sir Edward Grey in December 1913, the waves of intense excitement over this command, which was agitating Petersburg, had reached London.

Meanwhile von Wangenheim had gone on leave and Councilor von Mutius was acting in his place. In consequence of a communication from Minister von Jagow, the German Chargé d'Affaires again urged me, between Christmas and New Years, to resign the command or exchange it for that of the Second Army Corps.

The former I would not and the latter I could not do. But I informed him, if it was thought necessary to yield for political reasons, that I wanted to be recalled to Germany.

To meet the wishes of foreign countries, H. M. the Emperor sought a way out by promoting me on January 14, 1914, ahead of time, to the grade of general of cavalry. Since according to the contract we were entitled to rank one grade higher in the Turkish Army than our grade in the German Army, I was appointed a Turkish marshal and had to give up the command of the First Army Corps which now passed into Turkish hands.

At the same time I was appointed Inspector General of the Turkish Army. That meant nothing special because as chief of the military mission I had the right to inspect all troops and fortresses.

During the few weeks of my command of the First Army Corps I had become aware of the internal conditions of the troops which were anything but pleasing. A mental depression had taken hold of the entire corps of officers.

One day in January 1914 Izzet Pasha failed to make his appearance in the War Ministry in which the offices of the military mission were located, and sent me word that he was sick. I visited him next morning in his konak and learned from him that he had to resign. I sincerely regretted the loss of this intelligent and most honorable co-laborer.

Next evening Enver came to my office in the Ministry; I had seen him but once before during German maneuvers. He wore a general's uniform and informed me that he was the new Minister of War.

The Sultan himself had not heard of the appointment of the new Minister of War much before I did. That morning he sat in his room reading the paper. Suddenly he dropped the paper and remarked to the only adjutant present: "It is stated here that Enver has become Minister of War; that is unthinkable, he is much too young."

I have this from the adjutant who was on duty and the sole witness of the event.

A few hours later Enver presented himself to the Sultan as Minister of War and as a general.

Enver quickly oriented himself in his high position, and his comtemporaries in the army complained that he hardly knew them and had become unapproachable. In the spring of 1914 he married a not very wealthy imperial princess, but soon began to live in princely style.

The manner of Enver's access to his high position makes it apparent how absolutely powerless the Sultan was as compared with the all-powerful Committee.

To me the Committee has ever remained a mystery. I have never learned of how many members it consisted or, excepting the well known leaders, who the members were. Later I learned from experience that it was perfectly vain to take action against an officer who belonged to the Committee.

Enver's first official acts were merciless proceedings against those Turkish officers in whom he saw political opponents.

Some 1,100 officers were suddenly dismissed in January 1914.

Under the terms of the contract of the military mission I was to be consulted in filling the higher offices. This proviso could not become effective unless I knew the nominees, but I thought it would have been the proper thing at least to inform me officially in each case.

So I asked Enver for the reason of this mode of procedure. He replied that they all were officers who had failed in the Balkan War, were inefficient or too old. This was a relative statement not warranted by facts.

Soon it became known that a number of officers were imprisoned in the cellar vaults of the War Ministry. They were men from whom Enver feared counteraction.

The military mission, of course, was never officially informed of such acts. It was much to be regretted that the mission came at the moment of a military-political crisis.

So it came that those who could judge things from the outside only and were without knowledge of the inward state of affairs, presumed that the military mission had in some way had a hand in this imprisonment.

In the provinces, too, arrests of officers were made. I received in those days a letter from a lieutenant colonel of the general staff who was unknown to me, was of Arab birth and imprisoned in Asia Minor. He had succeeded in getting his letter out through a confidential party. He wrote that he had been arrested in his office by Enver's orders without statement of charges against him and had been taken straight to prison. He urgently besought help since he feared that he might be simply made to disappear.

I personally handed this letter to Enver and requested information. He showed some embarrassment and declared that the matter would be thoroughly sifted. The German Embassy had received the same letter and was amazed at the way I dealt with it. At any rate I had succeeded in procuring for this officer a hearing and initiation of legal process.

Soon thereafter Enver abolished the Superior War Council which up to that time had been a permanent institution of the Turkish Army. In the contract of the military mission it was expressly stipulated that I was to be a regular member of the Council. But neither the other members nor myself were officially notified of the abolishment of this highest military authority.

Soon friction arose between Enver and myself because we had divergent views as to the interpretation of my rights and duties. I will state but one of the points of controversy then arising. I had inspected troops of the 8th Division in Tschorlu which I found in the most wretched condition. The officers had not received pay in six or eight months and they and their families were compelled to get their subsistence from the troop messes. The men had not seen pay for years, were undernourished and dressed in ragged uniforms. Of the company sent to the railway station at Tschorlu as guard of honor, a considerable part wore torn boots or shoes, others were barefooted. The division commander explained that he could not hold large exercises because the men were too weak and could not march with such defective footgear. I informed Enver in writing of my finding and requested remedial action, whereupon Enver dismissed the division commander, Colonel Ali Risa Bei. On learning of this I went to Enver and informed him that any military activity on my part in Turkey was impossible, if those officers were dismissed who told me the truth. After more or less talk Enver reinstated the division commander. Subsequently Ali Risa Bei made good during the World War and in the fall of 1918 was still a corps commander.

Other means were now taken to deceive me. When I was going to inspect troops, the Intendant General expressed new clothing to these troops with orders to return them after my departure. When I discovered that I was inspecting the same clothing over and over again, I gave as brief notice of my inspections as I reasonably could. But it was not only clothing that was sent around, men themselves were exchanged for the inspections. The sick, the weak, the poorly trained were concealed so that the German general might not see anything ugly or unpleasant to complain of.

In the interior service of the troops everything was deficient in those days. The officers were not in the habit of looking out for their men and of controlling them. In many organizations men were infested with vermin. Bathing arrangements nowhere existed in the barracks. A regular airing of rooms was unknown.

The cooking arrangements were the most primitive imaginable, this service was unregulated and left much to be desired in the way of cleanliness. I was on the point of ordering a model cooking apparatus from Germany when Lieutenant Colonel Nicolai, the German commander of the 3d Division, accidentally discovered one carefully boxed up in the large Selimje barracks. Five years before the German Emperor had made a present of it to the Turks. But the War Ministry had turned it over to the troops without specific orders to unpack it and so it remained boxed up for five years.

The condition of the horses of the mounted troops was terrible. A large part of them were still suffering from farcy contracted in the Balkan War. There was no care of hoofs. Saddles, bridles and harness were in a corresponding state of neglect. The clothing rooms of the troops were empty.

The interior of the many large public military buildings, well known to every visitor to Constantinople and admired for their beautiful locations and grand dimensions, offered a lamentable picture of desolation with rubbish heaps in every corner.

It is one of the great merits of Enver during the time before the World War that he supported unreservedly and with all the means at the command of the War Minister, all suggestions the correctness of which he recognized. A just critic must recognize and acknowledge that.

At the beginning whenever we suggested changes and improvements, the commanders invariably replied that no funds were available. That was a convenient excuse. The fact was that there was less a lack of funds, than of a sense of order and cleanliness and diligence.

In those days the Turk disliked to be called on by the German officer to exert himself and used excuses in the attempt to prolong his musing existence. In their innermost thoughts the majority of the older Turkish officers considered it improper for higher officers to meddle with such details as we did.

Vigorous action on our part, however, was indispensable in laying the fundaments for further work and we gradually received effective support from an ever increasing number of Turkish officers.

In all Turkish military centers, including the general staff college, there prevailed in those days an excess of theory, while practical terrain exercises were neglected. In consequence the general staff officers as well as the higher troop commanders suffered from lack of practical training and therefore of practical judgment. Thus we had to make changes everywhere and build anew.

Alarming conditions existed in all Turkish military hospitals. Dirt and every imaginable bad odor made the overcrowded rooms unsanitary and almost intolerable abodes. Internally and externally sick lay confusedly mixed, often in the same bed when there was one. In many cases the sick lay in dense rows in the hallways, some on mattresses, some on blankets. In the absence of suitable treatment a large number of these wasted soldiers died daily. When at the inspection of such hospitals I expressed my indignation at such conditions and reported the responsible Turkish medical officers to the War Ministry for punishment, efforts were made to prevent further complaints by other means. Now I would sometimes find several rooms in the hospital locked and the surgeons conducting me would state that the keys were lost. When I ceased to accept this excuse and insisted on having the rooms opened, I discovered that these dark rooms had been filled with the seriously ill and with moribund patients in order to hide them from me.

The education of Turkish medical officers—insofar as it had been accomplished in Turkey—was entirely different from what we were used to. The majority confined themselves to a daily inspection of the sick from a respectful distance and to unlimited prescriptions of medicine. When there was one thermometer for taking the temperatures of about 300 patients, we had to be content.. Very few of the medical personnel could read and write and were capable of using the thermometers. Usually sick officers were the only persons whose temperatures were taken. For the ordinary soldier it was not considered worth while. The sense of duty, of devotion to the service without distinction of person, was foreign to most of these gentlemen. They were used to being supervised and watched and needed it.

The senior medical officer of the military mission, Professor Dr. Mayer, an energetic man, soon effected far reaching improvements in the Turkish military hospital service. It was due to him in the first place that later during the World War the Turkish military hospitals were fully and completely up to requirements. In saying this I do not wish to be understood as minimizing the merits of Suleiman Numan Pasha, the intelligent and highly educated chief of the Turkish military medical service.

That the vigorous action of the military mission in all departments of the military service made many enemies for us was unavoidable. On the other hand there were many men of judgment who recognized that we were progressing out of the decline of the army following the Balkan War.

CHAPTER 2

ADMIRAL LIMPUS AND GENERAL BAUMANN; THE DIPLOMATIC CORPS IN CONSTANTINOPLE

When the German military mission arrived in Constantinople, a British naval mission under Admiral Limpus had been there for some time. I am not in a position to judge whether subsequent criticisms of their work were justified or based on calumny. In the orient any calumny is possible and false rumors, in passing from mouth to mouth, grow after the manner of an avalanche.

Since the activity of the German military mission was limited to the army and had no essential points of contact with the British naval mission whose activity was confined to the navy, there was no friction. I except the case of combined military-naval maneuvers which were several times suggested and which I could not approve on principle. In June 1914 when the tension between Turkey and Greece had become such that hostilities seemed possible, a conference was held by Enver which members of the German military mission and of the British naval mission attended.

Among the higher foreign officers, besides Admiral Limpus, there was the French general, Baumann, who had charge of the entire Turkish police. According to the contract of the military mission, foreign officers could not be appointed to the army without my approval. Hence there should have been some understanding as regards General Baumann and the many foreign officers serving with the Turkish police. The police comprised more than 80,000 men of select troops. To forestall a conflict, the Turkish Ministry found a way out by detaching the entire police from the land army a few days after the arrival of the military mission and placing it under the Ministry

13

of the Interior. My personal relations with General Baumann, who invariably was pleasant to me, were and remained good throughout.

Marquis Pallavicini, the Austro-Hungarian Ambassador, was the dean of the diplomatic corps when I came to Constantinople in December 1913 and he was still at his post on my return from Syria after the Armistice in November 1918. He held the responsible post of Austro-Hungarian ambassador for twelve years and enjoyed great respect and the real confidence of the Turks. Being a diplomat of the old school he made an impression of complete harmlessness on those who did not know him well. Every important piece of news appeared to be a surprise to him though no one was better informed than he was or had better insight into the tangles of Turkish politics. His connections reached everywhere and he was not limited, as were other diplomats, to the reports of a few political agents. He was not the pessimist the German Emperor took him to be and he early and correctly judged the Turkish politics and military developments and foresaw the logical course they would take.

Most people in Constantinople and Therapia knew the amiable gentleman riding by on his snow white horse and saluting his friends with a cheerful double "servus," but not many suspected in him the far seeing diplomat weighted during the war with wide reaching cares.

During the five years of my service in Turkey there were five successive German ambassadors there, the first of whom, Freiherr von Wangenheim, died in the late fall of 1915 and was buried in the honor cemetery of Therapia. It was Freiherr von Wangenheim who originated and brought about the request for a German military mission as well as the German alliance with Turkey. He was an energetic and impulsive man and knew how to gain his ends in Turkey. In my opinion, however, he was too optimistic in his views of internal Turkish conditions and in his estimation of the prospects of a speedy restoration of order by the Young Turks.

During the illness and leave of absence of Freiherr von Wangenheim in the summer of 1915 Prince Hohenlohe acted as ambassador until Count Wolf-Metternich was called to this important post. This very sagacious and far seeing diplomat, who may have seemed somewhat reserved to the Turks, was recalled after a little more than a year in consequence of German intrigues hatched in Constantinople. In the fall of 1916 Enver with some German officers from the embassy and from Turkish headquarters had visited the German headquarters in Pless and had there expressed a wish for a change of ambassadors without having instructions to that effect from the Turkish government. This wish was complied with.

His successor, von Kuhlmann, knew Turkey from his youth and had a full understanding of Turkish mentality; he became the object of the same German intrigues which might have scored another success had not von Kuhlmann been called home to become Minister of Foreign Affairs.

In following up these German intrigues in Turkey one always gets on the tracks of the same persons. Their names were known in Constantinople to every one but nothing could be done to them as they resided in Constantinople permanently, controlled the telephone and telegraphic connections to the German authorities and, when needed, were protected by the name or signature of Enver.

I am calling the expression of fault finding and disparaging criticisms of the highest responsible officials and officers serving abroad "intrigue" because it consisted in sending home secret reports without the knowledge of the parties concerned. Moreover the actors were persons standing in rank far below those whom they were criticizing. To protect its official occupants of the highest positions it was incumbent on the German government or Army Direction to give these men their unlimited confidence and to be guided by their judgment to the exclusion of any other.

In the fall of 1917 von Kuhlmann was succeeded by Count Bernstorff who still held the office at the time of the Armistice.

It is plain that such constant changes, particularly in a country like Turkey, a correct judgment of which presents such great difficulties, were bound to be detrimental to the cause. During a war additional difficulties might be expected to arise for the ambassadors because the military and naval attachés went their separate ways in making their reports. These last—with the exception of the intelligent and tactful military attaché, Colonel von Leipzig who unfortunately lost his life by an accident in returning from the Dardanelles in June 1915—have caused much harm to Turkey and with it to Germany. It is due to their reports to the home authorities, and to the reports of individual German officers at the Turkish headquarters that wholly incorrect ideas were conceived and held as to Turkey's military capacity.

These gentlemen never saw Turkish troops except at short-cut inspection trips of Enver and had no conception of the real inner conditions of the new Turkish Army, its unstable condition and especially of its corps of officers.

The German Army Direction, receiving as it sometimes did, military reports from seven different sources which were bound to involve contradictions, was overburdened with more immediate and pressing tasks and was not always in position to make the proper decision because so far from the scene of action. General Ludendorff himself acknowledged these difficulties to me during my visit to German headquarters in Kreuznach in November 1917.

Since Germany had created a great military mission in Turkey with extensive military powers, it would have done better from the beginning to make it the center for all military reports. Officers of the military mission who were spread over the whole empire and working within the Turkish Army were beyond doubt in position to make more pertinent reports based on their own experience and views than the informants of military and naval attachés.

In no other way could uniformity of responsible military

reports be secured that might have been of immense value to the German central authorities.

The most reliable reports to the highest authorities holding the final decision, will ever be those which originate with the men responsible for the acts. Any other reports made directly by advisory personages or official spectators bring with them grave dangers, because in the final analysis they cannot be held accountable for their accuracy and because they may be influenced by personal views. This holds good for abroad much more than for home because of the difficulty of verifying the reports. A manifold system of reports, as we had in Turkey, is bound to arouse unpleasant animosities under which the great common aims have to suffer.

The foregoing criticisms are supported by a long chain of facts extending through five years and it is well to make them public in order that we may learn from the past for the future.

The first requisite for our position abroad in future is a conscious and unified coöperation of the Germans under energetic representatives who are not afraid of responsibility; but they must be assured of backing at home. I believe that on this point we have much to learn from other countries.

It was plain before the war that the relations of the officers of the German mission with the embassies of the Entente could not become close. But they were correct throughout. For instance on the birthday of the King of England in June 1914 a number of us attended the reception at the British Embassy to present our congratulations.

The Russian Ambassador also, von Giers, had dropped his opposition, after the command of the First Turkish Army Corps had passed back into Turkish hands.

The Italian Ambassador, Marquis Garroni, remained well disposed toward the Germans after Italy had declined in August 1914 to take an active part with the Triple Alliance.

With the American Ambassador at the Golden Horn, Mr. Morgenthau, and after him Mr. Elkus, we came in social contact only. Their wives with their large wealth did charitable work on a grand scale which gained them the sympathies of the Turks.

Many of our officers frequented the houses of the Dutch, Swedish and Bulgarian Ambassadors both before and after the beginning of the war.

CHAPTER 3

THE MILITARY MISSION UP TO THE BEGINNING OF THE WORLD WAR

When Enver became Minister of War he at once appointed himself Chief of the Turkish General Staff, in order, he said, to eliminate the never ceasing conflicts between the Minister of War and the Chief of Staff.

As assistant in the latter capacity he asked me for Colonel Bronsart and I had to accede to the request though not without some hesitation. Most of the important positions in the great general staff of the Turkish Army remained in the hands of Turkish officers, which was quite in keeping with the sense of the contract of the military mission.

The German general staff officers were to act as advisers and instructors to direct and instruct the Turkish general staff officers in their various duties in the expectation that with this added preparation they would be able later to function independently for the benefit of their army.

Provision for a permanent stay of the mission had not been made, hence the training of the Turkish officers for subsequent independent work had to be our foremost objective.

After the beginning of the war the number of German officers originally provided had to be exceeded in some cases because of the necessity of promptly placing completely trained officers in the most important positions at headquarters and in the special arms. But these extended limits were later still further exceeded through the use of too many German officers in the Turkish general staff, in the Turkish Army and in the zone of communications.

The German officers, unfamiliar with the language and with but superficial understanding of the country and of the Turkish

Army, should never have been made to shoulder the responsibility for conditions strange to them to the extent that it was done.

The consequences were bound to be what they logically became. At Turkish headquarters the elimination of Turkish general staff officers in many important positions caused dissatisfaction among these officers and sometimes passive opposition and in the end led to direct concealment of many Turkish affairs from the German officers. This patent lack of German-Turkish collaboration gave rise to unpleasant Turkish criticism. Finally when defeats were incurred, the Turks ascribed to the German officers the responsibility for many things in which they had had no share whatever.

Enver possessed neither the experience, judgment nor training to properly settle these important questions of German collaboration.

He fully recognized the value of the German work, but later was unable to recognize the salutary limitation that should have been imposed on it in his army where a different religion, language and interior organism required special considerations.

Before the opening of the Dardanelles Campaign he began to dispense with my advice and did so more and more as he increased the number of German officers on his staff.

A statement of this fact is necessary to a full understanding of the recital of events to be discussed later.

In the course of the first half of the year 1914 before the war, the number of German officers not only was increased to the number of forty-two specified in the contract, but had to be increased to seventy because the work of organization steadily increased the burdens imposed on staffs and troops in the provinces. Still the number cannot be considered excessive for the reorganization of an army as large as the Turkish.

It should be stated right here, however, that toward the end of the war the military mission handled the personal papers of more than 800 German officers, medical officers and officials present in Turkey. In consideration of the great prior losses of officers in the World War it may be readily understood that among such a large number there were bound to be some not suitable for employment abroad.

In addition to the work of the German officers in the military centers and with the troops in the first half of 1914, it may be mentioned that the school of fire in Constantinople for infantry, field artillery and coast artillery, and the cavalry non-commissioned officers' school in Ajas Agar were given German directors and instructors, that their programs were extended and that we established an officers' school of equitation and a school for the instruction of the trains.

An extensive exercise under my direction, with debarkation of troops, was planned for the beginning of September between Gallipoli and Rodosto. Shortly after these maneuvers I meant to direct the great general·staff journey on the west coast of Asia Minor.

But the World War began; Turkey at first remained neutral but mobilized its troops.

CHAPTER 4

PERIOD OF TURKEY'S NEUTRALITY IN THE WORLD WAR

On one of the first days of August 1914 I was asked to come to the German Embassy in Therapia that evening. There I met the ambassador, Freiherr von Wangenheim, and Enver. They informed me that they were considering the plan of a secret alliance between Germany and Turkey and desired my advice as to the employment of the military mission in case Turkey entered the war. I invited the attention of the gentlemen to the stipulations of the contract of the military mission providing for the recall of the German officers in case Germany should become involved in a European war. The ambassador replied that they were only considering the case of our being left in Turkey.

In case the military mission was ordered to remain in Turkey and that Turkey entered the war, I advised that the German officers be assigned to positions that would give them real influence on the conduct of the war.

The passage relating to the military mission was at once translated into French and the military mission was assured an *"influence effective sur la conduite générale de l'armée."*

I was not informed of any other details of the projected treaty of alliance. At the beginning of September I asked the ambassador in writing for these details, but in a communication of September 5, Freiherr von Wangenheim refused my request. I mention this specifically as the best proof that the military mission was not informed of political decisions.

As I was taking early leave that evening from the ambassador and from Enver, the latter informed me that he would assume the position of vice-generalissimo should Turkey enter the war, and asked whether in that case I would be willing to become his

22

chief of staff. I declined and stated that I would prefer the command of troops.

The most contradictory rumors now began to circulate about Turkey's entry into the war or its maintenance of neutrality. The military mission received no official information of the state of the negotiations either from the Turkish or the German side. The situation was most painful for the German officers as the war at home had begun. After a few days it was given out that Turkey would remain neutral.

Then, on August 11, I sent an explicit telegram to H. M. the Emperor inviting attention to the provision of the contract referred to and requesting prompt recall of all German officers to the German Army.

On August 22 a telegram brought the decision of the Emperor that for the present we were to remain in Turkey and that we should not suffer any disadvantage thereby as our service here would be counted as though we were in the field with the German Army.

I at once called the German officers together and there was much gloom among them when informed of the decision. All believed that the war would not last long and would be fought without us. Hardly any one in those days counted on Turkey entering the war, as it was known that the majority of Turkish Ministers were in favor of neutrality.

In September I once more tried for the recall of all German officers and received from the Chief of the Military Cabinet a telegram beginning,

H. M. the Emperor and King charges me again to remind Your Excellency that Your Excellency should consider your employment in the present capacity as any other employment in war. It is the positive order of His Majesty that Your Excellency subordinate any views diverging from the policies of the Imperial Ambassador as approved by His Majesty, etc.

The Turkish mobilization of 1914 was accomplished without much difficulty quite in contrast to that for the Balkan War.

This was due to the mobilization regulations prepared by the military mission in collaboration with Turkish general staff officers which prescribed general rules only and eschewed details which would simply have served to create confusion in view of the varying conditions prevailing in different parts of the large Turkish empire. Again, time was not pressing this time and the mobilization was merely a precautionary measure. It much benefited the war-like training of the troops which now could be trained in organizations of sufficient strength; and the active as well as the mobilized officers learned to habituate themselves to the methods of command and to the leading of full strength organizations.

Heretofore training had been badly hampered by the low strength of organizations. It is true that units of the First Turkish Army Corps in Constantinople, constantly open to inspection of foreign spectators, were of normal strength, but in the provinces the strength, particularly of infantry organizations, had been very variable. Thus in the summer of 1914 I found infantry companies with no more than twenty men for duty.

The Turkish headquarters when mobilized gave orders as early as August for the formation of several armies. I was given command of the First Army with headquarters in Constantinople; it was to consist of five army corps located in and near Constantinople, in Thrace, on the Dardanelles, near Panderma and to the south of it. The Sixth Army Corps stationed in Aleppo was gradually moved up to the vicinity of San Stefano.

Djemal, Minister of Marine, was given command of the Second Army with headquarters in Constantinople. To it were assigned two army corps to be stationed on the Asiatic side.

A Third Army was to be formed west of the Caucasus, approximately in the vicinity of Erzerum.

This division of the armies was a sensible one. It should be noted, however, that in the course of the war Turkey nominally

organized nine armies, which was contrary to good sense.   It
happened later on that armies existed by numbers with complete staffs and hardly any troops.   Authentic instances are the
First Army in 1917 which, besides some replacements and
militia, hardly comprised an infantry regiment; also the Second
Army in 1918 the infantry of which barely numbered seven
effective battalions.   In 1918 none of the so called three armies
on the Palestine front comprised as many combatants as a
single Turkish infantry division had at the beginning of the war.

This division of the army was made for the sake of appearance,
but it rendered the issuing of orders difficult and was positively
injurious because according to Turkish usage these many and
numerous staffs with their trains required a large number of
officers, men and horses which could have served a much better
purpose at the front.

Although I should have been consulted in these matters as
chief of the military mission, I was unable to exercise the least
influence on these decisions of the Turkish headquarters.

In the second half of August when the *Goeben* and *Breslau*
had been in port for a while, a military conference took place in
Enver's office in which participated the German Ambassador,
Admiral Souchon who had come in with the *Goeben*, the military
and naval attachés, Enver's chief of staff and other high officers,
among them myself.   The question was considered whether
action against the Suez Canal would be advisable in case
Turkey joined in the war.   The representatives of the navy
warmly advocated such a step.   In view of the then existing
situation on the German-Austrian front I considered a landing
in force of Turkish troops between Odessa and Ackermann more
timely as it would take the pressure off the southern wing of the
Austrians.

In view of the low estimate of the efficiency of the Russian
Black Sea fleet and on account of the presence of but few trained
troops in the district of Odessa, such an enterprise appeared
technically practicable enough if carried out with swiftness and

boldness. The Russian fleet of course would have to be defeated first to secure the supply of the army subsequent to the
landing. According to a former positive statement by Admiral
Souchon this might well be accomplished with the help of the
Goeben and *Breslau.*

No one shared my views and all were convinced of the great
effect produced by a swift descent on Egypt. Neither then nor
later could I understand how it could be thought possible to
conquer Egypt with the limited means of the Turks and in view
of the very poor communications. Having command of the sea
the British were able at any time and quickly to ship large forces
to Egypt from India, from the colonies or from the mother
country. The British positions on the Suez Canal were equipped
with every kind of modern arms. Four railway tracks on both
sides of the canal and ample rolling stock permitted prompt
concentration at threatened points. The effect of the long
range guns along the canal, the mighty calibers of the British
guns on the war vessels and on the floating batteries on the
canal reached far out into the flat desert.

The importance of the security of the Suez Canal to England
had been explained some time before by Lord Cromer in his
well known memorandum at the time the cession of Cyprus was
being discussed. He explained that since India was the center
of the imperium, every step in practical British politics must be
based on the idea of the security of the Suez Canal, that
possession of the land on both sides of the canal was indispensable and that the minimum requirement was the control of
Egypt and of the Sinai peninsula from the Gulf of Akaba to El
Arish. With these military-political principles in mind it would
be foolish to indulge in military illusions.

While the British were already in, and based on, Egypt, a Turkish expedition could not reach the canal except by traversing
the desert of El Tih requiring at least seven days' marches.
For such a march water for men and animals would have to be
brought across the desert by camels just as would artillery

projectiles. Such an enterprise might come as a surprise and thus be crowned by temporary success, but it never could be of decisive character because any expeditionary force advancing across the canal, unless of great strength, would face destruction. But in the first place how could Turkey with its totally inadequate communications assemble a great force at a base of operations against Egypt and keep it supplied there? It seems to me that very hazy ideas must have been entertained at home about the possibility of conquering Egypt. This so called fatal spot of England evidently was the subject of fantastic mischief in Germany and the navy was not without a share in it, though it should be stated in extenuation that the navy was wholly ignorant of the conditions surrounding a land expedition on Turkish soil in Asia.

The highest German authorities immediately received reports of my views, which diverged from those of the leading authorities in that there was but limited chances of success in an Egyptian campaign and that I considered other operations more timely. In consequence the Imperial Chancellor directed me on September 17 through the German Ambassador to put aside my views and on September 17 I received direct telegraphic instructions from the German chief of staff of the field army stating:

In the common interest an undertaking against Egypt is of great importance. Therefore Your Excellency should subordinate to this idea any doubts you may entertain as to the operations proposed by Turkey.

For a proper understanding of the lines of communication in Turkey it is necessary to insert here a few words about the condition of Turkish railroads during the war.

The so called Oriental Line, the only one connecting Constantinople with Europe, had failed completely in the Balkan War. So far as possible, repairs were made during the last few months before the war and also during it, so that the railroad was able to meet the most pressing requirements. The

construction of this single track railroad with its steep grades
and sharp curves limited its capacity.

The other great railway line of Turkey—the Anatolian and
Bagdad railway—was the only effective communication between
Constantinople and the interior and the periphery of the empire
and was controlled by German-Swiss influence. At its head
stood two men of intellectual eminence who had resided in
Turkey for many years and knew the country perfectly. They
were the directors, Huguenin and Privy Counselor Gunther. It
must be conceded that nothing within the power of man, certainly nothing capable of accomplishment under Turkish
conditions, was left undone by the direction and civil administration of the railroad. Of course the efficiency of this single
track railroad cannot be compared with that of our great European railways; the supply of locomotives and rolling stock was
entirely inadequate. To this is due the fact that the great
Taurus tunnel, the vital nerve of any further communication
with Syria, Palestine and Mesopotamia, was not completed
before the war and was only finished at the time of the military
collapse of Turkey at the end of September 1918.

Thus no train could go all the way through to Aleppo before
October 1918. Till the end of the war trains had to be unloaded
north of the Taurus and the cargoes transferred to wagon,
camel and auto truck for transportation across the mountains.
Later when the tunnel had pierced the mountain, though with
small profile, a dummy line was built and the cargoes were then
transferred from the main trains to the dummy trains. Similar
work was necessary south of the Taurus in order to use the
railroad.

Equal distribution of the rolling stock between the north
and south of the Taurus was impossible. Like difficulties
existed at first at the Amanus mountains, but they were overcome more quickly.

The lines south of Aleppo to Syria, Palestine and Hedjas
never reached a really effective state during the entire war.

They could not be systematically enlarged to meet increased demands, nor were sufficient improvements made for them to withstand heavy traffic.   Rolling stock was lacking everywhere. At Rajak the gauge changed.   Add to this the never ceasing calamity of lack of fuel for the locomotives.   Coal was supplied from Constantinople either not at all or in insufficient quantities, and even the procurement of wood was beset with great difficulties in a country so devoid of forests.

There is no doubt that from the beginning of the mobilization the Turkish headquarters never accorded proper consideration to the vital point of the communications to the south and southeast of the empire, that is, to through communications over the Taurus and Amanus mountains.   Instead of concentrating from the beginning all available personnel and material resources at these points for the completion of the railroad, a pernicious scattering of these resources took place.   Otherwise it was impossible to begin the line to Angora-Sivas, or that to Diarbekir or to make the Kizil-Irmak river navigable or to begin other large works.   In the case of the first named railroad it was certain from the first that the bridges for crossing various water courses could not be brought from Germany before the end of the war and it was equally certain and well known that several Turkish potentates had considerable pecuniary interests in this railroad.   So far as the present war was concerned this line had no strategic significance.

My report of October 25 to German headquarters contains a statement of these conditions.

It is well known that the Bagdad railroad could not be extended anywhere near to the seat of war in Mesopotamia.   The main line of communications of the Sixth Army in Mesopotamia coincided with that of the troops in Syria as far as Aleppo; from there it either continued down the Euphrates toward Bagdad, or followed the railroad to its terminus at Ras-el-Ain, thence 350 kilometers to Mosul by roads over country where in wet weather progress was greatly impeded by the heavy clayey soil and by marshy stretches. From Mosul it was a further 350 kilometers to Bagdad the last stage of which was covered by the Samara-Bagdad dummy line. The difficulties of exerting successful German influence, through military organs, on the operation of Turkish railroads were largely underestimated throughout the war both at home and at the Turkish military center.

Among the officers were too many who would not accommodate themselves to the peculiarities of the country and of the Turkish administration, and thought all that was necessary was to apply German standards and German methods to Turkish conditions.

A considerable number of Turkish officers, employed in the management of military railroads and with whom the Germans had to collaborate, were pursuing their own pecuniary advantages. They were not in the least interested in the introduction of German order and control.

It is well known that branch lines of the great railways in Turkey were but slightly developed. That is due to oriental indolence and to the former views of those in power who believed that facilitation of railway communication into the interior of the country constituted a danger to the existence of the state.

The most important of other existing lines, the Aidin-Kassaba railroad built by an English company and the Panderma-Manissa line built by the French, were of secondary importance in the Turkish conduct of the war.

CHAPTER 5

TURKEY'S ENTRY INTO THE WORLD WAR

On one of the last days of October 1914 the German military attaché, Major von Laffert, appeared at the headquarters of the First Army, then quartered in the military school of Pancaldi in Pera, and requested to see me on an urgent matter. He was excited and reported the *Goeben* and *Breslau* had had a successful encounter with Russian naval vessels in the Black Sea near the mouth of the Bosporus; that the Russian ships had withdrawn after a mine layer had been sunk; that the *Goeben* and *Breslau* and several small vessels of the Turkish Navy were en route to Sevastopol to bombard the Russian coast and that Turkey now certainly would give up neutrality and join in the war. On October 30 the military mission received the following communication from Turkish headquarters:

Fleet Commander reports at 11.15 p.m. October 29:

"On the 27th and 28th the Russian fleet followed all the movements of the Turkish fleet and interfered with its exercises. The Russian fleet began hostilities today. The Russian mine layer, three torpedo boats and a coal tender advanced today toward the Bosporus with hostile intentions. The *Goeben* sank the mine layer, took the coal tender, heavily damaged one torpedo boat, took three officers and seventy-two men prisoners and successfully bombarded Sevastopol.

"The mine layer carried 700 mines and 200 men. Using our torpedo boats we saved three officers and seventy-two men who will arrive in Constantinople on the 30th. It has been learned from prisoners that the Russians intended to mine the entrance to the strait and destroy our fleet. At Novorossysk, east of the entrance to the Sea of Azov the *Breslau* has destroyed fifty petroleum depots and fourteen military transports, etc."

The news of this action was a surprise to me because I had heard neither from the German Ambassador nor from Admiral Souchon, with whom I had had no conversation since our differences over the prospects of a Turkish attack on Egypt;

and that, in the existing tense situation, the Turkish fleet would enter the Black Sea.

Several weeks before, about the 20th of September, having heard from a reliable source that Freiherr von Wangenheim intended to send the *Breslau* and *Goeben* into the Black Sea under the German flag, I had hurried to Therapia to dissuade the ambassador.

I maintained that having nominally bought the *Goeben* and *Breslau* and announced the fact to the world, the Turkish government would be placed in an awkward position the inevitable consequences of which would fall on the Germans in Turkey. At a naval review at the Princes Islands before the Sultan on the 17th of September, the German ships had appeared under the Turkish flag. Their names had been changed to *Yawuz Sultan Seliur* and *Midillu* and the German naval officers and men wore the fez. Hence, in my opinion, they could not resume action as German ships at the end of September. The ambassador neither acknowledged nor denied his intention. At any rate the ships did not sail then.

The present engagement had taken place under the Turkish flag, so it is probable that the Turkish Minister of Marine, Djemal Pasha, had given his consent to the departure of the ships.

He is perhaps the Turkish Minister who in those days made a decisive change in his political convictions in favor of Germany and whose changed attitude was not without influence on the final decision of the Turkish government to relinquish neutrality.

It was known that Enver was wholly for Germany and that Talaat had certain leanings in that direction; Djemal, however, had heretofore shown quite pronounced sympathies for the Entente. Shortly before the beginning of the war he had attended the French naval maneuvers as guest of the French government and had been shown marked attention. As late as August 9th he had gone on board of those Entente vessels which were carrying the French back to their home country and in addressing them had wished them a happy journey and military glory.   On September 6 Enver had told an officer well known to me that Djemal would not favor a relinquishment of neutrality until the final decision of arms was in favor of Austria and Germany as against Russia.   Djemal certainly was one of the leading persons in Turkey, and his joining the Germanophile Ministers was of great significance.

The Turkish cabinet accepted the warlike collision in the Black Sea as basis for giving up its neutrality and Turkey joined the side of the Central Powers.   In those days it was stated in Constantinople that even after the action with the Turko-German ships in the Black Sea, Russia was willing to recognize Turkish neutrality, provided the German military mission and the officers and men of the *Goeben* and *Breslau* were at once returned to Germany; and that the Turkish government declined.   I cannot answer for the correctness of this information.

At any rate within a few days Turkey was in a state of war with Russia.

The entrance to the Dardanelles had been mined at the end of September; still this action, just like the mobilization of army and navy, might have been considered as a precautionary measure.   The Turkish government regarded forcible action of the Entente fleet against Constantinople as possible and meant to prepare for it.

Colonel Djevad Bei, commanding the Dardanelles, told me later that the above defensive measure was caused by the unfriendly conversation of the commander of a British destroyer with the commander of a Turkish torpedo boat which had gone outside the mouth of the Dardanelles.

Late in the fall Admiral von Usedom, known from the campaign in China, had reached Constantinople and had been made inspector general of coast artillery and mines.   Later he was given supreme command of the fortified straits of the Bosporus and of the Dardanelles with headquarters in Constantinople.   The immediate commanders of the two groups of fortifications were Turkish officers and so remained for the present.

The entry of Turkey into the war did not at once bring on extensive military operations. The *Goeben* and *Breslau* with a few torpedo boats would sometimes go into the Black Sea and bombard the Russian coast. The Russian fleet showed itself several times and exchanged long range shots with the Turkish ships, but nothing decisive happened, and by using certain precautions the Turks were able to maintain communication by sea with Trebizond.

The Turks never were able to completely close the Black Sea as later the Russian fleet became more active. There always remained certain little back doors that could be opened with gold. Thus during the ensuing years of the war the large brewery of Bomonti in Constantinople received many shiploads of barley by way of Roumanian ports and the Black Sea, which however faced variable and unpleasant additional costs whenever the Turkish Intendant General, Ismail Hakki Pasha, succeeded in laying hand on them when they arrived.

Greater events were in preparation in the Caucasus and on the Egyptian front. Toward the middle of November the Turkish government threw into the scales of war what formerly was the strongest arm of Islam and solemnly declared a holy war. The Turkish Ministry expected this measure to produce an overwhelming effect on all Mohammedans in the world.

For the deeply religious Anatolian soldier a holy war was not necessary; he would face death faithfully and bravely for his padishah without it.

With the Mohammedan Arabs under the Turkish government the holy war failed to remove the deep seated opposition between Turks and Arabs or the general dissatisfaction with the Turkish administration which had existed and grown for generations.

In the borderlands of Islamitic religion, whose assistance was counted on, the positive power rested in the firm hands of states belonging to the Entente, or, like Persia, they were wholly incapable of a general national rising or war-like activity on a large scale.   On March 8, 1915, a statement was made in the Italian Chamber that in the whole of North Africa the Fetwa nowhere had produced the slightest effect.

Moreover, in the case in point, the holy war bore the appearance of unreality because Turkey was allied with Christian states and German and Austrian officers and men were serving in the Turkish Army.

The lack of logic here is the same that appears in a speech of Lloyd George in the summer of 1919 when he spoke of General Allenby's crusade in Palestine, for in conjunction with the general referred to, many thousand Mohammedan Arabs intermixed with British officers and, equipped by England with all modern means of war, had fought for the conquest of Palestine under the command of Sherif Faisal.

The holy war received expression in Constantinople in November 1914 through the apparatus customary in all national demonstrations.   The processions, as usual, were arranged by the police and the participating Hamals and other available persons received a fee of a few piasters.   Hence the participants of such processions in Constantinople—no matter what their object—are generally about the same.   This time they paraded with green flags, appeared before the embassies of Turkey's allies and wound up November 20 by breaking all the windows and mirrors of the hotel Toklatian, the proprietor of which was of Armenian birth and had recently become a naturalized Russian.

Not much value was attached to these demonstrations except by foreigners, and in consequence of press exaggerations, in Germany.

The really worth while Turk with his formal reserve does not go in for noisy expressions of his feelings.

It may be that sometime in the future the holy war will have a more serious meaning and find its final expression in massacres of Christians, if the Entente holds the reins too tight in Turkey. Today Turkey is no longer assisted by allied Christian states which would check from the beginning, any extensive outward movement of Islam.

For Turkey today it is only a question of Christian enemies and this might lead to consequences which the Entente in the final analysis does not seem to estimate at their true significance. Otherwise no such concessions of Turkish territory, already granted or intended, would be made to the Greeks who are entirely different in character from the Turks and are looked down upon by the latter as beneath them in military worth.

The Turk is not going to forget that in the World War no Greek succeeded in gaining a foot of Turkish soil by force of arms.

CHAPTER 6

FIRST CONFLICTS IN THE CAUCASUS AND ON THE SUEZ CANAL

In November 1914 the Third Army came in conflict with the Russians in the Caucasus.

The Third Army was commanded by Hassan Izzet Pasha. His chief of staff was a German officer, Major Guse. Several other German officers had been assigned to this army and others were endeavoring to bring order into the very difficult communications in rear of the Third Army. Another German officer, Colonel Posseldt, had taken over the command of the so called fortress of Erzerum. He was assisted by a German artillery officer and a German engineer. A report from them arrived in Constantinople on November 23 which painted the condition of the totally neglected fortress in the darkest colors. Orders for the improvement of the insufficient defenses were of course issued at once by the Turkish headquarters, but, as always in Turkey, the available means were limited and could not be procured without great delays.

In the first conflicts with the Russians in November, on the road from Erzerum to Kars, approximately in the vicinity of Köprikiöj, the Turkish troops fought well and success and failure were fairly balanced between the opposing forces. The Russian advance had certainly been brought to a complete standstill by Hassan Izzet's action. As compared with Turkish performances in the Balkan War, a considerable gain in efficiency was noticeable.

This comparatively satisfactory beginning kept Enver's ambitions stirred up. On December 6 he appeared at the offices of the military mission in the War Ministry to inform me that he was going to sail the same evening for Trebizond to join from there the Third Army. The Intendant General, Hakki Pasha, would act as Minister of War and Talaat Bei, Minister of the

37

Interior, would act for him in other capacities. I specially
mention this, because characteristic of Turkish ideas and as a
proof, in the face of the many incorrect reports of the foreign
press, that quite independent of military rank German officers
at the central offices were never, not even in an acting capacity,
accorded a look into the interior of the Turkish government
mechanism.

Map in hand Enver sketched to me the outline of intended
operations by the Third Army. With one army corps, the
Eleventh, he meant to hold the Russians in front on the main
road, while two corps, the Ninth and Tenth, marching by their
left were to cross the mountains by several marches and then
fall on the Russian flank and rear in the vicinity of Sarikamisch.
Later the Third Army was to take Kars.

I had heard of this intended march several days before from a German officer at headquarters and studied its feasibility. My conclusion was that the operation was difficult, if not wholly impracticable. According to the map and everything else I could learn of them, the roads in question were narrow mountain roads or trails over high ridges. At that time they were probably deep in snow. It would require a special study how to effect the supply of ammunition and food with the available Turkish means.

I called Enver's attention to these grave objections as was my duty; he replied that they had already been considered and that all roads had been reconnoitered or were being reconnoitered. At the conclusion of our conversation he gave utterance to phantastic, yet noteworthy ideas. He told me that he contemplated marching through Afghanistan to India. Then he went away.

Soon after him appeared his chief of staff, General von Bronsart, to report his departure; he was to accompany Enver. I called his attention also to the great difficulties of the march as planned and to the responsibility that would rest upon him as a German chief of staff.

The operation, for which Enver took personal command of the Third Army, ended with the destruction of that army, the first one of the Turkish armies to enter the arena of the World War. The leading Russian troops in advance of Olti were surprised and certain successes were gained. Soon, however, the terrible difficulties of the terrain and of the Russian winter began to decimate the Turkish troops whom Enver was driving forward by forced marches. Only small portions of the two army corps which had entered upon this march reached the enemy at Sarikamisch. They gained a few small successes by surprise, were totally defeated on January 4 and had to retreat at once, pursued by the enemy.

The Eleventh Turkish Corps advanced by the main road, fought at the frontier for several days bravely and devotedly to make possible the retreat of the remainders of the other two corps via Hassan Kale, but finally had to give way.

According to official reports only 12,000 men of the original 90,000 of this army came back. The others were killed, captured, died of hunger or froze to death while camping in the snow without tents. Spotted fever now broke out among the returned soldiers who were much debilitated and took many victims.

After this lamentable catastrophe Enver with his staff started overland for Constantinople. Before his departure he gave the command of the ruined Third Army to Hawis Hakki Pasha, who beyond doubt was one of the most prominent Turkish general staff officers and was considered an ambitious competitor of Enver.

Though without deep knowledge he was of great intelligence and quick conception; he never bared his judgment completely and always kept back something with which to meet objections. The German who stood up for his convictions with unreserved openness, he considered foolish. He appeared to me as a typical representative of the educated upper stratum of the Far East.

Within the last six weeks he had advanced, from lieutenant colonel and section chief in the general staff, to general and army commander. Enver valued his conspicuous energy, but at the same time he was no doubt glad to know him far from Constantinople.

The extent of the heavy defeat was kept secret as much as possible. It was forbidden to speak of it; violations of the order were followed by arrest and punishment.

So far as I know very little leaked out in Germany.

Unfortunately I had several serious frictions with Enver in consequence of his disastrous campaign.

Before his departure from the Caucasus Enver had given telegraphic orders to send the Fifth Corps at once by ship to Trebizond to reënforce the Third Army. This corps, under my orders as army commander, was located around Skutari on the Asiatic side of the Bosporus. I was of the opinion that the corps could no longer be of use in the Caucasus, but might be urgently needed near Constantinople if a British-Russian attack were made there. It was not impossible that after the great Turkish defeat the Entente might entertain more far reaching plans. I therefore remonstrated against the despatch of the corps giving my reasons. Having the support of the embassy in this instance I was successful and the Fifth Corps was not sent to Trebizond. Enver resented my action as was natural.

The next conflict was somewhat sharper and remarkable for its truly Turkish method of adjustment. During his return trip from Sivas, Enver had sent telegraphic orders to all armies that the troops were to obey his orders only and that orders from other sources were without force. In somewhat awkward translation from the Turkish the wording of the order was as follows:

Besides me no one, for no reason, may give orders to these troops (fleet, armies). They will not be carried out except orders given by me.

I do not know what was the motive for this peculiar order, but it was made impossible for me to command a Turkish army so long as the order stood. As it was a purely Turkish matter, it had to be settled in Turkish fashion, hence I made written complaint to the Grand Vizir on January 21.

The Intendant General, Ismail Hakki Pasha, acting Minister of War, was sent to see me as mediator.

This much abused and maligned Intendant General was one of the most remarkable men among the leading Young Turks. His features inclined to the Mongolian type and the keen alert eyes betrayed the shrewdness of the Chinese trader. The whole person in spite of a certain restraint breathed inflexible energy. In Jemen where Ismail Hakki Pasha had lost a leg in action— he used a wooden leg—the Arabs nicknamed him "Kara biber" i.e., black pepper.

In a country of the vast extent of the Turkish empire with its inadequate lines of communication and transport facilities, he was charged to clothe and feed the armies fighting at the outermost frontiers. How to do it was his own affair. He knew that he was lied to and robbed right and left and could not afford to be scrupulous in the choice of his means. He, his officials and agents, distributed over the whole country, commandeered everything they could lay their hands on.

For example, Ismail Hakki Pasha requisitioned an automobile, a present from the German Emperor to Enver, on its arrival in Constantinople. Once on a short visit to the Dardanelles he left me a present of six bottles of wine which he had requisitioned from a friendly gift addressed to me.

Working under totally disordered conditions and in view of the constant transfers and splitting up of troops under orders from Turkish headquarters, he did what was humanly possible under Turkish circumstances.

So far as known, he was treasurer of the committee and had to make Enver's purchases of supplies and beyond a doubt he was merely the middleman in many financial transactions which were falsely ascribed to him for his own enrichment.

At any rate most of those that were ever ready with accusations and charges were not in the least able to judge the difficulties with which this man had to contend. He was one of the few who worked daily in the War Ministry until late at night, after the building had been empty for hours, since the others had left long before, after, at most, six hours of work.

In mediating my complaint Ismail Hakki Pasha maintained at first that the telegram surely was incorrectly translated. Though the translation of a piece of Turkish writing, made by two different persons, is never exactly alike, I was able to show that the translations I had received from the First and Second Army (also then under my command) were of the same tenor. I insisted that the order be rescinded. The Intendant General was unable to give a definite assurance and soon took his leave with expressions of deepest respect. He had left a big box on my desk. I sent it after him by my adjutant, but he sent word back that the contents were intended for me. The box contained the Grand Cross of the Osmanje Order. No other adjustment of my complaint was made. Enver's order was not carried out of course.

A third conflict ensued after Enver's return. As chief of the military mission I thought it expedient for the preservation of the authority of the German officers that, after the disastrous failures, Enver's chief of staff, General von Bronsart, should take a command. I wrote in that sense to Enver and reported at the same time to the home authorities. Enver insisted on keeping his chief of staff and from Germany I never received a reply. No change was made.

In November it was definitely decided at Turkish headquarters to form an army in Syria from which an expeditionary corps against the Suez Canal was to be formed while the army at the same time guarded the coasts of Palestine and Syria. Djemal Pasha, Minister of Marine and commander of the Second Army, was designated as the chief of this Fourth Army. He asked for Colonel von Frankenberg as chief of staff and immediately left for Damascus with a large retinue. Colonel Freiherr von Kress, a most excellent and efficient officer who in September had been assigned to the Eighth Army Corps in Damascus, was at the disposal of Djemal Pasha. As chief of staff of the Eighth Army Corps he directed the extremely difficult preparations for the advance to the canal and later made a splendid record as leader of the expeditionary corps. I have stated on a former occasion that the undertaking was condemned to failure from the beginning. Egypt cannot be taken by 16,000 Turkish troops. That the expeditionary corps traversed the desert El Tih in seven marches and reached the Suez Canal near Ismailia with its leading troops will forever stand as a great feat. The marches were entirely made at night and had remained unknown to the British on account of the precautions taken. Through their far spread espionage the British of course knew of the concentration of Turkish troops east of the desert, but their small number could not alarm them. They never thought that such a small force would dare to advance against Egypt.

The scouting officers of the expeditionary corps saw British officers calmly playing football when the leading Turkish troops were within twenty-five kilometers of the canal.

On the night of February 2/3 the attacking troops in proper formation and equipped with boats were successfully moved

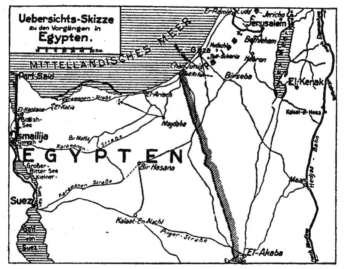

forward as far as the eastern bank of the canal. When the small British post there opened fire, a panic seized upon the Arabian soldiers. Part of the men already embarked jumped from the boats, others dropped the boats and rafts they were carrying.

British reënforcements quickly arrived after fire had been opened. About two Turkish companies had reached the west bank of the canal; some were killed and some captured. In half an hour the Egyptian bank of the canal was so strongly occupied, that further attempts at crossing had to be given up.

British armored trains with revolving guns arrived and five war vessels were delivering flanking fire from Lake Timsah and Great Bitter Lake.

The expeditionary corps managed to hold its ground till evening on February 3. A British attack on the right was checked. At 4 p.m. February 3 the commanding general of the Eighth Army Corps (who originally had intended to renew the attack next morning with the Tenth Division) decided to order Colonel von Kress to withdraw that evening because the British were constantly bringing up more troops.

The break away from the enemy and the withdrawal to a camp ten kilometers east of Ismailia were made in good order.

On the side of the enemy the Indian and Soudanese troops had not shown much initiative.

The retreat of the expeditionary corps was made without noteworthy losses. In the first part of the war the British always lost much time with their preparation for their movements. As the movement through the desert had been unexpected, the pursuit was not provided for in the English program and it was some time before it materialized.

As reconnaissance in force the enterprise was of value for the Fourth Turkish Army. It showed what difficulties the troops would have to meet after traversing the desert.

The commander of the Fourth Army now decided to maintain advanced troops on the line El Arish-Kalaat-en-Nachle and to harass the canal continuously with mobile columns in order to hinder the passage of ships.

Of the main forces the Eighth Army Corps was to take post in the vicinity of Chan Junis and Gaza, the Tenth Division in Birseba, and the Hedjas Division at Maan.

Now that the Turks had demonstrated the possibility of reaching the canal, the British soon took more extensive measures. Any subsequent attempt at reaching the canal would therefore meet with greatly increased difficulties. It is a fact that thereafter only small patrols and a few bold individuals succeeded in getting as far as the Suez Canal.

At the beginning of the winter of 1914–15 the first military special missions reached Constantinople. One was to go to Afghanistan, another to the mouth of the Schatt-el-Arab. Later a mission for Persia arrived. They had in common far reaching but ill defined plans and great sums of money. Their mission was originated by the Ministry of Foreign Affairs in Berlin and came within the scope of the German Embassy, or its military attaché. Though these missions consisted almost exclusively of officers, the military mission had not been consulted in the matter nor did it ever receive any kind of communication about them.

It appeared to me a mistake from the beginning to send these missions and I would have urgently advised against them had I been asked. A few persons, though they might have once travelled in those countries, could never produce a useful effect for the war unless accompanied by troops. Turkey alone was in position to furnish troops for this purpose and a request to that effect would entail dependence on Turkey whose interests did not entirely coincide with German views. Moreover the eyes of the Turks, already sufficiently occupied by the defense of their own country, would be directed into obscure and phantastic courses where no success was probable. Thus it came that not one of the missions accomplished anything of real value in spite of much devotion. As to events in the Turkish theatres of war at the end of 1914 and the beginning of 1915, there is nothing else to be reported except that in the middle of January Turkish troops had entered Tabriz, which was Persian territory and therefore neutral. Meanwhile the British had taken Basra in Irak, moved forward to Gurna (Korna) at the confluence of the Euphrates and Tigris and took post there on December 9, 1914.

It may be stated here in advance, that British troops seized the city of Amara on June 3, 1915, by an unexpected advance and that in those days the German consul in Bagdad was doubtful whether the German colony would be able to remain in Bagdad.

CHAPTER 7

THE PERIOD BEFORE THE DARDANELLES CAMPAIGN

At the beginning of 1915 general attention was more and more directed toward the Dardanelles. Reports as to enemy intentions, movements of ships and of transports of troops were coming in from various directions, chiefly from Athens. A successful attempt of the Anglo-French fleet to force its way to Constantinople was not considered an impossibility.

The then organization of the Dardanelles as fixed by Turkish Headquarters was not sufficiently lucid. As previously stated Admiral Usedom had supreme command of the fortifications on the Dardanelles and on the Bosporus. The German Admiral Merten was at Tschanakale (*Chanak*) as delegate of Turkey. The Dardanelles were under command of Colonel Djevad Bei who controlled the troops in the southern part of the Gallipoli peninsula as well as the troops guarding the strait on the Asiatic side. The units in the central and northern part of the peninsula belonged to the Third Army Corps, i.e., to the First Army commanded by me. In addition Turkish headquarters had reserved to itself certain rights of command.

As chief of the First Army on the spot I had made such preparations against an attempt of the Anglo-French fleet to break through as would at least have made its prolonged stay off Constantinople very difficult. From San Stefano to the Serail point, on the Asiatic side and on the Princes Islands, numerous batteries had been erected whose fire crossed on the sea. Flying detachments kept guard over these parts of the coast. Reserves were established.

It was to be assumed as a certainty that the *Goeben* and *Breslau*, in conjunction with the Turkish fleet, would attack the allied fleet, weakened as it would be during its passage, before it could reach Constantinople.

Even in case the allied fleet forced a passage and won the naval battle in the Sea of Marmara, I judged that it would be in a nearly untenable position so long as the entire shores on the Dardanelles strait were not held by strong allied forces. Should the Turkish troops succeed in holding the shores of the strait or in regaining them, the regular supply of food and coal would become impossible. But for a successful landing of troops near Constantinople where they might avail themselves of the resources of the country, the defensive arrangements left little hope of success.

A decisive success could not be won by the enemy unless the landing of large forces in the Dardanelles was coincident with, or antecedent to, the passage of the fleet. A landing subsequent to the passage would have to be made without the assistance of the guns of the fleet, as the latter would be confronted with new problems after forcing its way through.

Perhaps there were certain chances for the capture of Constantinople by an Anglo-French fleet if at the same time large Russian forces were landed to one side of the Bosporus and if this coöperation of the three allies accomplished the capture of Constantinople.

All defensive arrangements that seemed necessary had been made against a Russian landing. The coast of the Black Sea on both sides of the Bosporus was defended by batteries and flying detachments and the Sixth Army Corps was in readiness near San Stefano to meet any Russian landing force. This army corps had been specially prepared for this duty by numerous exercises on a large scale; the night alarms incident thereto at first caused considerable friction.

Thus as early as December 27, 1914, I was able to reply to an inquiry from German headquarters that the rumors of anxiety of the Turkish military authorities, in consequence of the threat to the Dardanelles, had no basis in fact and that all necessary measures had been taken.

Among the high German officers in Turkey who were not

within the control of the military mission, there was, besides the admirals, General Field Marshal Freiherr von der Goltz. He arrived in Constantinople December 12, 1914, exchanging his post as governor general of Belgium for that of adjutant general to the Sultan. The general field marshal was well known in Turkey and highly respected. He spent eighteen years of his life there as military instructor. Many of the high Turkish officers had been his pupils. The field marshal himself named Enver as his young friend.

For a man as active as Freiherr von der Goltz the position of adjutant general to the Sultan could not be but transitory. He soon arranged an office for himself in the War Ministry and took part in the conferences of the Turkish general staff.

Enver was still nourishing his resentment over my protests on the occasion of the disastrous campaign in the Caucasus. He wanted to remove me from Constantinople and in the middle of February 1915 he offered me the ruin covered area of Erzerum and the command of the Third Army. Hawis Hakki Pasha had died of spotted typhus on February 12.

The small remnants of the Third Army had been augmented by about 20,000 recruits. Operations in that section were unthinkable for many months. I firmly declined that command and so reported to Germany. The German Ambassador shared my view.

The soundness of my judgment of the moral and physical consequences of the winter catastrophe persisting for months, is proven by the following reports: On March 2 consul Dr. Bergfeld reported from Trebizond:

> Spotted typhus is raging in all the hospitals of the city. The extent of the epidemic is approaching a catastrophe. With an average sick report of 900–1,000 soldiers the daily death rate is between thirty and fifty.

The Red Cross surgeons, Dr. Colley and Dr. Zlocisti, reported on March 3 from Ersindjan:

> Lack of sanitary arrangements and of sufficient medical help is decimating the ranks of the Turkish soldiers in a manner unthinkable under German conditions.

Major Guse, chief of staff of the Third Army, wrote on May 25;

Only a small part of the replacements sent to the army from the recruit camps reaches its destination. Sickness, poor rations, desertions on the march, deplete the ranks terribly.

In a telegram of June 2, 1915, the German consul in Erzerum expressed apprehension that a third of the troops assembled in the camps there for training had fallen sick and that another third had deserted on the march to the army. Other reports were of similar tenor. It was fortunate that after the collapse of the Third Turkish Army in the Caucasus, the Russians on their part were likewise prevented by many causes from continuing operations during the ensuing months.

On January 29, soon after the return of Enver from the Caucasus I made a short inspection trip to see the defensive arrangements on the coast of Asia Minor between the Dardanelles and Smyrna. My first objective was Edremid, which I reached by auto from Balikesri. It was probably the first time that an auto had passed over this mountain road of Asia Minor. There were numerous bridges of the most primitive construction, some of them spanning deep clefts in the rocks. Soon thereafter German pioneers had to improve or reconstruct them because the pioneer expert, Major Effnert, declared that they would not even support the weight of marching field artillery. After the inspection of the troops in Edremid, we were for the first time quartered in a Turkish home, that of a wealthy oil manufacturer. There I saw for the first time the strange custom of the grown sons of the house waiting on the table in honor of the guest.

On the journey next morning to Aivalik we passed the Keme River, the bridge over which had been carried away by a flood some time before. True to genuinely Turkish custom no civil authority had troubled itself for the restoration of the bridge. German pioneers soon thereafter built a new and better one.

We crossed the obstacle on high buffalo carts and our auto was pulled through the river by spans of buffaloes. The rest of the day's journey led through glorious olive forests, which make this part of Asia Minor one of the most fertile of this blessed section. We passed through rich Greek villages in which grown-ups and school children in holiday dress lined the streets.

These Greeks were subsequently robbed of much of their wealth by the senseless harshness of the Turkish government, which compelled all those who were reported as unreliable by the police to move away from the sections near the coast.

In Aivalik, later so frequently mentioned and which I then was visiting for the first and only time, I inspected more troops. In explaining to me the obstructions laid to close the harbor as we entered it, the port commander quite ingenuously pointed out an unobstructed lane left open by the authorities in order that smuggling to and from Mitylene and other islands might be continued.

On the return journey we were overtaken by a blizzard and we crossed the mountains between Edremid and Balikesri with considerable difficulty. For many hours we marched on foot through deep snow and it took all the resources, cheerfully proffered, of the country people along the road to bring on our autos.

When we finally reached the railroad at Balikesri it turned out that it had been rendered impassable by landslides. It was necessary to carry on the train working detachments to clear the road. In Panderma on the Sea of Marmara we failed to find our ship for the return trip to Constantinople because all ships had fled this poor port before the force of the storm to avoid being stranded. We reached Constantinople several days late.

I have given a description of this short inspection trip in order to show the confused conditions obtaining in the best parts of Turkey at the beginning of 1915. The transient visitors of Constantinople who, sitting in the Pera Palace Hotel, were writing articles on the great improvement of communications, could not of course appreciate the bad conditions elsewhere.

The inspection trip had a peculiar sequence, which showed to me to what senseless attacks a German in Turkey could be exposed.

During the Dardanelles battles in the summer of that year, I received a communication from the German Ambassador in which King Constantine of Greece made inquiry whether I had in fact stated to the mayor of Edremid "that all Greeks had better be thrown into the sea." I had not seen or talked with the mayor of Edremid or any other personage during my brief stay in that city where I had nothing whatever to do with the Greeks and where I had, of course, made no utterance about Greeks. Hence I was able to rebut this shameless invention in a few words. Any German in a military position in Turkey was liable to such calumnies. No one there attached the least importance to such lies as they merely served as weapons of opposing parties. Being a Turkish general I was an offense to many fanatical Greeks.

On February 15, in the palace of Dolmar Bagtsche, the Sultan consecrated the colors of the 3rd Division and turned them over to the troops who then marched past the sovereign who sat at a window. It was rather painful to all of us that Enver, the vice-generalissimo, was late and compelled the aged and ailing monarch as well as the whole assembly to wait for more than an hour. The Sultan was frequently exposed to similar want of consideration on the part of the Young Turks. Talaat alone, a wise and naturally tactful man, was a commendable exception.

Meanwhile the Anglo-French fleet had gradually assembled and found suitable bases in the islands of Lemnos, Imbros and Tenedos. During the winter flying stations for land planes and hydroplanes had been erected on the last two islands together with other military establishments.

The guns of the enemy fleet were at first directed against the old works and batteries of Seddulbar (Sedd el Bahr) and Kum

Kale which closed the entry to the Dardanelles; the ships with their modern heavy artillery remaining beyond the range of the older Turkish guns. The available means in this conflict were too unequal to leave the outcome in doubt. After a few bombardments the Turkish batteries were silenced and part of the fortifications destroyed.

Repeated attempts of the enemy to land marines and take Seddulbar (Sedd el Bahr) by surprise were unsuccessful because in spite of the bombardment small Turkish bodies had remained in places not reached by the artillery fire and repulsed the landing.

By the end of February Turkish headquarters rather counted on the enemy fleet breaking through and all sorts of preparations were made for the Sultan, for his court and the treasury, and for the military and civil authorities. They were to be taken care of on the Asiatic side. These precautions were justified. On the other hand those military preparations, which the Turkish headquarters had ordered between February 20 and March 1 to meet a successful passage of the allied fleet through the Dardanelles, might have been fatal.

Had these orders been carried out, the course of the World War would have been given such a turn in the spring of 1915 that Germany and Austria would have had to continue the struggle without Turkey, because these orders exposed the Dardanelles to a hostile landing!

The orders of February 20 changed the organization of the First and of the Second Armies, splitting up the units of the First Army Corps. Furthermore, and that is the essential point, it was ordered that in case of a successful passage of the hostile fleet, the First Army was to defend the north coast, the Second Army the south coast of the straits and of the Sea of Marmara. The line separating the spheres of the two armies was drawn from the mouth of the Dardanelles through the Sea of Marmara from west to east as far as the mouth of the Bosporus in the Black Sea. It did away with any defense of the exterior coast of the Gallipoli peninsula with its dominating heights; it did away with the defense of the Asiatic coast at the mouth of the Dardanelles. It was the feeblest imaginable defensive measure.

I wrote to Enver on February 23 bringing to his attention the incalculable disadvantages of the measures he had ordered. I explained that one Turkish Army was needed for the defense against an Anglo-French landing in the Dardanelles, and another near Constantinople to prevent a Russian landing. That the fronts were west and east, not south and north. On February 25 I received a reply from Enver that he could not concur in my view, without a word of explanation.

On March 1 an order was prepared at Turkish headquarters directing the withdrawal of the Second Army Corps from Adrianople to the lines of Tschataldja, and of the transfer of the Fourth Army Corps from the section Panderma-Balekesri to the Gulf of Ismid. The Second and Fourth Army Corps were the troops nearest to the Dardanelles and the first to be called on in case of a hostile landing on the side of the Dardanelles.

I could not acquiesce in these unfortunate and fatal orders of Enver, and in order to secure a different decision I addressed myself at once on March 1 to the ambassador and to the Chief of the Military Cabinet of H. M. the Emperor.

I am unable to say what was done by these two German authorities to back up my view. Something was done, however, for the execution of these faulty measures was deferred for the present.

In the month of March the action of the allied fleet against the straits of the Dardanelles reached its apex and terminated with the attempt of March 18 to break through.

On March 1 five British battleships with numerous tropedo boats entered the anterior southwestern portion of the strait and engaged the Turkish howitzer batteries on the heights of Erenköj (Eren Keui) and Halil Eli from noon till 6 p.m.

The batteries referred to belonged to the 8th Foot Artillery

Regiment commanded by Colonel Wehrle and had been detached from the First Army under my command to strengthen temporarily the artillery defenses of the Dardanelles straits. The regiment, variously grouped on the heights of the Asiatic and European shores, gave splendid support to the artillery of the fortress and with its brave commander earned much praise. The hostile ships directed their fire not only against his batteries, but against dummy positions he had constructed and frequently changed.

Beginning March 1 the partial attacks of the hostile fleet, mostly made by four or five battleships, were renewed almost daily and there was great activity at night to remove the mine obstructions.

On March 18 the allied fleet made its great attempt to break through. According to Colonel Wehrle's report sixteen battleships took part; they began at 10.30 a.m. to enter the straits in two echelons, in order to silence the guns of the fortress and the batteries. The artillery battle lasted until 7 p.m.

In spite of the expenditure of enormous amounts of ammunition the hostile fleet accomplished no great results. The damage to the forts and batteries but little diminished their fighting capacity, though their ammunition supply had been reduced. According to the statements of Colonel Djevad Bei, the commander of the fortress, the losses in men did not reach 200.

The enemy suffered serious and weighty losses. Insofar as could be observed by Colonel Wehrle and his subordinates, the *Bouvet, Irresistible* and *Ocean* had been sunk and several other battleships were seriously damaged. Several smaller ships, engaged in salvage work, had also been sunk. The fire of Fort Hamidje under Captain Wossidlo was mentioned as particularly effective. It may be assumed that the mine field in Erenköj (Eren Keui) Bay laid at night by the Turkish mine expert, Lieutenant Colonel Geehl, contributed its share to the result.

At any rate the allied fleet had to withdraw and give up the attempt. The 18th of March is and remains a day of honor for the Fortress Dardanelles and for the commander of the straits. The attempt was not renewed by the Entente during the war.

The allies now probably recognized that the road to Constantinople could not be opened by action on the water alone. It was equally clear to me that they would not relinquish such a high prize without further effort. It would not have been in keeping with British tenacity or energy. Hence a large landing had to be counted upon.

As early as March rumors began to circulate of the concentration of a large expeditionary force for that purpose. These reports coming mostly from Athens, Sofia and Bucharest contained many contradictions, which was natural. Once it was 50,000 men, then again 80,000 British troops were being assembled on the Islands of Imbros and Lemnos; another time 50,000 French were named as participants in the expedition. The arrival at the Dardanelles of General Hamilton who was to assume command, and of the French General d'Amade on the cruiser *Provence*, were duly reported. It was known that a landing pier had been constructed in Mudros and that equipment and subsistence were being unloaded there daily. On March 17 four British officers had arrived at Piraeus and bought forty-two large lighters and five tugs for cash.

Now at last, on the 25th of March, Enver decided to form a separate army, the Fifth, for the defense of the Dardanelles. My constantly renewed efforts to bring about such a decision of Turkish headquarters had of late received effective support from the German Embassy and Admiral Souchon; Admiral von Usedom, however, after his experiences in China, would not yet believe in the probability of large landing operations.

CHAPTER 8

First Part of the Dardanelles Campaign

Late on the afternoon of March 24 Enver requested me to wait for him in my office. He came soon afterward and asked if I were willing to take command of the Fifth Army to be organized for the defense of the Dardanelles. I assented at once and informed him that the troops now there would have to be reënforced at once as we had no time to spare.

On the evening of the following day, March 25, I left Constantinople by boat for my new destination. I was not to see the capital again for ten months. As time was short, I could take but a small part of the staff of the First Army with me. Among these officers were the chief of staff, Kiazim Bei, and my two German aides, Captains Prigge and Muhlmann. The rest of the staff was to follow. With the exception of Captain Von Frese, commandant of headquarters, all the officers were Turkish.

The staff of the military mission remained in Constantinople. General Field Marshal Freiherr von der Goltz took over from me the command of the First Army.

On the morning of March 26 we landed at the port of Gallipoli where the headquarters of the Third Corps had been for some time, and established temporary headquarters there.

Myself, and the gentlemen of my immediate entourage, were quartered in a house which I was afterward told was that of the French consular agent. The only furniture in my two rooms was a round table and a wall mirror. All other things had no doubt been stolen. The kaimakan had to borrow for us the necessary beds and other indispensable furniture in the town. When I left the house about four weeks later, the greater part of my linen had disappeared. I was all the more surprised later on when I was accused by Greeks of having robbed and plundered the house. I had something better to do than to carry away the round table and the wall mirror.

The town of Gallipoli was then a fairly prosperous town, though several Greek families had previously been expelled by the Turkish authorities. At the end of the Dardanelles Campaign it was largely a pile of ruins due to hostile bombardments.

Days full of work ensued since the grouping of the troops and the guarding of the important stretches of coast had to be changed completely.

The Fifth Army numbered but five divisions, which were distributed on the European and Asiatic sides as coast guards; the divisions numbered 9–12 battalions, the battalions 800–1000 men. The British gave me four full weeks before their great landing. They had sent part of their troops to Egypt and perhaps also to Cyprus. The time was just sufficient to complete the most indispensable arrangements and to bring the 3rd Division under Colonel Nicolai from Constantinople.

The exterior coasts on both sides of the mouth of the Dardanelles were the first places where a landing might be expected.

The littoral region of the Asiatic coast consisted of fertile undulating hills and large flats with meadow land, traversed by the numerous windings of the Mendere River. Seaward the lowland is terminated by a ring of low coastal elevations. In case of a landing these elevations would be the natural artillery positions of the enemy whence his guns, in combination with the long range artillery of the fleet, could dominate the open country to the east. The Mendere River and the marshy stretches were not such as to seriously impede an army with modern equipment in spring and summer.

The narrow peninsula of Gallipoli which bounds the straits on the north on the European side, is pronounced mountainous terrain with precipitous ridges, the slopes of which are rent by deep ravines and sharp clefts.

A few low pine woods, a few bushes on the ridges and on the

banks of the creeks and coulees, formed the sole natural covering of the generally waste landscape.

The cultivation is dependent on the water supply and limited to the surroundings of the few villages, which are all on low ground. It is only the valleys around the small town of Maidos, the latter lying directly on the straits, that show some higher cultivation. Here are olive and mulberry plantations.

Toward the upper part of the Gulf of Saros (Xeros) the interior of the peninsula contains considerable plains which are open and more fertile.

The important question was where the hostile landing should be expected. On it depended the grouping of the troops, which were rather inconsiderable in comparison with the great extent of the coast.

Technical feasibility for the landing of large bodies of troops existed in many parts of the coast. All could not be occupied. The decision therefore must be made on tactical grounds.

The most important works and batteries dominating the straits of the Dardanelles, lay on the southern, Asiatic coast. The Island of Tenedos, occupied by the enemy, lay right in front of this shore, and the large and small Bays of Besica (Bashika) were particularly suitable places for landings. It was possible here to place large forces on the Turkish shore. As the works and heavy batteries of the fortress were arranged only for a struggle for the possession of the waterway, an advance and attack against our rear after his landing on the Asiatic shore, offered excellent chances to the enemy. Road communications here were tolerably good. Hence this was the place of greatest danger.

On the Gallipoli peninsula there were three places that had to be considered as specially important and in danger.

The first was the southern point of the peninsula at Seddulbar (Sedd el Bahr) and Tekke Burnu, because this terrain could be covered by the guns of the enemy's ships. After a successful landing at the southern point there rose before the enemy the widely conspicuous, bald height of Eltschitepe (Altchy Tepe) (Achi Baba) as the next decisive objective, up to which the gently rising ground offered no great terrain obstacles. From the top of the Eltschitepe (Achi Baba) ridge a part of the Turkish works and batteries along the coast could be taken under direct artillery fire.

The second place suitable for a quick decision was the coast line on both sides of Kabatepe (Gaba Tepe). From here a broad plain, broken only by a flat elevation, led directly to the town of Maidos on the straits. From the heights on both sides of Maidos the batteries of the fortress could be silenced with certainty. North of Kabatepe (Gaba Tepe) the steep heights of Ari Burnu lay close to the coast with a well protected landing place. If the enemy directed his main attack on Maidos by way of Kabatepe it was necessary for him to hold the heights of Ari Burnu because they flanked the plain mentioned.

The third specially important place for a landing on the European side was the vicinity of Bulair on the upper Gulf of Saros (Xeros) where the peninsula is not more than five to seven kilometers wide. It afforded no direct artillery effect against the fortress, and the grounds for deciding the question of a landing here became strategic. There the peninsula could be cut in two and shut off from communication with Constantinople and Thrace. If the enemy occupied the narrow ridges between the Gulf of Saros (Xeros) and the Sea of Marmara, the Fifth Army would be cut off from every land communication and the communications by water become endangered as soon as British long range guns, assisted at night by search lights, commanded this narrow part of the Sea of Marmara. The hostile submarines had devoted their attention to the mine field since the beginning of December and attempted to enter the Sea of Marmara; they would be instrumental in completing this separation. Conformably to the degree of danger I formed three groups. The 5th and 7th Divisions were stationed on the upper Saros (Xeros) Gulf, the 9th and newly organized

19th Division were ordered to the southern part of the peninsula and the 11th Division was stationed on the Asiatic side together with the 3rd Division which soon arrived by boat.

The positions of the five existing divisions up to March 26 had to be altered completely. They had been posted on different principles and distributed along the entire coast, somewhat like the frontier detachments of the good old days. The enemy on landing would have found resistance everywhere, but there were no reserves to check a strong and energetic advance.

I ordered the divisions to hold their troops together and to send only the most indispensable security detachments to the coast within their sectors.

Whatever might be in store, in view of our weak forces, our success depended not on sticking tight, but on the mobility of our three battle groups.

The next step necessary after getting the troops in their new positions—they had grown stiff in their coast guard positions— was to make them as mobile by marches and exercises as we wanted them to be at the decisive moment. To expedite the movements of troops at the proper moment without loss of time, boats were assembled in suitable ports of the straits and the labor battalions were at once set to work constructing direct communications between sectors. So far there was hardly a through road on the peninsula. There were only foot paths and pack trails for the movement of pack animals in single file.

The new positions were taken up by night marches to conceal them from hostile aviators.

The Fifth Army had not a single aeroplane. The few aeroplanes in Tschanak-Kale (Chanak) belonged to the fortress and were barely able to serve its purposes.

In those days the planning of troop exercises called for some caution, because hostile ships were cruising everywhere and firing on any detachment that became visible. Much to our surprise the ships fired even on such single horsemen or pedestrians as they caught sight of.

For the improvement of the field fortifications of the most
endangered stretches of the coast all available men were put to
work and mostly at night. The available Turkish means of
obstruction were as short as were the tools, but we did the
best we could. Torpedo heads were used alongside with the
regular land mines and the fences of gardens and fields were
stripped of their wood and wire. At places particularly suitable
for landings barbed wire was stretched under water.

Enemy's newspapers later frequently stated that the British
aviators had not correctly seen and reported the positions of the
Turkish troops before the landing. This probably is not quite
correct. It would appear that the landing plan was based on
older reports of aviators and in view of the precautions we took
the new grouping effected in the last few weeks had not become
apparent to the enemy.

At the end of March the Fifth Army took over from the
fortress the destroyed forts of Seddulbar (Sedd el Bahr) and
Kum Kale, so that the fortress had to defend only the interior
of the straits.

On the 24th of April the 11th Division had a maneuver based
on a hostile landing in the small Besika (Bashika) Bay. Late
in the afternoon I returned to the town of Gallipoli.

At 5 a.m. of April 25th reports were received in rapid succession at army headquarters of extensive landings of troops
made or about to be made. From the south, beginning on the
Asiatic side, the 11th Division reported the concentration of
hostile war vessels and transports in, and off, the large and
small Besika (Bashika) Bays, threatening a landing.

A little farther north, at Kum Kale, the advanced troops of
the 3rd Division were heavily engaged with French troops
which had been debarked there under a heavy fire of numerous
French war vessels.

At the southern point of the peninsula of Gallipoli at Seddulbar (Sedd el Bahr), Tekke Burnu, at the mouth of the Sigindere
(Zighin Dere) and in Morto Bay the advanced troops of the

9th Division were contending with heavy British forces for the possession of the landing place. All of these stretches of coast and the country in rear were deluged with a frightful fire from the large caliber naval guns of the British.

At Kabatepe (Gaba Tepe) and to one side of the formerly mentioned place of Maidos, and at Ari Burnu troops were being debarked from British war vessels and transports, while a semicircle of hostile battleships was deluging the shore and the ground in rear with fire from the heaviest calibers.

Nearest to us, in the upper Saros (Xeros) Gulf, numerous war vessels and transports were approaching the coast. Soon we distinctly heard a continuous roar of artillery fire from that direction.

From the many pale faces among the officers reporting in the early morning it became apparent that although a hostile landing had been expected with certainty, a landing at so many places surprised many and filled them with apprehension. My first feeling was that our arrangements needed no change. That was a great satisfaction! The hostile landing expedition had selected those points which we ourselves considered the most likely landing places and had specially prepared for defense.

It seemed improbable to me that extensive landings would take place at all of these places, but we could not discern at that moment where the enemy was actually seeking the decision.

After alarming the 7th Division in the town of Gallipoli and instructing it to march at once in the direction of Bulair, I rode ahead to the heights of Bulair with my German adjutants.

On the narrow ridge of Bulair where neither tree nor bush impedes view or gives cover, we had a full view of the upper Saros (Xeros) Gulf. About twenty large hostile ships, some war vessels, some transports, could be counted in front of us. Some individual vessels were lying close in under the steep slopes of the coast. Others were farther out in the gulf or were still underway. From the broadsides of the war vessels came an uninterrupted stream of fire and smoke and the entire coast including our ridge was covered with shells and shrapnel. It was an unforgettable picture. Nowhere, however, could we see any debarking of troops from the transports.

After a while Essad Pasha, commanding the Third Army Corps, arrived on our heights and brought some detailed reports. The reports stated that British landing attempts at the south point of the peninsula had so far been repulsed by the 9th Division, but that the enemy was tenaciously bringing up more and more troops. At Kabatepe (Gaba Tepe) things were going well; the enemy had not been able so far to get a footing. But at Ari Burnu the heights along the coast were in the hands of the British, though the 19th Division was on the march to recapture the former. No detailed reports had yet been received from the Asiatic side.

I directed Essad Pasha to find any ship he could and go to Maidos to take command of the southern part of the peninsula.

I myself had to remain for the present at Bulair because it was of the utmost importance that at this point the peninsula be kept open. The troops on the Asiatic side I knew were in the safe hands of Colonel Weber.

This was the beginning of the Dardanelles Campaign which was to last eight and one-half months and which, counting both sides, brought together over three quarters of a million men for battle on the Gallipoli peninsula.

The preparations of the enemy were excellent, their only defect being that they were based on reconnaissances that were too old and that they underestimated the powers of resistance of the Turkish soldier. Hence they failed to bring in the first few days the decisive results which would have converted this grand operation into a decisive and swift military achievement.

According to our estimation the enemy was using 80,000 to 90,000 men in trying for the first success, while the Fifth Army numbered at the most 60,000 men, from which total certain deductions should be made for troops guarding other places. Moreover the superiority of the enemy's artillery was so immense as to defy estimation. His means of transportation seemed almost unlimited. On April 25 the various posts of observation along our coast counted nearly 200 ships—warships and transports.

That General Hamilton did not consider his task an easy one, is shown by his address previous to the landing which, in translation, reads:

General Headquarters,
21st April, 1915.

Soldiers of France and of the King

Before us lies an adventure unprecedented in modern war. Together with our comrades of the Fleet, we are about to force a landing upon an open beach in face of positions which have been vaunted by our enemies as impregnable.

The landing will be made good, by the help of God and the Navy; the positions will be stormed and the War brought one step nearer to a glorious close.

"Remember," said Lord Kitchener when bidding adieu to your Commander, "Remember, once you set foot upon the Gallipoli Peninsula, you must fight the thing through to a finish."

The whole world will be watching your progress. Let us prove ourselves worthy of the great feat of arms entrusted to us.

IAN HAMILTON, *General.*

Even his enemy recognizes that the troops of General Hamilton fought with the utmost bravery and tenacity in this landing and did honor to his confidence.

In the course of April 25 the transports in the Gulf of Saros (Xeros) repeatedly put out boats which sought to approach the coast but retreated under our fire. This action appeared to me to indicate a demonstration. It was noted that the transports were not deep in the water as could be seen on the sides of the ships. The decks of all transports were lined with dense rows of vertical branches so that it could not be seen whether there were troops on board. But the artillery fire of the warships continued without interruption.

In the afternoon the chief of staff sent word from Gallipoli that according to the reports received all enemy attempts to land in Besika (Bashika) Bay had been repulsed, and that perhaps it might be a demonstration.

Soon a telegram came from Essad Pasha from Maidos, that in the southern part of the peninsula at Seddulbar (Sedd el Bahr) and at Eski Hissarlik in Morto Bay there was pressing need of reënforcements; that the enemy had gained a footing there and was constantly being reënforced; that Colonel Sami Bei, commanding the 9th Division, had put his last available troops into the fight. As the impression of a demonstration in the Gulf of Saros (Xeros) was more and more confirmed, I ordered the 7th Division, which I had stopped at the road fork southwest of Bulair, to embark that evening two battalions in the harbor of Gallipoli and despatch them during the night to report to Essad Pasha. At the same time I ordered the 5th Division, which stood in readiness at the eastern edge of the Gulf of Saros, to send at once three battalions to Scharkeui and to get them to Maidos during the night. All such shipments had to be made at night because enemy submarines had gotten through the straits and into the Sea of Marmara. On the forenoon of the 25th they fired at us on our height of Bulair from the rear.

On the Gulf of Saros (Xeros) I considered myself strong enough even if the enemy should attempt a landing during the night.

Late in the evening a report was received that all attempts of the enemy to land at Kabatepe (Gaba Tepe) had been repulsed and that the 19th Division had driven back the enemy troops, Australians and New Zealanders, advancing via Kodjadere (Koja Dere) and were now contending with them for the heights along the shore.

Considering a night landing in the Gulf of Saros (Xeros) still possible, I remained on the heights of Bulair until next morning. But the night remained quiet excepting for artillery fire; the ships frequently changed position. As the concentration of the hostile ships in the upper Saros Gulf was fully recognized as a demonstration by morning of April 26, I ordered that forenoon that further units of the 5th and 7th Divisions should be transported to Maidos by boat during the next night and that the field artillery of the two divisions march to Maidos by land. I placed Lieutenant Colonel Kiazim Bei, chief of staff of the Fifth Army, in command on the upper Saros Gulf with instructions to start all the remaining troops of the 5th and 7th Divisions for Maidos, if no landing was made during the next twenty-four hours.

This turned out to be the case, hence the upper Saros (Xeros) Gulf was almost completely denuded of Turkish troops while the enemy war and transport vessels continued their demonstration to detain troops there. Finally Lieutenant Colonel Kiazim Bei had only a depot pioneer company and a few labor battalions which he made pitch their tents on the edges of the ridges to indicate the presence of troops. The withdrawal of all troops from the shores of the upper Saros Gulf was a serious and far reaching decision for me as responsible leader. But it had to be risked on account of the great superiority of the enemy in the southern part of the peninsula. Had the British noticed this weakness, they probably would not have hesitated to take decisive advantage of it.

The British ships bombarded Gallipoli from the Saros (Xeros) Gulf with indirect fire from their heavy calibers and destroyed a number of houses, chiefly near the harbor.

When the reënforcements from the 5th and 7th Divisions reached Maidos early on the morning of April 26 Essad Pasha sent them at once to the south group at Seddulbar (Sedd el Bahr) because there the fighting was most severe. Some small detachments of the 5th Division had to be sent to Ari Burnu to reënforce the 19th Division.

In the first few days after the landing it was difficult to preserve the organizations intact because the degree of danger determined the use of any reënforcements.

On arriving with his division Lieutenant Colonel von Sodenstern, commanding the 5th Division, took command at Seddulbar (Sedd el Bahr) and I placed Essad Pasha in command of the front at Ari Burnu.

I myself with my two German companions, the Captain of Cavalry Prigge and Veterinary Captain Thieme, took quarters in the tents of Essad Pasha at Maltepe, a hill four and one-half kilometers from the battlefield of Ari Burnu. The staff of the Fifth Army remained for the present in Gallipoli.

After severe and bitter fighting for four days with varying success, the 3rd Division under command of Lieutenant Colonel Nicolai inflicted heavy losses on the French who had landed at Kum Kale and had advanced to Yeni Shehr—colonial troops and 175th Infantry Regiment—drove them back to their ships during the night of April 29 and rid the Asiatic side completely of the enemy. In view of the general situation this was of great value. In the first place the fortress was no longer menaced on its most sensitive side, and the 11th Turkish Division could now be withdrawn to the principal disputed points in the southern part of the Gallipoli peninsula.

The Division started at once to march to Tschanakale (Chanak) in successive detachments, crossed the straits to the European shore by boat during the ensuing nights, and joined the front at Seddulbar (Sedd el Bahr). The 3rd Division, after detaching various troops to the battlefields of the peninsula, remained alone now in guarding the Asiatic shore south of the mouth of the Dardanelles.

In order to understand the following brief description of the battles of the Gallipoli Campaign, it should be stated here that they were fought almost exclusively by troops of the Fifth Army and that the Turko-German Navy could not take much part in them.

I have found that quite erroneous ideas existed in Germany where it was frequently maintained in speech and in writing that in the Gallipoli Campaign, which was so important for the outcome of the war, the Turkish Army and Navy took equal parts in the fighting.

The Turko-German fleet took no direct part except that it furnished to the Fifth Army two machine gun detachments with about twenty-four machine guns which were of great benefit. The *Haireddin Barbarossa* and *Tourgout Reis*, the old *Weissenburg* and *Woerth*, assisted in the first few weeks after the landing with indirect fire from the straits against the British landing places and ships near Ari Burnu. The movements of a Turkish torpedo boat in the lower part of the straits during the night of the 12th of May and the, unfortunately very brief, activity of the German submarines will presently be discussed. The *Goeben* and the *Breslau* did not ever throughout the campaign of eight and one-half months, come into the Dardanelles.

The separate German naval detachment under Admiral von Usedom was tied to the works and batteries of the Dardanelles fortress and of the Bosporus and had no direct part in the many battles and engagements of the Fifth Army on the Gallipoli peninsula. The tasks of the special detachment all lay on the interior of the straits, while the big battles were fought on the exterior coasts, except those of the south group which took place on the inner coast. The guns of the fort of In Tepe on the Asiatic shore did valuable work against the landing place and the camps at Seddulbar (Sedd el Bahr), and against the communications leading thence northward, but could do nothing against the battle fronts farther north on account of the distance and the intervening terrain.

A frequent and prolonged bombardment of the coast at Seddulbar (Sedd el Bahr), and of the Bay of Morto from the Asiatic side could not be kept up till autumn on account of lack of ammunition for the guns of the fortress.

I have no doubt that the bombardment from In Tepe frequently proved harrassing to the enemy and that he sometimes assigned special ships to bombard these batteries. But all this remained secondary in comparison with the great battles on the peninsula.

Later Enver ordered several heavy batteries of the fortress to be attached to the Fifth Army which had no heavy guns of any kind.

Soon after the landing Enver Pasha wired urgent orders from Constantinople to drive the strong British landing force at Seddulbar (Sedd el Bahr), Tekke Burnu and Morto Bay from the peninsula. That was the aim of the Fifth Army also but the execution exceeded our powers.

The naval guns of the enemy completely covered the southern part of the peninsula with their fire from three sides. As seen from the position of Sodenstern's group, the dense lines of the gray ships and the confusion of masts and smokestacks suggested the idea of a great harbor. The leader of the naval machine gun detachment, the brave Lieutenant Boltz, gives the following account of his impression on reaching the battlefield of Seddulbar (Sedd el Bahr) on the evening of May 3rd:

The battle field presented a grand and awful spectacle. The point of the peninsula was surrounded by a circle of war ships and transports. The ships' guns, assisted by great search lights, maintained a terrible fire against the Turkish lines.

The enemy ships protected the landed troops in the fullest sense of the word. We on our side in those days had nothing but field artillery, which was badly needed to repulse the enemy's land attacks and which even then had to economize its ammunition. Their power and range precluded any action against the ships.

Nothing remained but to drive the landed troops back to their ships by night attack. On orders from the Fifth Army Colonel von Sodenstern made the attempt during three nights.

Reënforcements now gradually arriving from Constantinople were attached to his force.   All three attacks were successfully carried forward during darkness, one of them got close to Seddulbar (Sedd el Bahr), but the purpose could not be accomplished.   In each case daybreak brought an overwhelming fire from the ships which compelled the Turks to withdraw to their positions.   Only a part of the captured machine guns could be carried off.

Painful as it was for me, I now had to give orders to abstain from further attacks on the Seddulbar (Sedd el Bahr) front and to remain on the defensive.   But not an inch of ground was to be yielded as the enemy was not far from Eltschitepe (Achi Baba) ridge, his next great objective.   I ordered the Turkish troops of the first line to entrench themselves as close to the enemy as possible.   A distance of a few paces between the hostile lines would inhibit the fire from the ships which would now equally endanger the troops of both sides.   This was explained to the leaders and to their troops.

Since the Dardanelles Campaign is the only great operation in the World War where a land army had to do steady battle against a hostile army and navy, it must be stated here that the artillery effect of the hostile battleships constituted a support of extraordinary power for the landing army.   No heavy land artillery can so easily change position and direct its fire on the enemy's flank and rear as was possible to the guns of the ships. Add to this that the ships' guns could direct their fire as on the firing ground without being under fire themselves, and that observation was assisted by captive balloons and aviators, in both of which the Fifth Army was wholly deficient.

At Ari Burnu we had likewise failed to drive the enemy from the coast.   On the 29th of April a strong Turkish attack was driving part of the landed Australians and New Zealanders from the ground they had gained and they were beginning to reembark when reënforcements hurriedly arrived and the arrival of battleships restored the situation.   It should be kept in mind that the enemy's base, the Island of Imbros, was not more than twenty kilometers from Ari Burnu where the British maintained ample reserves of troops and ships.

Later the Anzac corps—Australians and New Zealanders—made several strong attacks on the Turkish lines after preparation by the heaviest kind of naval bombardment. They invariably failed with heavy loss.

After the first two weeks of the bloody battles it became imperative to order Essad Pasha to abstain from any extensive attack until further orders, and to defend our positions on the ridges obstinately; to use every bit of favorable ground and every dark night to push our foremost lines to within a few paces of the enemy. In this way we here also deprived the British of the support of the ships' fire against the foremost Turkish trenches.

Thus on both fronts which had remained in the enemy's hands after his great landing, the mobile war gradually assumed the character of a war of position in the first third of May.

The few villages of the peninsula situated in the sectors of the two battle fronts or in their rear, suffered severely from the fire of the British ships. The prosperous port of Maidos went up in flames on April 29 under the fire of the British ships. The first building to become the victim of British naval shells was the large local hospital which was crowded with wounded. In spite of every effort many Turks and some twenty-five wounded British became victims of the conflagration, which spread with irresistible force. Many peaceful inhabitants likewise perished. Men, women and children, who were trying to save their most indispensable possessions, had to be removed from their houses under a rain of projectiles. From Kilid Bay they were transferred to the Asiatic side to save their lives. In Maidos, which was not fortified or occupied by staffs or troops, not a single house or wall remained intact.

Similarly other Turkish villages, for instance Kodjadere (Koja Dere), were levelled to the ground, and others like

Bulair, Kara Burgas, Jenikeui and the town of Gallipoli, were heavily damaged. With the same moral right with which the reconstruction of the destroyed parts of Belgium and northern France is insisted on, the Turks might ask for the reconstruction of all those places on the peninsula of Gallipoli which were destroyed though they were of no military value.

Similarly to the villages in the interior of the narrow peninsula, Ak Bashi and Kilia, ports of the Fifth Army on the European shore of the Dardanelles, were subjected to heavy indirect fire. They were the debarking ports for most of the food and military supplies.

The bringing up of food to the Fifth Army was especially difficult. The railroad station in Usunköpri (Uzun Kupru) in Thrace was seven marches distant and the means of transport were very limited. In those days the armies in Turkey had no auto trucks and it was with much difficulty that the columns of camels, pack animals and Turkish ox wagons managed to get a few tons to the front. Hence the Fifth Army had to depend for its supplies almost completely on water transport through the Sea of Marmara where British and French submarines tried to close this line. It was fortunate that the submarines could not do it, otherwise the Fifth Army would have died of hunger.

In judging the action of submarines it should be noted that in the narrow and open Sea of Marmara four or five submarines operating at the same time were unable to stop transportation by boat. Several Turkish ships were torpedoed, but the majority came through and reached their destination by steaming at night from etape to etape. Various things came to the debarking stations by sailboat and towed mahones.

Meanwhile Colonel Weber became available on the Asiatic side and on May 5 took over the command of the south group from Colonel Sodenstern, who had been severely wounded in the knee and had to be sent to Constantinople. The front of the south group stretched about one and one-half kilometers south of Kirte (Krithia) approximately east and west across the narrow peninsula from the Aegean shore to that of the Dardanelles. Both sides began to construct complete systems of field fortifications in three and more lines, with numerous dugouts and many kilometers of approaches. The tools with which the two sides worked were sadly different. The enemy controlled all the resources of the world and possessed the most modern war material, the poor Turks had few entrenching implements and frequently had to capture the tools for the construction of their field works from the enemy. The wood and iron for the dugouts were collected from the destroyed villages. Not even sand bags could be procured in anywhere nearly sufficient quantity. When a few thousands of them arrived from Constantinople, there was danger of their being used by the troop leaders for patching the ragged uniforms of their men. It was due solely to the stoic calmness of the Anatolian soldier and to his freedom from wants that all these difficulties were overcome.

The officers no longer had the same nerve as the soldier. I received repeated and urgent suggestions from various parties during the ensuing weeks to move the battle front of the south group back to the Eltschitepe (Achi Baba), because the plain south of Kirte (Kritha) afforded no natural positions. After acrimonious discussions I declined all these suggestions as they would have completely broken down my principle of a step by step defense. It was plain that the farther I withdrew to the north, the more troops were required for the defense, because the peninsula broadened out in that direction. Furthermore a line of defense abreast of the Eltschitepe (Achi Baba), visible from every direction, would have offered an excellent target to the overwhelming fire of the naval guns. The events justified me.

On the front of Ari Burnu, commanded by Essad Pasha, the much rent mountainous terrain afforded to the Turks better conditions for their field works than was the case on the south front. Since the line of defense ran north and south, the ships' guns could fire in one direction only or at best at a slightly flanking angle. It was one of the reasons that on this front the enemy's progress, in spite of all the bravery of the Australians and New Zealanders, was limited, so that in some places the British positions were but 800–1200 meters inland from the landing.

The reënforcements reaching the Fifth Army about this time comprised the 4th Division, followed by the 13th, 15th and 16th Divisions, i.e., the Fifth Army Corps whose detachment to the Caucasus I had once prevented.

In addition to these fresh troops we gradually received some heavy artillery though of old or antiquated models. It was needed because the opposing army was putting more and more heavy guns of various calibers on land and in position.

The ammunition supply of the Fifth Army was difficult. There was plenty of infantry ammunition, but artillery ammunition was inadequate from the beginning. As there were no efficient artillery ammunition factories in Constantinople and as neutral countries would not permit the passage of German ammunition, the Turkish batteries had to economize ammunition from the beginning of the battles. Considering the many other difficulties of the Turks this was hard in comparison with the unlimited ammunition of the enemy.

In the spring Captain Pieper (German Navy) established an artillery ammunition factory in Constantinople; the relief was slight because neither the machines nor the materials were of the proper standard.

On observing the effect of this ammunition we soon came to the conclusion that the British did not think much of it. Prisoners stated that of twenty shells on an average but one would explode. But this help was nevertheless welcome for it happened that some batteries had to fire blank ammunition to make the infantry believe that it was supported by artillery fire.

In May the headquarters were brought up from Gallipoli

and placed in camp about five kilometers behind the Ari Burnu front and three kilometers from the village of Boghali. The camp was so well fitted into the terrain among low pines that it was never discovered by the enemy's aviators. Precautions were taken to prevent roads leading to it from becoming visible. That it was nevertheless bombarded several times was an accident and due to the fact that the whole of the narrow peninsula was sometimes deluged by the enemy's naval guns.

On the 10th of May the well trained 2d Division arrived from Constantinople; I placed it in rear of the Ari Burnu front in order to drive the enemy from this part of the coast by a last decisive attack. During the night from the 18th to the 19th of May it advanced against the center of the enemy's position, broke through the first lines and penetrated the second. But the British armament for close combat and the reserves were so strong that a decisive result could not be gained. On both sides the losses were so great—our brave 2d Division lost nearly 9,000 in killed and wounded—that the local British commander requested a brief suspension of hostilities to bury his dead, which I granted for the 23rd of May. This is the only instance where battle action in the Dardanelles was suspended for a brief space of time.

I feel that the attack was an error on my part based on an underestimation of the enemy. Its preparation by our artillery, weak in numbers and deficient in ammunition, was bound to be insufficient for the purpose.

We now gradually gathered the impression that the enemy was seeking the decision on the south front at Seddulbar (Sedd el Bahr) as he constantly increased his reënforcements and renewed his severe attacks. At Ariburnu (Ari Burnu) on the other hand there were few combined attacks during the first few weeks and action was somewhat desultory. Small actions succeeded each other day and night, sometimes increasing somewhat, in various places.

In the month of May the Turko-German fleet brought us some

temporary relief by its action against enemy war vessels. On the evening of May 13 the Turkish torpedo boat *Muavanet-i-Miliet* under Lieutenant Firle sank the British battleship *Goliath* in the southernmost part of the Dardanelles near Morto Bay by a few torpedo discharges. The attack was so well prepared and so sudden that the Turkish torpedo boat was able to withdraw through the straits without damage.

On the 25th and 27th of May the recently arrived German submarines scored two great successes in that Lieutenant Hersing torpedoed the British battleships *Triumph* and *Majestic* off the outer coast of the peninsula. The enemy now temporarily withdrew the greater part of his battleships to the protected ports of Imbros and Lemnos and during the next few weeks the artillery support of the landed army came chiefly from the destroyers and torpedo boats. At the same time, however, all the effective means of defense against submarines were put in operation by the enemy who had at his disposal every kind of material he wanted. Thereafter the German submarines were unable, during the next seven months of the campaign, to score any success against the hostile fleet, except that they torpedoed a transport.

As early as June 16th I had to telegraph to the naval chief, Admiral Souchon in Constantinople, that the enemy was again using his large transports unhindered in transferring and relieving his troops. On June 20 I telegraphed him that the enemy war vessels had begun the same activity with their artillery as before the success of the submarines. On June 29th I informed him that in a large attack on the preceding day against the right flank of the south front, they had strongly coöperated with their fire and were doing the same on June 29th in the still continuing battle on the south front. The idea expressed in German papers, that the coöperation of the submarines had broken the backbone of the attack against the Fifth Army on the Gallipoli peninsula, was therefore quite erroneous. At home such erroneous statements led to a false estimation of the efficiency of the submarines.

In the very hot summer of 1915 the invariably calm sea and the clear steady air greatly assisted the artillery fire of the hostile fleet and facilitated the direction of artillery fire by means of aeroplanes and captive balloons. The roar of the guns on the coasts of the peninsula never ceased day or night. When the land batteries ceased firing, the ships' guns began, and *vice versa*. In all the attacks the guns on land and on shipboard coöperated.

The only German organization which took a part in the Dardanelles campaign on the Gallipoli peninsula joined the Fifth Army toward the end of June. It was an extemporized German pioneer company whose non-commissioned officers and men had gotten into Turkey as travellers by various routes. This pioneer company with a strength of 200 men was attached to the south group at Seddulbar (Sedd el Bahr). In consequence of the torrid climate and Turkish subsistence to which they were not used and of severe losses in battle, its numbers were soon reduced to forty men. They were now distributed on both fronts to act as foremen. In this capacity they rendered valuable service.

No other German unit reached Gallipoli during this campaign. Individual German officers and non-commissioned officers, the latter mostly from the artillery, were employed at the various headquarters and with the troops of the Fifth Army.

On account of severe losses and the constant battles, part of the Turkish troops on the south front had to be relieved. They were relieved by fresh troops of the Second Turkish Army and the chief of the Second Army, Wehib Pasha, relieved Colonel Weber in command of the south group at Seddulbar (Sedd el Bahr). Wehib Pasha was the younger brother of Essad Pasha who was in command at Ari Burnu. It was a good thing that these closely united brothers were the chiefs of the two battle groups. It eliminated jealousy and lack of coöperation so common among Turkish general officers. In this position Wehib Pasha, an energetic man, proved himself in every way a determined and far seeing leader and this commendation applies equally to the older brother at Ari Burnu, the knightly and valorous Essad Pasha, the celebrated defender of Janina in the Balkan War.

Just as the troops at Seddulbar (Sedd el Bahr) were being relieved by those of the Second Army on July 13, a heavy Anglo-French attack materialized which was repulsed with difficulty and not without the use of the last reserves. It was fortunate for us that the British attacks never lasted more than one day, and were punctuated by pauses of several days. Otherwise it would have been impossible to replenish our artillery ammunition.

During the second half of July rumors were increasing that another great landing was imminent. A report arriving via Salonika on the 16th spoke of the concentration of 50,000 to 60,000 men on the Island of Lemnos alone and gave the number of war and transport vessels assembled there as 140. Other sources named higher figures. The probability of another landing lay above all in the fact that the heavy battles of the past months had not brought the enemy sensibly nearer to his objectives. At that time the English Minister Churchill stated in a much quoted speech that the final success of the landed army was now in prospect.

Along the front there were hardly any indications where this landing might be expected. Both flanks of the south front rested on the water, on the west the sea, on the east the Dardanelles. There the front might be reënforced, but it could not be extended.

On the Ari Burnu front both flanks were open. The British southern wing had made several attempts to gain ground. The only result was that the Turkish left was slightly bent back. On the British north flank a detachment, little more than a battalion, had been detached from the flank and pushed some distance to the north. It appeared to me of some significance, but Essad Pasha did not see any danger in it. Several attempts to drive this detachment back—adding even the headquarters guards to the attack,—met with strong resistance and failed.

These were the only indications which pointed to an intention to extend the front in that quarter. The indications were rather insignificant. There was the possibility of an attack against the narrow isthmus on the upper Saros (Xeros) Gulf to cut the peninsula completely from Constantinople. The prior failure on the Asiatic shore precluded a renewed landing in that quarter.

The open space between the Ari Burnu front and the south front was the source of the greatest anxiety of the Fifth Army because a landing in that space would have endangered the rear of the south front.

When in consequence of the relief of some troops from the south front and of the arrival of reënforcements, a few units became available, the 3rd Division under Colonel Kannengiesser was pushed into the open space to the western slopes of Kajal Tepe Hill.

To the north of Essad Pasha's troops, from Anafarta Sagir on the Azmak Dere to Suvla Bay, the coast was guarded by a detachment of three battalions, one squadron and four batteries under command of the Bavarian Major Willmer. The infantry consisted of the gendarmery battalion Brussa, the gendarmery battalion Gallipoli and parts of the 33rd Infantry regiment. On the upper Saros (Xeros) Gulf the 7th and 12th Divisions were placed in readiness.

In the midst of these preparations for an expected new landing I was surprised by instructions from the chief of the general staff of the German field army to come to the German headquarters for a conference. 1 realized at once what this recall from a hot battle front to a far distant headquarters meant. I here quote verbatim the communications concerned so that every one may form his own opinion:

General Headquarters 8th July 1915. In receiving my report of the events on the Dardanelles H. M. the Emperior charges me to express to

Your Excellency His warmest appreciation of your work. H. M. knows that Your Excellency has fully realized the extent of the task confided to you in its relation to the course of the war and firmly relies on your superior leadership, etc.

Sgd. VON FALKENHAYN.

General Headquarters 22nd July 1915. To the military attaché. From reports received here it seems probable that at the beginning of August a strong attack will be made on the Dardanelles, perhaps in connection with a landing in the Gulf of Saros (Xeros) or on the coast of Asia Minor. It will be well to economize ammunition.

Sgd. VON FALKENHAYN.

General Headquarters 26th July 1915. General von Falkenhayn identically to the Turkish government, Enver Pasha, and General Liman von Sanders—In order to inform the chief of staff of the German field army of the situation at the Dardanelles His Majesty the Emperor would appreciate it with thanks if the Turkish government would send General Liman von Sanders to the general headquarters. Field Marshal Freiherr von der Goltz is available to take his place in command of the Dardanelles. If desired the military attaché, Colonel von Lossow, could be designated as his chief of staff."

Thus at this critical moment a change of command was intended which I had not foreseen after the first telegram. My answer addressed July 28th to the German Chief of the Military Cabinet is as follows:

It has been requested that I be sent to general headquarters to inform General von Falkenhayn of the situation at the Dardanelles. This instruction is issued after I have led the Fifth Army for three months in uninterrupted battles, after Enver has frequently expressed to me his thanks and confidence, at a moment when heavy enemy attack is imminent, while General von Falkenhayn has nothing whatever to do with these operations. I stress that it is not His Majesty that has ordered me to a conference. At the same time Field Marshal Freiherr von der Goltz is suggested as my successor and as his chief of staff the military attaché whose duty it is to render the required reports. Since my recall is certainly not requested by the Turkish government or by Enver, I request information whether it is the desire of His Majesty the Emperor that I request my discharge and separation from the Turkish service. Liman von Sanders.

Within two days I received the reply that for the present my recall was deferred, but that it was the desire of general headquarters that Colonel von Lossow be attached to my staff. He arrived shortly thereafter, but did not stay long, as I had absolutely no official work for him.

Soon thereafter I heard from Constantinople confidentially and in detail the circumstances of this affair which had originated in Constantinople and in which Enver had no part. I will say no more about it here in order not to interrupt the account of the severe and heavy struggles with the recital of political intrigues.

Less serious than the foregoing affair was alarming news from Constantinople about an imminent new great landing. I will quote but one. The adjutant of the military mission informed me from a reliable source that the success of this new enemy enterprise was counted on with such certainty that already windows were being rented in Pera Street for the entry of the British troops and that the British Embassy was being put in order and the beds newly covered. I merely replied that I requested him to order a window for me too in Pera Street.

Other sources reported of impending landings at Aivalik and Smyrna, etc.

CHAPTER 9

THE SECOND PART OF THE DARDANELLES CAMPAIGN

On the evening of August 6 the new grand operations of the enemy began, during which gradually five fresh British divisions—among them a dismounted cavalry division—were landed on the Gallipoli peninsula between Ari Burnu and the north end of Suvla Bay. At the same time severe attacks were made on the south group at Seddulbar (Sedd el Bahr) and on the left wing of the Ari Burnu group.

Essad Pasha at first believed that the decisive attack was directed against his left wing. But on the evening of the 6th it was discovered that from the beach at Ari Burnu the enemy was moving northward along the coast and that still farther north strong forces were being disembarked at various points. This was the decisive moment.

The first reports were received at the headquarters of the Fifth Army toward 9 p.m. Kiazim Bei, the chief of the general staff, had gone late in the afternoon to Ari Burnu for a conference with Essad Pasha and was unable to return during the next few hours because the entire country in rear of Ari Burnu was under severe fire.

Immediately upon receipt of the foregoing report I telephoned to the 7th and 12th Divisions on the upper Saros (Xeros) Gulf, ordering that they be alarmed and made ready to march at once. About an hour later orders were sent to start both divisions at once in the general direction of Usun-Hisirli east of Anafarta Sagir. Essad Pasha that evening alarmed the 9th Division and ordered it to march northward.

As the division approached the Kodjaschimendag (Koja Chemen Tepe) mountains, a report came that British infantry was ascending the mountain from the north. The first of the enemy's riflemen had reached the top when the advanced parts of the 9th Division were still climbing the last part of the acclivity. After a brief engagement the Turks occupied the height and drove the British back to the northern slopes. The brave leader of the 9th Division, Colonel Kannengiesser, was shot through the breast as he reached the top at the head of his troops.

This was the first crisis that we had to overcome in the Anafarta battles. It was of great importance because the whole Ari Burnu front would have had to be drawn back, had the enemy been able to retain possession of the summits of this massive height. It dominated the Anafarta valley to the north, and on the south afforded artillery positions toward the straits of the Dardanelles a long stretch of which was in full view.

In the Anafarta valley north of the dry bed of the Azmak Dere the British had taken the Mastan Tepe hill on August 7 which was defended by a company of the gendarmery battalion Brussa and the 2d Battalion of the 33d Regiment. They failed, however, to gain the summit of Ismail Tepe which joins on to the Mastan Tepe on the east.

On the morning of August 7th reënforcements were sent to the important Kodjaschimendag (Koja Chemen Tepe). The first to be sent was the 4th Division under Djemil Bei from behind the right of the south group, reënforced on his own initiative by Wehib Pasha from his own division though he himself was heavily attacked several times that day.

On the afternoon of August 7th the commanding general of the Sixteenth Corps, consisting of the 7th and 12th Divisions, reported to me the arrival of the corps, to my great surprise. He stated that the troops had made a double march on that day.

I therefore in person gave this commander orders to attack in the Anafarta plain on both banks of the Azmak Dere at daybreak on August 8.

The British divisions continued to extend northward.

The weak coast guard of Major Willmer fought splendidly but they could not forever resist an enemy who was constantly being reënforced. The more British troops landed, the more risky became the situation in the Anafarta valley. Hence it was necessary that the 7th and 12th Divisions attack without delay.

On August 7 orders had also been given to Mehmed Ali Pasha, commanding the troops on the Asiatic side, to send all battalions not in the first line, to TschanakKale (Chanak); they were to cross the Dardanelles by boat to Kilia and Ak Bashi during the next night.

On the morning of the 8th of August I rode before daybreak to the ground where the Xeros Corps was to form for attack in the general direction of Gr. Anafarta (Anafarta Sagir). I found no troops there. Finally I saw the general staff officer of the 7th Division who reported that he was selecting an outpost position. I heard from him that large portions of the two divisions were far in rear and were closing up and that certainly no attack could be made that morning. I now ordered the attack for the evening beginning at sunset. This would have the advantage that in the darkness the fire of the hostile fleet would not have much effect.

When toward evening I learned from Major Willmer that the troops of the Sixteenth Corps had not yet reached the assembly place designated by me, I called the commanding general to account; he replied that the fatigued state of the troops did not yet permit of an attack.

That evening I gave command of all the troops in the Anafarta section to Colonel Mustapha Kemal Bei, commander of the 19th Division, which was farthest north on the Ari Burnu front.

Mustapha Kemal, who earned his first military laurels in Cyrenaica, was a leader that delighted in reponsibility. On the morning of April 25th he had attacked with the 19th Division on his own initiative, drove the advancing enemy back to the coast and then remained for three months in the Ari Burnu front tenaciously and inflexibly resisting all attacks. I had full confidence in his energy.

On the morning of August 9 he took command of the thrice ordered attack on both sides of the Azmak Dere and pushed the enemy back toward the coast in several places. But the Mastan Tepe remained in the hands of the enemy. The lost twenty-four hours could not be made up. In the meantime considerable British forces had been disembarked.

This was the second crisis of the Anafarta battles. At the very last moment the advance of the enemy in the Anafarta valley had been definitely checked.

In the forenoon of August 10th Mustapha Kemal personally led an attack undertaken chiefly with reënforcements from the south group, against the British infantry next to the peak of the Kodjaschimendag (Koja Chemen Tepe) and the adjoining Jongbahir heights and drove them back a considerable way on the northern slopes. Possession of this dominant mountain was thus definitely secured for the Turks.

On August 15th came the third crisis on the northernmost part of the new landing front, on the steep and bald ridge of the Kiretch Tepe which runs northeast from the Suvla Bay and abruptly terminates the peninsula toward the Gulf of Saros (Xeros).

The position of the gendarmery battalion Gallipoli, with two guns on the Kiretch Tepe, had been attacked lightly on August 8 and more severely on August 9th by troops landed in Suvla Bay. The brave battalion had held its post. In the following days I sent all available parts of the 5th Division and some small detachments from the coast guard at Edje Liman (Ejelmer Bay) to this point and gave the separate command on the Kiretch Tepe to Major Willmer.

On August 15th the British attacked with strong forces. They were successful at first and advanced beyond the middle of the ridge. In this action the Gallipoli battalion was destroyed and its brave commander, Captain Kadri Bei, received

a mortal wound. On the 16th the attack was renewed with stronger forces. We estimated the enemy at one and one-half divisions.

The Turkish battalions from the Asiatic side were approaching from Kilia and Ak Bashi but had not yet reached the mountain. They were quickly brought forward after they had deposited their packs. The ascent of the Kiretch Tepe was difficult and the advance on the bald ridge was still more difficult because several war vessels in the Gulf of Saros (Xeros) opened a severe flank fire on this very conspicuous target, while at the same time the enemy in front held the Turkish troops under a heavy fire.

In the end, however, these troops were deployed by the side of the already deployed battalions of Major Willmer. In the evening the enemy had been pushed back beyond the middle of the ridge and the former position was again in our hands.

From now on the British were confined to the western portion of the ridge and its slopes and did not gain more ground in spite of many small attacks.

Thus the third crisis in our outer wing was successfully overcome.

If on August 15th and 16th the British had taken the Kiretch Tepe they would have outflanked the entire Fifth Army and final success might have fallen to them. The ridge of Kiretch Tepe and its southern slopes dominated the wide Anafarta plain from the north. From its eastern end a decisive attack could easily be pushed through the great depression extending toward Ak Bashi clear across the peninsula.

As it was, the landing troops had been checked not far from the coast and all dominating elevations in rear were in the hands of the Turks. Instead of pushing across the peninsula, driving back the Turks of the Ari Burnu and south fronts, or cutting them off completely, the result was merely an extension from the Ari Burnu front to the north.

There can be no doubt that in view of the great British superiority success would have been possible. The British knew where they wanted to land and could make the most explicit preparations. The Turks had to hold their troops in readiness for various eventualities and could only gradually concentrate them against the section selected by the British. The heavy British naval guns were available from the first moment in any desired strength, while the Turks were deficient in long range and heavy guns and the few that were available, could not be brought up except with much delay. On the British side all modern means of combat were available.

We all had the feeling that after the various landings beginning August 6th, the British leaders had delayed too long on the shore instead of advancing from the landing place at any cost.

The opponent of course does not know the reasons of the enemy. Since the weakness of the Turks in the Anafarta section was known, the British leaders may not have thought that reënforcements could be brought up so quickly, the more as large forces were tied to the two battle fronts by heavy attacks simultaneously made on them. Perhaps they had difficulty getting their young troops quickly forward over the cut up rocky terrain where there was hardly a road.

I mention the Kiretch Tepe as one of the most sensitive points of the Turks which would surely have fallen into British hands by a rapid advance from the shore during the first two days. It would have been impossible for the Fifth Army on the evening of the 6th of August and on the 7th to get reënforcements to this point, the distances being too great. The British possessed the means for such an advance on their extreme flanks, in their great transport fleet protected by war vessels. The British however began on their inner flanks and did not advance in force from the outer flanks until connection with the inner flanks was established by a continuous battle line.

The Fifth Army succeeded in parrying the Anafarta landing only by taking all available troops from adjoining fronts without regard for any dangers that might be threatening them. Thus for the second time the Saros (Xeros) Gulf was completely denuded of troops and on the whole Asiatic coast there were but three battalions and a few batteries left as coast guards. In order to deceive the enemy the batteries during the next few days were required to make marches in various directions which could be observed from the enemy's observing station on the Island of Tenedos. After dark they were invariably returned to their stations.

The decisive orders from the headquarters of the Fifth Army had been issued without delay, yet in the three crises the decision often hung on a knife edge.

The Anafarta landing was an enterprise planned on a grand scale, intended to open the Dardanelles to the Allies by land action while at the same time cutting the Fifth Army from its communications. If the Anafarta landing served to bring the Dardanelles Campaign to a tactical decision as desired by the British, the batteries of the fortress on the straits would have been quickly silenced as they had little ammunition. The mine-fields in the straits could then be removed and no further difficulties would lay in the way of combined action of the victorious British Army and the Allied fleet. In this case the lines of Tchataldja (Chalalja), not far from the gates of Constantinople, which had saved the city in the Turko-Bulgarian War, would be of little value, because both flanks would have been under the fire of the enemy's fleets. A Russian landing would no doubt have coincided with the Anglo-French operations. At that time many reports from Bucharest and Athens mentioned the concentration of troops and ships in Odessa.

Secure communication between the Western Powers and Russia would have been established and Turkey would have been split off from the Central Powers. In that case it is more than improbable that Bulgaria would have relinquished her neutrality and precipitated herself into such an unpromising military situation.

Thus the Anafarta landing, which in point of time lies approximately in the middle of the Dardanelles Campaign of eight and one-half months, was its political-military summit.

In the great Anafarta landing our fleet could give us no assistance except through the machine gun detachment formerly mentioned; they were first used on the Ismail Tepe. Submarines were not there. *Haireddin Barbarossa*, on the way to us with munitions and stores, had been torpedoed off Gallipoli by a British submarine on August 6th and had gone down. The fortress and the special naval detachment could take no part in the heavy and decisive battles on the distant exterior coast of the peninsula.

On the 21st of August the enemy combined all the troops recently landed on the new front in a grand attack on, and on both sides of, the Anafarta plain. It led to severe and bloody fighting but was repulsed by the Turks who had to use their last reserves including the cavalry. Various English papers stated the enemy's (British) losses as about 15,000 killed and 45,000 wounded. Between the 22d and 26th of August we had to transport 26,000 wounded to the rear. Most of them were sent by water to Constantinople because all the new hospitals established on the peninsula were inadequate on the days of great battles. The Turkish hospitals were assisted by the German Red Cross sanitary missions—the hospitals of Major von Trützschler, of Count Hochberg, who had organized splendid hospitals with his private means, and of Dr. Stutzin; but they were inadequate to meet such extraordinary demands. Nor did the hospital ships or the small steamers temporarily fitted up for the transport of the wounded suffice, though they were on the way day and night. It was great good fortune that the Fifth Army was not visited by any epidemic throughout the war.

After all effective troops had been withdrawn from the upper Saros (Xeros) Gulf on the 6th and 7th of August to reënforce the Fifth Army, the protection of the upper Saros Gulf, in the middle of August, was entrusted to the First Army commanded by Field Marshal General Freiherr von der Goltz. The field marshal transferred his headquarters to the town of Gallipoli.

Neither on that front nor on the Asiatic side was there any further fighting during this campaign. The fire of individual ships sometimes entering the upper Saros Gulf could do no real damage to the well protected troops any more than to the troops left on the Asiatic side.

The entire fighting power of the enemy was concentrated on the three main fronts of the peninsula of Gallipoli.

On the south front at Seddulbar (Sedd el Bahr) the enemy's advanced line had pushed forward to within about 1,200 meters south of Kirte (Krithia). The many attempts of the enemy to get a footing in Kirte—the village was a pile of ruins—were again and again repulsed. The right front of the allied group at that point consisted of two French divisions while three British divisions constituted the center and left wing. There was much shifting of sectors and in the distribution of troops.

On our side the south front under Wehib Pasha was held by five divisions, sometimes by four.

The enemy landed more and more batteries, but on the Turkish side we also had been able to improve the artillery. It was well and energetically led by the Turkish Lieutenant Colonel Assim Bei. The fighting on the south front remained severe throughout.

After the Anafarta landing the Ari Burnu front under Essad Pasha had been prolonged southward toward Kabatepe (Gaba Tepe) by a combined division because the enemy on his part tried hard to advance his lines and outflank us.

A small intermediate group on the Kajal Tepe maintained the connection with the south group and secured for us the possession of this ridge which flanks Maidos from the south.

The newly created Anafarta group under Mustapha Kemal defended the ground from the northern slopes of the Kiretch Tepe to the Kodjaschimendag (Koja Chemen Tepe) inclusive, closely connecting with the right flank of the Ari Burnu front. It consisted of six divisions. In this front, which crossed the Anafarta plain and was parallel to the coast, all command-

ing heights were in the hands of the Turks and crowned by
Turkish artillery. Unfortunately the artillery was not numerous nor modern, barring the field guns, and ammunition was
short. Otherwise the British would not have been able to
remain long in the lower portions of this front.

The extreme Turkish right on the Kiretch Tepe—made into
the 11th Division under Major Willmer—frequently received
flank fire from ships in the Gulf of Saros (Xeros), in addition to
the fire from the front. The only long range 8.8-cm. battery
and a few 15-cm. howitzers were sometimes pushed forward
after dark and surprised and drove away the ships, but these
mostly remained beyond our range.

Suvla Bay was the supply station for the northern part of the
British front and frequently we counted twelve or fifteen ships
lying there. It was protected by nets against submarines.
The broadsides of the war vessels lying there were frequently
directed not only against the 11th Division, but against our
positions of the 12th Division which adjoined the 11th on the
south.

The 12th Division, commanded by Colonel Selaheddin Bei
and later by Lieutenant Colonel Heuck, had established its
defensive line on the low ground in order to remain close to the
enemy. In rainy weather which was frequent in the fall, the
bottoms of their trenches were covered with water. The division had the slim satisfaction of knowing that the British on the
other side, and who were still closer to the coast and to the Salt
Lake, were at least as badly off.

Toward the south the 9th Division prolonged the line to the
Azmak Dere, its center of defense being the Ismail Tepe. South
of the Azmak Dere were three more Turkish divisions which
prolonged the line to the right of the Ari Burnu front.

From the Ismail Tepe and Kiretch Tepe the splendid artillery
commander of the Anafarta sector, Major Lierau, who had distinguished himself in the very first days of the landing, sank
many a British ship by the fire of his artillery. Many months

after the departure of the British any visitor could see hull after hull strewn along the northern coast line.

In September the entire artillery of the Fifth Army was placed under the command of Colonel Gressmann who had arrived from the western front; Colonel Wehrle had several weeks before assumed command of the heavy artillery of the Fifth Army.

The severe partial attacks of the enemy were frequently repeated in September and October without accomplishing any worthwhile result.

On the 4th of September we received one of the astounding reports from Turkish headquarters in Constantinople, which might have caused apprehension to weaker souls. I am stating it here verbatim as it may be of some interest to see what queer communications may reach a leader in war even officially.

General Headquarters
    No. 1478
                                Constantinople, 4 Sept. 1915
It is reported that the following is being planned:
While the large naval vessels at the mouth of the Dardanelles hold the attention of the forts and provoke the Turks to a great expenditure of ammunition, everything is to be in readiness to build rapidly a track, with material now there or en route, across the isthmus of Gallipoli (Bulair) for the transport of 200 naval boats from the Gulf of Saros (Xeros) to the Sea of Marmara. It is believed possible for these 200 well equipped boats to force Constantinople. Fifty of these boats hardly have the value of a crusier, so that even if a number of them, whose component parts were en route to the Dardanelles, should be lost in the attack on Constantinople, the loss would be small in comparison with the expected result.

Of course there was not a word of truth in it.

I made a note on the paper, "This is probably taken from the 'journey around the world in eighty days.' "

Several well known British papers had published such incorrect statements on August 23 about great British progress on the Gallipoli peninsula and false statements about the relations between the German and Turkish officers, that four weeks later when I learned of it, I sent the following telegram to the German headquarters to contradict the press, the contents of the telegram giving the view prevailing at our headquarters:

Camp at Boghali, 23 Sept. 1915

The Anafarta operations undertaken by the British in great strength may be considered a total failure. As at Ari Burnu, so in the Anafarta section and in Suvla Bay the British hold but a narrow strip directly on the coast where they are entrenched and have been able to maintain themselves under the protection of the fleet. Everywhere the British camps are directly on the coast. All elevations commanding this narrow strip of land in front are in possession of the Turkish Army. The communications on the peninsula are completely open and nowhere interrupted. All British attacks have been repulsed with enormous losses. The news of discord between Turkish and German officers are pure inventions. The dirty source, which is spreading such news from Constantinople, would like to spread discord and is unable to do so. Present relations between Turkish and German officers are the best imaginable. Both are proud of the continued success of the brave Osman Army.

Sgd. LIMAN V. SANDERS.

Among the funny things in those serious days was a letter received from a German-American who wrote me as follows:

Honored General,

Having read in the papers that you were wounded, then sick, that you had been murdered by Turkish officers, that you had fallen in disfavor with the Sultan and that you had been killed in battle, I now learn to my great joy from my friend, General Eisentraut in Cassel, that you are well, and am sending you my best wishes, etc., etc.

When Bulgaria joined the Central Powers in September, the Fifth Army hoped for an early opening of through transportation from Germany to Constantinople in order to get German war materials, particularly good artillery ammunition. The hope was not realized until November after the way had been opened through Servia.

The troops of the Second Army were gradually withdrawn from the south front in the second half of September and in the first half of October, in order to be prepared in Thrace, for other employment in conjunction with other troops. They were replaced on the south front by divisions of the First Army stationed on the Gulf of Saros (Xeros). They were for the most part of Arabian birth. Neither their training nor their prowess was sufficient for the continued heavy fighting on the peninsula. It soon became necessary to intermix with them good and proven troops, for instance the excellent four battalions of the fire regiment, to give them some backbone in defense. For the attack they were unfit.

The withdrawal of the Second Army at that moment was neither a necessary nor a happy measure. The enemy's pressure on all fronts continued so strong that the troops should have been regularly relieved, as was the case with the British. The decision of the Dardanelles Campaign was still in the distance and strong reserves were desirable to enable the Turks to resume the offensive at suitable points. In February 1916 the Second Army was still in Thrace and nothing had been done. With this change of troops Djevad Pasha, heretofore commanding the Dardanelles fortress, took over the command of the south front from Wehib Pasha.

About the middle of October Field Marshal General Freiherr von der Goltz was sent to Mesopotamia to command the Sixth Army. The Turkish headquarters placed Colonel Back in command of the army corps on the upper Saros (Xeros) Gulf.

The scouting of the Turkish troops improved greatly in the course of the campaign. There always were many volunteers for the many scouting parties. It is a mistake to say that the training of the Anatolian soldier is impossible beyond a certain degree. The only trouble is that it takes a long time before he assimilates and comprehends the training for offensive purposes. Under good enterprising non-commissioned officers he will meet all requirements in the war of position, in short attacks and in scouting. Later in Softatepe we found British orders commending the scouting of the Turks.

It seems that in the late fall the British authorities were no longer sanguine about a favorable ending of the campaign, as is evidenced by a telegram of Secretary Chamberlain of October 21st to the Viceroy of India in which he says "our situation and our prospects in Gallipoli are very uncertain."

A new landing on Gallipoli was once more announced from Germany on November 1st. It materialized no more than did the passage of the fleet through the Dardanelles announced from Berne on November 24th.

At last in November the long coveted German artillery ammunition reached the Fifth Army. Its arrival increased the hope of a successful ending of the campaign. The Turkish artillery was in excellent training and its firing was good, but with its poor ammunition it could not produce more than limited results. From now on it was different.

The first troops from the Central Powers arrived in Gallipoli November 15 for our active support. It was an excellent Austrian 24-cm. mortar battery which was posted on the left of the Anafarta front and soon opened a very effective fire against the Mastan Tepe. An equally good Austrian 15-cm. howitzer battery, which followed in December, was attached to the south group. No other non-Turkish troops reached Gallipoli before the withdrawal of the British. The total of all Germans employed there, officers, non-commissioned officers and soldiers, had increased to about 500.

Toward the end of November the Fifth Army began to work on a plan for an attack in force. It was planned to pierce part of the Ari Burnu front and the adjoining right wing of the Anafarta front and thus to force back the outer parts of these two fronts. Reënforcements for this purpose from the Second Army were promised by Turkish headquarters. Technical troops for the purpose were to be drawn from Germany. Under instructions from German headquarters Colonel von Berendt, Liuetenant Colonel Klehmet and Major Lothes came to Gallipoli to gather the requisite information and make preparations.

The divisions selected for the attack were taken out of the front and practiced for the attack on the instruction works erected behind the front.

The enemy anticipated the execution of the attack by his withdrawal from both the northern fronts. The withdrawal was due in the first place to Lord Kitchener as we learned later. He had in person visited all the fronts of Gallipoli in November and accurately informed himself of the conditions of the present offensive and of its chances if continued. After this inspection he deemed it best to give up the attack and stated that the withdrawal from the peninsula was feasible without great losses. Before this some other British leaders had considered a withdrawal from the peninsula very difficult. The events justified Lord Kitchener.

Since the aim of the Anafarta landing had not been accomplished, there was no prospect for the enemy to carry the attack to a successful ending with the means at hand. During the last few weeks the enemy's progress on all the fronts had been very limited and dearly paid for in blood. All dominating heights were in the hands of the Turks. The best plan probably for the British was to give up the attack. Though the first and innermost reason therefor was the hopelessness of success, there was the reflection that reënforcements would hardly be able to change the course of events after the Central Powers had opened the way to Turkey.

We of course knew nothing of the intended withdrawal and did not learn of it up to the last minute. Its possibility had been considered by the Fifth Army and all leaders had been called on in writing for special watchfulness in that direction. But the very skilful beginning and execution of the withdrawal prevented its being seen from the front line of the Turks.

On the night of the 19/20 December a dense fog covered the peninsula and the coast. The fire along the fronts continued in customary volume till midnight. Then it became a little weaker. The enemy's naval guns were firing from several directions. On the afternoon of the 19th a heavy attack on the south front had been repulsed. During the night the British withdrew from the Ari Burnu and Anafarta fronts.

The events on the side of the Fifth Army were as follows:

Between 1 and 2 in the morning the enemy had exploded a mine in the Ari Burnu front. The Turkish troops advancing according to instructions to seize the crater, found no resistance.

When the adjoining Turkish companies were feeling their way toward the foremost enemy trenches, there were a few shots and then firing ceased. The trenches were occupied by the Turks. Reports were despatched to the higher commanders. There was some natural delay before they could arrive and give instructions for further action, since no special instructions had been issued for such a case, and the fog prevented vision. Where the way led through the enemy's trench system, there were obstacles to be removed everywhere. In several places mines exploded when stepped on and caused confusion and loss. In this way the rearmost troops of the enemy had gained a good start. The fire of the ships covered the ground traversed by the advancing Turks. Though the road to the coast was short, the descent through the steep rocky hills of the coast in the dark foggy night was troublesome. When the leading troops reached the coast, the enemy had disappeared. The ships at once changed their aim to the beach.

The withdrawal on the Anafarta front was similar except that contradictory reports caused difficulties in the issuing of orders. In several places where the fog was less dense, red lights were visible on the shore and some of the subordinate leaders conjectured another landing.

The first reports that reached me at the headquarters camp at 4 a.m. were written in this dubious style. I at once ordered a general alarm and the turning out of all reserves including the cavalry. Each unit in its own sector was to advance in a direct line to the shore. But orders do not circulate as fast as one hopes, particularly when two languages are involved.

The troops of the Anafarta group encountered mine-fields which caused much loss. At some points short engagements took place with the rear points of the enemy, as in case of the Turkish 126th Infantry Regiment. Here too the enemy had embarked with hardly any loss. The withdrawal had been prepared with extraordinary care and carried out with great skill. The hostile artillery had been removed except a small number of guns which now fell into our hands. This removal had been possible because all British land batteries lay close to the shore.

One or another artillery commander had noticed that in the last few days some batteries had fired with one gun only or not at all, but no importance was attached to the fact which therefore was not reported to superiors. It had happened several times that the batteries paused one or two days in their firing, particularly when changing positions. On such occasions the fire from the ships became heavier.

Immense stores of all kinds were abandoned by the British on their withdrawal. Between Suvla Bay and Ari Burnu five small steamers and more than sixty boats were abandoned on the beach. We found large quantities of material for dummy rail lines, telephones and obstacles, piles of tools of all kinds, medicine chests, medical supplies and water filters.

A great mass of artillery and infantry ammunition had been abandoned and whole lines of carriages and caissons, hand arms of all kinds, boxes of hand grenades and machine gun barrels. Many stacks of conserves, flour, food and mountains of wood were found. The tent camps had been left standing and sacrificed. This probably served better than anything else to mask the withdrawal. Several hundred horses which could not be embarked were killed and lay in long rows.

How sudden the order for withdrawal must have come to the last troops on the peninsula appears from the fact that in some tents freshly served food stood on the tables. From the written orders found in the camp it appeared that a large part of the troops not in first line had been embarked during the past two nights and carried away. These captured British papers informed us of other interesting matters.

On the Anafarta front we found foot paths lined with whitewashed sandbags so as to be visible on a dark night. They had shown the last troops the way of carefully avoiding the minefields.

It should be taken in consideration in the entire withdrawal that the distance from the front lines to the shore was short, varying between one and four and one-half kilometers. Hence the British withdrawal from Gallipoli cannot be compared with the great rearward movements on European fronts, as has been done by some.

The enemy continued to hold the position at Seddulbar (Sedd el Bahr).

On the forenoon of December 20 orders were given by the Fifth Army to bring the best batteries of the abandoned fronts to the south group. In like manner it was ordered that the best grenade throwers, scouts and pioneers be at once put in march to the south group.

There was some possibility that in Seddulbar the enemy wanted to keep a base for further operations. The position there was particularly strong and well protected by the fire of the ships. The authors of this idea spoke of a second Gibraltar supplementary to the Salonika position. No such idea was entertained by the Fifth Army. It was thought possible, however, that the enemy might hang on for some time. That could not be permitted.

Hence a plan of attack on the enemy's position at Seddulbar was at once taken in hand, giving due consideration to the technical troops expected from Germany. An attack was prepared on the entire south front by the four divisions there and eight others to be brought up. No troops had to be taken from the Second Army since on the other fronts our own troops had become available and because only limited troops were needed to guard the coast. Superfluous units were ordered by the Turkish headquarters to march to Thrace.

New Year's Eve 1915/16 I sent to the military attaché in Constantinople a telegram for German headquarters, proposing that after the complete withdrawal of the British from Gallipoli, an army be constituted from our troops and pushed via Demotika and Xanthi against the right flank and rear of the enemy army at Salonika, while German and Bulgarian troops attacked from the front. From our point of view the Salonika Army of the Entente remained a constant reservoir for menacing the Turkish coast and threatened our only land communication with Europe, our sole bridge to the Central Powers. We were aware of course, that there were other considerations for the German head-quarters to weigh and that ours was merely a suggestion of Turkish cooperation in an attack on the Salonika front. No reply was received.

During the first days of January 1916 it appeared as though the fire of the land artillery at Seddulbar (Sedd el Bahr) was becoming weaker. But one gun was firing from several bat-teries, frequently changing its position, while the fire from the ships, including the largest calibers, sometimes grew to great vehemence. The removal of guns was observed from the Asiatic side. The scouting parties which were pushed forward against the hostile front at all hours of evening and night, invariably met with strong resistance. Of the troops designated for the attack, the 12th Division had arrived in rear of the south front. The division was designated to capture a section of trenches projecting northward opposite the extreme Turkish right, from which the British artillery could have flanked the great attack we were planning.

In the midst of these preparations the Turkish headquarters ordered on January 5 that nine divisions of the Fifth Army were to be withdrawn at once and put in march for Thrace. Several of these divisions had been designated for the attack. The situation on the south front had not become sufficiently clear for such a step nor was there any necessity for it, as the complete Second Army stood in Thrace. I explained the situation to Enver by telegraph and requested my discharge from the Turkish Army because his wholly unwarranted order was at the last moment jeopardizing the final result of the Dardanelles Campaign. He withdrew his order by telegraph. Like many other things in Turkey I have never been able to ascertain whether this matter, as was subsequently stated, was a misunderstanding due to another incorrect Turkish translation or whether the orders were actually issued in the form in which they reached me.

On January 7th I ordered the 12th Division to carry out the attack planned on the extreme Turkish right after two hours of preparation by the heaviest artillery fire and explosion of mines. It met with strong resistance, but was partly successful in that we gained some of the ground at the projecting point.

The Turkish troops on the south were cautioned again and again to watch attentively for any indication of a withdrawal during the night. Bridges were everywhere placed in readiness to enable the artillery to cross the enemy trenches quickly. A field artillery battalion of the 26th Division on the Asiatic side, under the command of Captain Lehmann, was ordered by the Fifth Army to push to the outermost point of land at Kum Kale, where during the night of 8/9 January it bombarded such ground at Seddulbar (Sedd el Bahr) as was within range. In like manner the fortress guns near In Tepe assisted by a heavy fire.

During the night from the 8th to the 9th of January the enemy withdrew from the southern sector. The Turkish troops pursued at once when the fire from the advanced trenches was no longer answered by the enemy. In some places there were bloody conflicts. But all in all the enemy here again was successful in his withdrawal in spite of all our watchfulness. A large part of the troops were not marched the longer way to the place of embarkation at the south point, but had reached the south shores of the peninsula by the shortest routes and were embarked at suitable points in every kind of war and transport vessels, while the last rear guard was still maintaining a heavy fire from the advanced trenches. Fireworks had been used to give the impression of lively firing and the artillery fire came from the ships.

The Turkish divisions reached the coast everywhere long before daybreak. In many places they had been delayed by fields of land mines which caused serious losses. One division had captured nine guns on the way to the coast.

When it became daylight, our artillery sank a loaded transport on the west coast. The hostile torpedo boats in the vicinity opened a heavy fire into the sea near the transport believing that it had been torpedoed by a submarine. Unfortunately none were present at the withdrawal.

The booty at the south group was extraordinary. Wagon parks, automobile parks, mountains of arms, ammunition and entrenching tools were collected. Here too most of the tent camps and barracks had been left standing, in part with all of their equipment. Many hundreds of horses lay in rows, shot or poisoned, but quite a number of horses and mules were captured and turned over to the Turkish artillery. Here as at the other fronts the stacks of flour and subsistence had some acid solution poured over them to render them unfit for our use. In the next few days the hostile ships made vain attempts to set the stacks and the former British tent camps and barracks on fire. It took nearly two years to clean up the grounds. The immense booty of war material was used for other Turkish armies. Many ship loads of conserves, flour and wood were removed to Constantinople. What the ragged and insufficiently nourished Turkish soldiers took away, cannot be estimated. I tried to stop plundering by a dense line of sentinels but the endeavor was in vain. During the ensuing time we saw the Turkish soldiers on the peninsula in the most incredible garments which they had made up from every kind of uniform. They even carried British gas masks for fun. ·

The tribute of tenacious and steadfast prowess cannot be withheld from the Turkish troops, of whom at the height of the fighting twenty-two divisions stood in the primary and secondary fronts or as reserves, under the command of the Fifth Army. They had held their ground in unnumbered conflicts with a brave enemy who ever renewed his attacks and was supported by the fire of his fleet.

The total loss of the Fifth Army in the Dardanelles Campaign is very high and corresponds to the duration and severity of the fighting. It amounted to about 218,000 men, of whom 66,000 were killed and of the wounded 42,000 were returned to duty. There were Turkish infantry regiments which in this campaign needed and received 5,000 replacements.

The Gallipoli peninsula remained under the command of the Fifth Army, the headquarters being transferred to Lule Burgas in Thrace toward the end of January. Djevad Pasha received the command of the peninsula.

Upon the completion of the Dardanelles Campaign I recommended to Turkish headquarters to place the Dardanelles, the only approach to Constantinople from the sea and a source of apprehension for centuries, on a different basis by constructing a canal west of Bulair. I stated that a second water way from the Sea of Marmara to the Ægean Sea would afford a secure exit to the Turkish fleet, which will always have to be based on Constantinople. The mouth of the Gulf of Saros (Xeros) is thirty kilometers wide and much more difficult to blockade than the narrow exit of the Dardanelles. As against the former, Tenedos was of no value and Imbros of partial value only. The north shore of the Gulf of Saros, to which could be brought all the resources of Thrace, would form one corner pillar after the erection of fortifications and shore batteries. The Asiatic coast of the Dardanelles could be made into the other pillar. The suggested canal was so far drawn back from the sea that if the north coast of the peninsula was properly protected, any hostile influence was precluded.

The economic effect of the construction of this canal for Turkey in Europe was bound to be considerable.   The site was located on the peninsula where the latter was but five kilometers wide, and its construction offered no technical difficulties as surveyed and attested by experts.   Perhaps the project will be resumed at some future time.

In the foregoing I have given a summary of the campaign in the Dardanelles from the point of view of the commander in chief, because little is known of the campaign in Germany.   A detailed description of battles must be left to the Turkish general staff.

CHAPTER 10

WARLIKE EVENTS ON OTHER TURKISH FRONTS DURING THE DARDANELLES CAMPAIGN

CAUCASUS

The Russians rested content with the complete defeat of the Third Turkish Army in January 1915 and made no further advance on the Sarikamisch-Hassan Kale road. Possession of the passes between Id and Olti gave fair protection to the left of the Third Turkish Army.

A detachment under Lieutenant Colonel Stange, operating from the extreme left flank and which had advanced as far as Ardahan, encountered superior forces near Artvin and had to withdraw. The detachment consisted of 1,000 regulars; attached to it were bands of volunteers organized by the committee of the *Défense nationale*.

In March 1915 the Russian Black Sea fleet became more active on the Turkish coast. The constructions at the coal mines of Songuldak and Eregli, and the harbor and city of Trebizond, were several times bombarded by Russian ships.

In April the bands of volunteers, which had been considerably reënforced, made a vain attempt on the fortress of Batum. The fortifications of Batum were not very modern and the garrison was small, but it was enough to repulse these irregular inferior units.

The Third Army, now under Mahmud Kiamil Pasha, whose able and energetic chief of staff, Major Guse, was the moving spirit at headquarters, had been reënforced to about 34,000 men by recruits, whose training left much to be desired.

In May the Russians became more active. They pressed the left flank of the Third Army back and the Turks had to relinquish Id. Near Tortum, about eighty kilometers northwest of Erzerum and situated among wild rocky mountains, the fighting continued with varying success until the middle of June.

More important was the Russian advance from their left in Armenia. There they took Tutak and Melazgerd in May and threatened Van and Bitlis. The insurrection of the Armenians had grown and the Turkish Vali had left his station in the city of Van. The Turks then sent a division to Bitlis which restored the situation but on July 12 it was attacked by the Russians and driven back. The indentation of the extreme right of the Turkish front became important later on.

In August the operations in these parts came to a standstill. The Turkish front extended from about the middle of Lake Van to the Turko-Russian frontier on the coast of the Black Sea. The snow had not left the high plateau until May and in September the first snows were falling in the mountains.

With the fall of the first snow the communications within the theater of operations became difficult because there were few constructed roads. Most of the roads on Turkish territory which appear on the map receive no official attention. Their breadth changed constantly depending on whether they went through open country or dwindled to narrow trails between walls of rocks and steep precipices. This must be kept in mind in considering any troop movements in and on the Caucasus. Most of the camps where recruits were trained for the Third Army, had been concentrated at Erzerum by fall. They averaged 20,000–25,000 recruits.

After communication by the Black Sea had become limited, the main line of communications of the Third Army was the Anatolian railway from Haidar Pasha as far as Ulu Kyschla. There it became a land line 500 kilometers long via Kaisaryeh and Sivas to Ersindjan (Ersingyan) whence it forked to the various sectors.

On the side of the Russians Grand Duke Nikolai had taken command in the Caucasus in the fall of 1915.

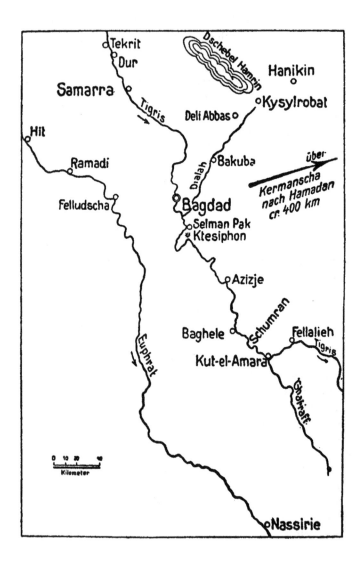

Between the Caucasus front and Mesopotamia the Russians occupied Urumia and Suj Bulak at the end of May 1915, driving away the Turkish troops. The Persians and Armenians at these places joined the Russians.

The operations of small detachments in this section were of no decisive importance.

IRAK

Subsequent to the occupation of Amara on June 3rd, 1915, the British took Kut-el-Amara on September 29th, after suffering considerable losses in driving back the Turks. General Townshend followed the Turks in the direction of Azizie. In the middle of November he began his advance on Bagdad. He had about 15,000 men for this purpose. It has been established by the commission investigating the events in Mesopotamia, that the advance was made with fatigued and insufficient forces, and that the organization of the transport lines was inadequate. The advance was checked November 22d at the battle of Ctesiphon. General Townshend had to fall back fighting to Kut-el-Amara which he reached on December 3rd, having suffered considerable losses. From Kut he was able to transport his sick and wounded by ship to Busra and on December 6th his camel brigade was still able to leave Kut. On December 7th the investment of the British troops in Kut was completed by the Turks.

The Turkish commander here was Colonel Noureddin Bei.

Field Marshal General Freiherr von der Goltz did not arrive in this theater until later. Soon after his arrival he prepared a general attack on Kut-el-Amara.

EGYPT

In February 1915 Colonel Freiherr von Kress had taken over the command in the desert. His problem was to keep the British stirred up by continuous small enterprises and to make preparations in the desert for a new expedition on a larger scale.

The course of political conditions in Syria and Palestine was even then being unfavorably influenced by Djemal Pasha. His harsh measures roused not only the Arabs, but also the Christian and Jewish population against the Turkish government.

In April Major Lauffer undertook an enterprise to interrupt traffic on the canal. The march was directed toward El Kantara and in the night of April 7/8 a mine was placed in the canal after great toil. But the anchoring was insufficient, the mine came to the surface and was rendered harmless by the British. Colonel Freiherr von Kress established his camp at Ibni, about eight hours' march from El Arisch. He was quite justified in his doubts whether in those days there was serious intention in Constantinople to renew the attack on the canal and whether in view of the campaign in the Dardanelles the Turkish headquarters was in position to supply the necessary means therefor. There was no doubt that without German help they could accomplish nothing here. There were needed in the first place German special troops, German aviators and German money. This support became more questionable in May after Italy had joined the Entente against Germany.

Between the 5th and 13th of May Colonel von Kress personally led a small enterprise against the canal without result as did other German officers who were leading scouting parties against the canal. The main objection to these small enterprises and of the flying columns ordered by Turkish headquarters was the fact that they all had to end in retreat and thus depressed the never strong morale of the Syrian troops.

There ensued a considerable pause in the operations in this theater of war. In those days the British could not without considerable risk withdraw large forces from Egypt or diminish their warships in the canal and at its entrances.

The climate of the desert soon became intolerable for Europeans.

On August 5th Colonel Freiherr von Kress assumed the

duties of chief of staff of Djemal Pasha commanding the Fourth Army, with headquarters at Ain Sofar in the Lebanon. Toward the end of August the headquarters were transferred to Jerusalem. The preparation for new and more extensive operations began with a demand for German general staff officers and other German assistance.

CHAPTER 11

THE MILITARY MISSION

At the beginning of 1916 the officers of the military mission and of those attached to it had reached the number of about 200. An order from the Military Cabinet of November 1st, 1915, invested the chief of the military mission with the rights and jurisdiction of a German Superior Army Commander and Councilor Gruetzmacher was assigned to the mission for the administration of German justice in Turkey. Dr. Collins, surgeon and senior medical officer, became the head of the German sanitary service in Turkey in December 1915. Through prolonged and indefatigable toil he raised the German medical institutions in Turkey to high excellence. His work was particularly beneficial in improving the very difficult sanitary conditions along the long line of communications. There he had to combat everywhere spotted typhus, malaria, dysentery and sometimes cholera, to the infection of which the German military persons were exposed in consequence of the filth customary in habitations, and of the numerous diseases within the Turkish Army, and of contact with the labor battalions stationed along the lines of communication.

As chief of the military mission, I had several unpleasant conflicts with Enver, of which I will mention a few to show the difficulties of a German in a high position in the Turkish Army.

As stated before I had asked Enver on January 6 to relieve me because his orders of January 5th had taken away from me the troops for the final great attack on the peninsula. As Enver rescinded the order I considered the matter closed. On January 22 I received a communication from him to the effect that he would lay my request for separation from the

Turkish service before His Majesty the Sultan. Strangely I received on the same day a telegram from the Chief of the Military Cabinet in Pless to the effect that H. M. the German Emperor considered it out of the question that in the present situation I, being chief of the military mission, should forsake the German officers in Turkey. This led to a conference with Enver in which he relinquished his intention of a report to the Sultan.

Other frictions followed in rapid succession. At the beginning of March I sent my adjutant, Captain Prigge—being absent myself—to the German Embassy with a written summary of the very poor sanitary conditions in the Fifth Army under my command. The sanitary situation was such that it seriously threatened the battle efficiency of the army. After the toil of the Dardanelles Campaign many thousands had to be sent to the hospitals. The death rate from debility was terrifying. There was urgent necessity to inform the highest German authorities in order to prevent false ideas of the value of Turkish troops and their further employment. On March 7th I received a communication from Enver in which he objected to any information being given out about the condition of the Turkish Army and demanded from me the punishment of Captain Prigge, because he had given such information to a "foreign embassy." I knew from Count Metternich that he had not spoken about this matter with any Turk, so I simply asked Enver from whom he had received official information of the communication sent to the German Ambassador by my order. Up to date I have received no reply to my inquiry. A mere request for the names of the persons involved sufficed to cause the matter to be dropped.

About the same time the Turkish headquarters requested the confiscation of a small publication, in which one of my adjutants had briefly described the fighting in the Dardanelles in which he had participated from beginning to end as a member of my staff. It had passed German censorship without objection,

and had been on sale in Germany for some time.   Enver himself
was presented with the first copy from the press and had been
informed of the intended publication in the preceding November.
He himself expressed to the author the wish that it might be
translated into Turkish and had presented his signed photo-
graph that it might be added to the book.   It was claimed by
Turkish headquarters that the book might give the enemy
useful information for renewed action in the Dardanelles.

The book stated facts long known from reports and newspaper
articles and contained a description of the terrain in part taken
from Baedecker.   Any one familiar with the circumstances
knew that the British had better information of the terrain of
the peninsula before the campaign than the Turks and that
British maps had a representation of the terrain superior to
that of the Turkish.   Even the Turkish staffs had provided
themselves as much as possible with British maps found on the
killed and wounded during the campaign.

The greatest conflict was caused in February 1916 by a
circular letter of Enver to all Turkish armies, wherein he
decreed that from then on he alone would give orders about the
employment of German officers in the Turkish Army, without
reference to the chief of the military mission, whom the contract
required to be consulted.   It was an illegal as well as an impossible order.   Neither Enver nor the Turkish headquarters
knew the qualifications of the German officers sent to Turkey
and neither could judge for what employment they were fitted.
In the Turkish personnel section, which in such a case would
have to handle the German personnel papers, there existed an
incredible confusion.   Sometimes it required months to ascertain with what organizations Turkish officers sought were
serving.   It happened that officers killed long ago were ordered
transferred.   The chaos was increased by the ever recurring
Turkish names which are personally selected and not family
names.   In the personnel section the names of German officers
were habitually so incorrectly written that they could not be

deciphered. According to German ideas care had to be exercised so as not to assign German officers to offices controlled by Turkish commanders who were inimical to Germany. This had previously given rise to much unpleasant friction and to unjust far fetched accusations against German officers.

For these reasons I firmly protested against Enver's order and submitted the matter to the Chief of the Military Cabinet for the Emperor's decision. When Colonel Freiherr von Kress refused to carry out Enver's orders before the matter was properly regulated from Germany, Enver threatened to remove this meritorious officer from the Turkish Army. When I repeatedly told Enver that I must have the decision of the German Emperor, before these violations of the contract could be carried out, he wrote me that unless I yielded at once, he would request the Sultan to relieve me from command in the Turkish Army. Thereupon on April 21, 1916, I addressed a request to the German Emperor for my recall to Germany, stating my reasons and so informed Enver. I prepared for my departure and was in hopes of escaping from this, to me, in every way, unpleasant situation. During my preparations for departure the chief of staff of the Fifth Army, Lieutenant Colonel Kiasim Bei, brought me a letter from Enver in which he formally apologized and requested an interview which I had to grant, as it was in line with the Emperor's wishes. The result of the long conversation was that in any change of position of a German officer the military mission would be consulted as heretofore.

This was very necessary for during the brief duration of the conflict he had given quite impossible orders. To quote one of them, I will say, that he had designated the senior German garrison officer of Constantinople who had been severely wounded and was capable of garrison duty only, as company commander in the Turkish Infantry Regiment No. 58 in the Dardanelles where all other company commanders were lieutenants or warrant officers. These and similar orders were now rescinded.

From the foregoing narrative, the written proofs for which are in my possession, any one may see that the victorious campaign in the Dardanelles did not raise sentiments of gratitude at Turkish headquarters, but caused the opponents of the military mission to join hands in efforts for the removal of the chief.

Though friction never ceased during the existence of the military mission, an improvement took place in the fall of 1916 when Colonel von Lenthe was sent to Turkey as chief of staff of the military mission. The home authorities also found ways to conserve and strengthen the position of the military mission.

ASIA MINOR

After a brief pause following the termination of the Dardanelles Campaign the enemy's intentions seemed to point to an attack on the coast of Asia Minor and Smyrna. I cannot judge whether such intentions really existed or were merely surmised without an actual foundation.

As early as the spring of 1915 there had been rumors of threatened attacks on Smyrna and in those days the British occupied the Island of Kösten which dominates the outer harbor The inner harbor had previously been mined by the Turks. In March 1916 the sector of the Fourth Army Corps assembled near Smyrna as well as that of the 57th Division in Aidin was turned over to the Fifth Army which now transferred its headquarters to Panderma on the Sea of Marmara. From then on the Fifth Army had to guard a sector which extended from Midia on the Black Sea through Thrace, the Gulf of Saros (Xeros), the Dardanelles and the whole west coast of Asia Minor to Adalia on the Mediterranean inclusive. The coast line to be guarded had an extent of more than 2,000 kilometers; and it is to be understood that all islands lying off this long coast were in the hands of the enemy and could be used by him as points of support for operations, while not a single Turkish war vessel was on the Asiatic coast.

THE CAPTURE OF THE ISLAND OF KÖSTEN

The British installed artillery on the Island of Kösten, established an aviation station and put out mine and net obstructions for the protection of their war vessels lying in the small harbors on the west side of the island.   There was a lively traffic between Kösten and Mitylene.   Taking position between the northeast coast of the island and the Menemen shore the hostile monitors frequently bombarded the antiquated fortifications of Smyrna, the fort of Yenikale and adjacent batteries.

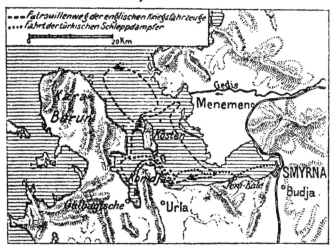

The high road from Smyrna to Urla along the sea coast was frequently bombarded and buildings and bridges were destroyed so that communication in day time was dangerous or interrupted.   Urla also, a town inhabited almost exclusively by Greeks, was several times bombarded by ships.   Numerous Turkish ships in the port of Urla, three kilometers from the city, were sunk by gun fire.   The few houses of this coast town had finally to be abandoned by the inhabitants because of the constant danger.

In case the Entente contemplated serious operations against

Smyrna, Kösten would be a valuable intermediate base.   Hence the first thing for us to do was to take the island.

In March 1916 the three divisions of the Fourth Army Corps were concentrated near Smyrna and neighboring towns.   As soon as the Fifth Army took charge here extensive changes were made.   The divisions were pushed to the north and northwest toward the coast of Asia Minor, and on the shores of the outer bay batteries were emplaced at night.

An attack on Kösten was prepared and based entirely on surprise.   In Smyrna it was particularly difficult to guard the secret of the preparations, because this city with a population of 400,000 was mostly inhabited by Greeks, and because enemy aliens were given full freedom of movement.   The Turks certainly cannot be charged with intolerance in that particular. By spreading misleading news and diverting attention in other directions, no intimation of our real intentions leaked out in the city.

We selected the time of new moon and during the dark nights of May 3/4 and 4/5 two old tug boats towed large lighters with guns and ammunition from the harbor of Smyrna to the promontory of Kara Burun opposite the British anchorage at the northwest end of the island.   The artillery consisted of a platoon of field artillery, a platoon of Austrian 15-cm. howitzers and a platoon of 12-cm. guns.   Infantry for their protection was sent there at the same time by night marches on the one existing trail.

Theoretically the trip of the very slow tug boats was impossible, because they had to pass close to Kösten which was held by the enemy, not to mention the probability of meeting hostile patrol boats.   Practically, however, it was successful.

About seven and one-half kilometers from the enemy's anchorage near Kösten the guns were unloaded at 3 a.m. on May 5th on the promontory of Kara Burun.   Careful preparations had been made to conceal them during the day, so that neither land observation nor fliers detected them.   During the night of 5/6 May they were placed in position.

At 4.45 a.m. on May 6th we suddenly opened fire. An enemy destroyer had just returned from patrol and taken station alongside of the two monitors anchored on the northwest side of the island. One of the monitors, *M30* according to British reports, was hit several times and a shell penetrated the ammunition chambers. There was a big explosion and the ship drifted slowly ashore, where it remained a total wreck. The other monitor escaped amidst dense clouds of smoke. The destroyer at once got under way, opened a lively fire and soon left the bay in the direction of Mitylene.

The next problem was the capture of the island with the support of this artillery. A tent camp and the aviation station were still visible for some time and lively communication was kept up with Mitylene at night. Enemy ships thereafter avoided the anchorage near the island for any prolonged stay.

The preparations for a landing on the island of Kösten were made in the bay of Gülbagtshe. A considerable Turkish boat flotilla landed during the night of June 4th on the south point of the island and discovered that the British had gone. The hangars had been abandoned and were still standing.

We occupied Kösten and erected batteries on the heights of the island. More guns were pushed forward to the north point of Kara Burun and to the opposite point of the Menemen shore, thus closing the entrance to the outer harbor. A bombardment of Smyrna and its vicinity was no longer possible.

Kösten remained in the hands of the Turks to the end of the war. The success of the operation is due to Major Lierau in the first place and to his faithful assistants Lieutenant Missuweit, First Lieutenant Diesinger and the Austrian Captain Manouschek. Several brave Turkish officers also distinguished themselves by their intrepidity and presence of mind.

The Turkish Army report made but brief mention of this brave deed. I read it in the only Turkish newspaper published in German, the *Osmanli Lloyd*. There it read, under item 5

Caucasus: "The island of Kösten has been occupied by us."
I consider it possible that the enumeration under the heading
"Caucasus" was a misprint.

During my visit to the extreme left flank of the sector of the
Fifth Army at Adalia in the spring of 1916 to inspect the defenses, I had a renewed chance of seeing the peculiarities of
Turkish roads in the interior of the empire. From Baladis, the
terminus of the railroad, it was 130 kilometers by country road
to the Italian sphere of influence of Adalia. The quality of the
road corresponded to the efficiency of the Turkish officials in
that section. Where they were efficient, the roads were in good
repair; otherwise they were neglected and barely passable
in bad weather. Over some of the ridges they were mere
trails according to our notions.

In Adalia we saw the unusual picture of a well kept Turkish
city. The local mutessarif kept exemplary order. He was not
in favor with the committee and had given offense when he
energetically protested against the confiscation of the property
of his wards. Shortly after our visit he was relieved and
conscripted as a common Turkish soldier. I succeeded in
saving him by having him detached to the miltary mission as
interpreter—he spoke excellent French.

DETACHMENT OF TURKISH TROOPS TO EUROPE

In 1916 Turkey began to take an active part in the European
theater of war.

During the summer the 19th and 20th Divisions were com-
bined as the Fifteenth Army Corps commanded by Jakob
Schefki Pasha and sent to the army detachment of Count
Bothmer in Galicia. In the fall, after Roumania had joined
in the war on the side of the Entente, the 15th, 25th and 26th
Divisions were combined into the Sixth Army Corps under
Hilmi Pasha and detached to the army of Field Marshal
General von Mackensen. Toward the end of the year the 50th
Division was sent to the Second Bulgarian Army on the Struma,

and the 46th Division was sent there in the middle of December. They were to form the Twentieth Turkish Army Corps under command of Abdul Kerim Pasha. In addition the 177th Turkish Infantry Regiment was part of the Beles detachment of Below's army group.

The first named divisions in Galicia, in the Dobrudja, and Wallachia were taken from the Fifth Army under my command.

I have always considered it a mistake to send troops to Galicia and still think so. In the summer of 1916 I had laid my serious misgivings before the chief of the military cabinet for H. M. the Emperor.

The detaching of Turkish troops to the Second Bulgarian Army I likewise consider a mistake.

It was different with the war against Roumania. There I deemed the detaching of troops justified in the interest of the defense of Turkish soil. In the absence of this detachment Turkey would have been forced at the beginning of the Roumanian campaign to organize an army in Thrace for the protection of the country. Hence it was better to take an active part in the decision of this campaign.

The considerations as to the first two detachments are quite different.

A full understanding of the entire situation in 1916, and perhaps earlier, made it clear that Turkey was no longer able to protect her own territories and frontiers.

The far distant theaters, where the Turkish troops were invariably facing far more numerous opponents, in the Caucasus, in Mesopotamia and on the Sinai peninsula, the protection of the extensive coast of Asia Minor and the direct protection of Constantinople, made such demands on the strength of Turkey that they could not be met for any length of time if the troops at home were to be kept in a usable and efficient condition.

Turkey entered upon the wrong road the moment she thought she had to help others when she could no longer help herself.

The Turkish troops at home now began more and more to become paper organizations rather than effective battle units. Germany should have avoided bringing about such consequences, even indirectly. They were against the interest of Turkey as well as against Germany's own interests.

The Turkish troops sent to Europe showed an entirely different appearance from those remaining behind. Before departure the less efficient officers, and in each division thousands of the physically less fit men were exchanged for the best officers and men of the troops remaining behind. The departing divisions received all the good clothing and equipment collected from the entire army. They were raised to full strength and in addition were given men from the reserve, while the strength, as well as the quality of the troops remaining behind, was diminished. The Turkish War Ministry likewise ordered that only the best officers and best men be sent to Europe in replacement.

The human material remaining in Turkey fell below all proportions. As early as August 1916 the ages in the infantry regiments varied between sixteen and fifty. I am convinced that maintaining a good, and therefore successful army in Turkey, would have served the larger ends of the war better than by dispatching comparatively insignificant reënforcements to Galicia and Macedonia. The decision of the World War, which alone could have justified such detachments in spite of their drawbacks, could hardly be looked for in the regions mentioned.

I believe I am in a position to express an opinion of the internal conditions of the Turkish Army in 1916, because the Fifth Army under my command had to detach in all twenty-two divisions up to October 12, 1916, and besides had to give up some 10,000 men for scattered details ordered by the Turkish headquarters. Upon my report on the condition of the troops General Ludendorff subsequently stopped further detachments to Europe. His telegram of November 28, 1916, reads:

In view of the situation in Turkey we forego the two additional divisions which Enver Pasha has offered for the European theater. Sgd. Ludendorff.

At that time the Fifth Army consisted almost exclusively of recruits and of the unfit left behind by the twenty-two divisions.

It was almost impossible to keep up the interest of the Turkish officers who were constantly being deprived of the men with whom they worked. The officers added nothing to their own knowledge because their duties were confined to recruit training and because company exercises, not to speak of larger units, were no longer practicable.

The depot regiments, many of them commanded by German officers, were unable to serve their full purpose in spite of the hardest work, because they had to contend with the most elementary difficulties. As an example I quote the beginning of a telegram sent on March 14, 1916, from Balikesri to the army department of the Turkish War Ministry:

Inspected depot regiment here today. Strength over 8,000, only 1,050 rifles of various patterns available. Not a single cartridge box, many men armed with rifles are without side arms or bayonets, etc.

As compared with these facts a telegram deserves notice which was sent to German headquarters in the spring of 1916 by two high German officers from the eastern front where they were travelling with Enver. They stated that the military situation of Turkey never had been better than now, and described the resources of Turkey as inexhaustible. In this way the German high command could not form a correct idea of existing conditions.

By telegram of June 25th to the chief of the Military Cabinet, I requested to be called to German headquarters for a report in person. I received a favorable reply, but the time was not stated, so the report was deferred for the present.

The following brief statements of events on the distant Turkish theaters of operation will show what the military situation in Turkey became in 1916. Among many others a report by Colonel Freiherr von Kress from Jerusalem dated January 19, 1917, shows the exhausted condition of the human material at the end of 1916, beginning as follows:

> They have sent me as reënforcements the 160th Infantry Regiment, of which 1,250 trained and healthy men were exchanged before departure to Syria for a like number of sick, feeble and untrained men of a regiment detailed to Galicia, etc.

CAUCASUS

On January 14 an unexpected Russian offensive began against the center of the Third Army. The attack began on the dominating heights north of the Aras River, followed by further attacks in the sections adjoining on the south. For some reason the commander, Mahmud Kiamil Pasha, happened to be in Constantinople just then and the German chief of staff was absent in Germany to recover from a case of typhus. Abdul Kerim Pasha led the army.

The Russians broke the center of the Third Army. The Turks withdrew at first to the nearby mountains to the east and northeast of Erzerum. The first Russian attack against the field fortifications at Erzerum failed; another from the northeast was successful. Erzerum fell February 15. To the west of Erzerum a Turkish division was surprised and destroyed.

Mahmud Kiamil returned and resumed command. He led the disorganized troops of the Turkish center across the Euphrates west of Mamakhatun. Reënforcements from the Fifth Army Corps arrived in driblets. The line of the Euphrates, where the river turns from north to south, and the heights of Baiburt were held after heavy fighting. The retreat caused the Turks great losses in men and war material.

Meanwhile Wehib Pasha had assumed command of the Third Army and established his headquarters at Ersindjan (Ersingyan). Quick support of the Third Army by large reënforcements was impossible, because after the withdrawal of the British from Gallipoli, Turkish headquarters had failed to push the Second Army, stationed in Thrace since October 1915, forward in successive echelons in the direction of the Turkish eastern front along the Anatolian railway at least as far as Ulukishla. The movement was advisable as the east front was bound to gain in importance to Turkey in 1916.

As the movement was not made, there was a peculiar situation in that in February three Turkish armies were assembled in Thrace where there was no enemey. The First Army under Essad Pasha was near Constantinople, the Second Army under Wehib Pasha and later under Izzet Pasha stood at Tschorlu (Chorlu), and the Fifth Army under my command was at Lüle Burgas, while at the same time in the eastern part of the empire the Russians and British were penetrating deeply into Turkish territory.

The offensive in January and February had gained the Russians closer connection with their left wing which had reached Lake Van some time before. Their next plan was to get their right wing forward and take Trebizond. The coast detachment on the left of the Third Army was twice defeated and driven back. Reënforcements received in March, particularly the 28th Infantry Regiment under Major Hunger, enabled the Turks to check the Russians at Sürmene, about thirty kilometers east of Trebizond, which city fell in April in consequence of a Russian landing in rear of the Turks. Though a whole Russian army corps was now landed in Trebizond, the Turks continued to hold the mountains south of the city.

With Trebizond the most important Turkish Black Sea port in the entire theater of operations fell into the hands of the Russians.

The loss of Erzerum was kept so secret by Turkish headquarters, that it did not appear among the army news and remained unknown for months even to the Sultan and his entourage.

The loss of the fortress and of the extensive Turkish territory appeared so important to Turkish headquarters that extensive operations were decided upon to give a decisive turn to the campaign. Thus originated the plan of using a whole army to strike in flank and rear of the Russians.

The Second Army was selected for this operation; it consisted of ten divisions organized in four army corps under the supreme command of Izzet Pasha and was to be assembled on the line LakeVan-Mush-Kigi. Thence the army was to advance toward Erzerum and to the east of it.

The time required by the troops from their departure from Haidar Pasha to the center and left flank of the army was estimated at forty days if expedited to the maximum. Using the railroad to the Taurus and through the Amanus, there remained some 550 to 650 kilometers to be covered by marching. The troops for the right wing were to use the railroad as far as Ras-el-Ain and advance from there via Diarbekir. The German headquarters directed that the German Auto-Truck Columns No. 510 and 514 be turned over for auto freight transportation between Diarbekir and Ras-el-Ain.

The assembly of the Second Army began in April and lasted until August. Its commander, Izzet Pasha, while in Malatia, and while the heads of the leading Third Army Corps (7th and 11th Divisions) were still approaching by marching, gave the following description of the Turkish situation on July 8th:

> The 5th Division is in the hills south of Bitlis from which place it had to withdraw; the 8th Division is in the hills south of Mush. They will form the 16th Army Corps under the command of the Second Army. Adjoining to the northwest are two mixed detachments as far as the valley of Elmalu, both in a long thin line. They also join the Second Army.
>
> In the Elmalu valley we gain touch with the right of the Third Army whose Cavalry Brigade No. 11 is posted there. The line of the Third Army runs from there northward leaving Ashkale on the west, and by a sharp westward curve reaches the coast of the Black Sea about forty kilometers west of Trebizond.
>
> My plan is to assemble the greater part of the Second Army at Diarbekir and the smaller part at Kharput, and advance from there toward Erzerum and to the east of it.

So far as known we are confronted by the reënforced Fourth Caucasian Army Corps.

The plan was clear, but it was not carried out. I will sketch the fate of the Second Army in a few words.

Turkish headquarters were of the opinion that in June the Russians were transferring troops from the Caucasus to Europe. For that reason headquarters urged offensive operations against the Caucasus front.

In the opinion of the army commander nothing serious could be undertaken with the Third Army Corps, the only one that had arrived and was still closing up.

The Third Army, the headquarters of which had been transferred to Gümüsh-Khane, had taken Mamakhatun on May 31. On June 21/22 it had made an attack from the southeast under Fewzi Pasha on the heights south of Trebizond, in which a mountain top was secured. But all these attacks were without sufficient support.

On July 7th superior Russian forces attacked the center of the Third Army and the Turkish right was hard pressed on the 8th. The Third Army requested assistance from the Second Army. A weak detachment was all that was available, and through lack of decision of its leader it did not get into action. The center and right wing of the Third Army had to fall back. Baiburt and Ersindjan (Ersingyan) were lost.

Between July 12 and 16 the 8th Division of the Second Army was attacked by the Russians on the heights south of Mush and on that day was pushed back thirty kilometers to the south.

The retreat of the center of the Third Army was thrown into disorder after two penetrations by strong Russian cavalry had produced a veritable panic in the rear. The right wing also had fallen back in disorder in the Elmalu valley.

Izzet Pasha now had to give up his former plan of a great offensive toward Erzerum and east of it. He decided to assemble the Third Army Corps and all troops approaching from the south and southwest, on the left of the designated place of assembly and to attack later west of Erzerum the flank and rear of the Russians. But this decision, which certainly was sound, was not executed.

The Third Army fell back farther and farther and stopped at last on August 8th on a line from Kemakh on the Euphrates, about thirty kilometers west of Ersindjan (Ersingyan) northward to the Black Sea coast. There the Russians ceased their pursuit.

Of the Second Army, the 1st, 14th and 53rd Divisions had been placed in the front as they arrived and gradually became engaged in conflicts which brought some results in August, but no decisive success. This fighting took place in the Ognot section.

On August 10th Izzet Pasha had to give up his second plan, and decided to take up a defensive position approximately on the line Kighi-Ognot—south of Mush.

This was the end of the great offensive of the Second Army planned as a flank attack.

Anticipating the decision of Turkish headquarters, the Russians had defeated the Third Army decisively, before the assembly of the Second Army was anywhere near completion. Up to that time no coöperation between the two armies had taken place.

The necessity of reorganizing their lines of communications and the flanking position of the Second Army had brought the Russians to a halt and stopped their further pursuit of the Third Army. The Second Army could not be neglected notwithstanding that other Russian troops contained that army in front.

In deciding to remain on the defensive Izzet Pasha had to consider some other difficulties which impeded the mobility of his army in that terrain.

The Second Army was deficient in mountain guns which alone in that mountainous terrain could reach the places where the infantry needed their support. The Second Army had but eighteen such guns and ammunition was short. There was a deficiency of pack animals and particularly of camel columns which could follow anywhere with subsistence. Nor did the fighting trains and baggage trains have sufficient pack animals; some had but a third, others two thirds, of the prescribed number of animals. The mobile sanitary establishments were wholly incomplete.

Turkish headquarters cannot be entirely absolved from blame for not having duly considered these things in organizing the great offensive, and not having made better provisions in good time. The contemplated purchase of oxen for ox carts in the assembly district could by no means balance the deficiency in pack animals, for on the narrow mountain trails ox carts could not follow everywhere. It was furthermore found that the statements of the civil authorities about the number of cattle in the assembly district were erroneous and exaggerated.

The lack of the requisite means of communication, for the supply of food on the snow and ice covered trails, subsequently brought about the lamentable conditions through which the Second Army lost a large part of its men and animals during the ensuing winter.

The ultimate cause of the failure of this campaign, as of all offensive operations begun in Turkey throughout the World War, lay in the long and imperfectly organized lines of communications.

The nature of the strategic flank attack implies a certain degree of surprise. But a surprise can hardly be expected, when the assembly of the army, as in this case, took three or four months. For a flank attack, moreover, a certain guaranty was needed that the enemy remained approximately in the same place where it was intended that the offensive should strike him on the completion of the long winded approach. At the very least the Third Army should have been reënforced to the extent that it could hold its ground, until this movement of the Second Army took effect. There is no question but that the strength of the Russians was underestimated by Turkish head-quarters.

Through its retreat and panics the Third Army had lost a great part of its strength, because thousands of men left the ranks without leave. About the middle of August the Third Army reported the capture of 13,000 deserters. The prefect of Sivas had engaged to apprehend and collect 30,000 deserters in a short time.

In September the Third Army was reorganized, the army corps became divisions, the divisions became regiments and the regiments became battalions. The designations of the units were also changed, and in this wise the First and Second Caucasian Army Corps came into existence on the front of the Third Army.

In October there were some disputes in the Third Army about the value of the Georgia Legion. This unit had about the strength of a battalion, exclusive of the Georgians of the Lasistan detachment, had had no part in the fighting and was stationed in Kerason on the Black Sea. The original purpose of its organization had been to gain a small reënforcement for the Third Army, and to put into the hands of the Georgian revolutionary committee something with which to make propaganda. The duties of the legion were more of a political than of a military character. Its organization, like that of all irregular formations and expeditions in Turkey, was under the German military plenipotentiary in Constantinople. Wehib Pasha distrusted the legion and wanted to treat it like any Turkish battalion. This caused numerous disputes. Ultimately the legion was dissolved in January 1917 without having been of any account in any direction.

Under the firm hand of Wehib Pasha order was quickly restored in the Third Army. Still he could not expect to use these troops in the near future for an effective offensive. Moral impressions persist for a long time with Turkish troops, and much time is needed to overcome moral depressions.

To assist the supply of the Third Army in its present position, German auto-truck columns had been established on the line of communications from Ulukishla to Sivas.

On account of insufficient food the condition of the troops became worse and worse after the early winter had set in in the Caucasus. The losses suffered in small engagements in the front were of little account, but hunger and cold rapidly decimated the ranks.

When in November the Russians had drawn back their advanced troops to a distance of twelve to thirty kilometers from the Turkish lines, and held only the dominating heights and passes, the Turkish headquarters decided to move a large part of the Second Army to places in rear, that offered better protection against the climate. This step by no means balanced the great deficiencies of the inadequate transport material. In a report of a division commander of November 29, 1916, appears the following description of the lamentable conditions:

Great losses are caused by lack of subsistence and lack of warm clothing. Many Turkish soldiers are dressed in thin summer garments, have no overcoats and no boots. The feet are mostly wrapped in rags from which the toes protrude.

Not more than a third of a ration can be issued here so that all men are badly undernourished.

No fodder is issued for the draft animals, saddle horses receive daily one or one and one-half kilograms of barley. The daily loss in animals is very high and the number of our means of transport, never sufficient or efficient, is more and more diminished.

No wonder that under such conditions whole detachments were found in caves dead from hunger and cold after blizzards or other heavy weather.

I do not believe that the heroism of these poor men was inferior to that of the celebrated cossack dying in the snow in the Shipka pass.

Under existing circumstances it was difficult to bring order into the sanitary conditions.   A German surgeon, Dr. Schilling, reports on December 16, 1916:

There are about 5,000 or 6,000 sick in Diarbekir and the authorities of the Turkish line of communication are apparently unable to cope with this mass of sick.   I saw a transport of 500 to 600 sick and exhausted in Mardin which started at 6 a.m. in empty German transport columns.   The sick were in the most lamentable and filthy condition, etc.

Dr. Niekau reports from Kharput on December 24, 1916:

The sick delivered here are in a lamentable condition.   Aside from filth and vermin the men are in a dangerous condition from undernourishment and enfeeblement.

And later:

With the help of the chief surgeon of the army I succeeded in having two places designated for the burial of the dead, monthly as many as 900.

Mass dying in the Second Army had begun.

The balance sheet for 1916 on the Caucasus was anything but gratifying.

IRAK

During the first few months of 1916 the British made several attempts to relieve the surrounded troops of General Townshend. Two divisions from France and some other troops were brought to Busra for the purpose.

The Turks had three entrenched positions, one in rear of the other, on either side of the Tigris.   In bloody fighting from the 7th to the 9th and on the 13th and 14th, the Turks were driven from their first two positions.   In the third position they withstood the enemy's attacks, which were repulsed with great loss to the British.

New British attacks with fresh troops were made at Es Sinn on March 7th and repulsed.

The Turks had then returned to the second Fellalieh position, where they were heavily attacked on April 9th and 22d. The British attacks failed.

According to Turkish reports only about 2,000 men of Turkish infantry had been left at Kut to maintain the investment. It is to be presumed that the condition of General Townshend's division had been so reduced by the long investment, that it was no longer capable of forcing a way through this weak force.

General Townshend capitulated on April 29th.

Field Marshal General Freiherr von der Goltz died in Bagdad on April 6th from spotted typhus. It was a tragic fate that prevented him from witnessing the victorious outcome of the last few months.

The grief for this highly honored and respected leader and instructor was universal in the Turkish corps of officers. On June 24, 1916, grand obsequies were held in Constantinople after which his body was transferred to the honor cemetery in Therapia in solemn procession, where the field marshal found his final resting place in one of the most beautiful spots in the world.

For the German interest there was further cause of grief over the death of the field marshal, through the loss of his great personal influence with the Turks. The surrender of Kut had taken place under the Turkish leader Halil Pasha, a very young uncle of Enver, who had held his command in place of the field marshal but a short time. His merits for the final result cannot be denied, but it raised the egotism of Halil and of the Turks to such a degree, that they were no longer receptive to German advice in that theater of war.

The influence of the field marshal was soon missed.

The first effect was that the success of Kut was not turned to account by again attacking the British and recovering the lost large section in Irak. Instead the Thirteenth Turkish Army Corps advanced into neutral Persia.

On July 11, 1916, I expressed my opinion in an official report which I quote here verbatim and to which I have nothing to add:

Intelligent leadership seems to be lacking in the Sixth Army in Irak. Halil Pasha is anything but an army leader. After the success of Kut-el-Amara, instead of attacking the British at Fellalieh and compelling them to evacuate at least a part of Irak, Halil Pasha ordered the very influential and shrewd, but tricky and German hating Ichsan Pasha, to advance to Kannikin and Kermanshah to reap cheap and exaggerated laurels against a few Russian cavalry regiments (about five) with a few battalions (two or three). The whole movement to Persia is a mere blow in the air, for success there cannot be durable and in the second place the pressure intended to be brought to bear on Persia, with its unreliable and unmilitary population, has not the slightest effect on the decision of the World War.

In consequence of Turkish inactivity, the British in order to have a secure base for a further advance against Bagdad were enabled to remain at Fellalieh to complete their intrenchments and gradually and systematically to improve their river and land communications.

A few weeks after the fall of Kut the heat became so great that large movements of troops were impossible during the ensuing months. When operations again became practicable in the fall climate, no troops were available on the Turkish side. Meanwhile the Thirteenth Army Corps had advanced to Hamadan and failed against the British.

The Sixth Army had only the 45th, 51st and 52d Divisions in the front and these were incapable of an obstinate defense.

In those days Persia played a great rôle in Turkish politics. Unfortunately Germany also has involved herself there to a degree that is not easily understood and which I have regretted.

During the winter of 1915 Germany had sent a large mission to Persia which was to organize military formations there with the assistance of the Turks. The German program of "liberation of Persia by Germany and Turkey without pursuing selfish political aims" may have been very laudable, but it certainly was not practical.

The only question to my mind was to win the World War, and every officer and man used for any other purpose meant a mistake.

The existing basis on which the organization of the new Persian troops, which were expected to drive the Russians out of northern Persia, had to be erected was entirely unfitting.

Up to that time the only troops in Persia were gendarmery troops whose training had been directed by efficient Swedish officers with great skill and devoted labor. They were unable to secure lasting results because the human material was unsuited for military purposes and because of the limited budget.

And now German officers were to form effective Persian organizations with the assistance of the Turks. They sought to recruit gendarmes and volunteers and found some military-political support in the former governor of Kermanshahan, the Persian Field Marshal General Saltaneh, which cost a great deal of German money.

In meeting the Russians the new formations proved of inferior quality as was to be expected. During April and May the Russians advanced toward the Turkish frontier from the east, in the general direction of Bagdad with a cavalry division and a few battalions, and the new Persian formations collapsed.

The gendarmes dispersed in all directions or went over to the enemy, and the German officers were ordered to withdraw to Bakuba north of Badgad. The affair was not calculated to raise the respect for German officers either among the Turks or the Persians.

There were plenty of intelligent German officers who advised against active participation of Germany in Persia, but their advice was not heeded, and the foreign office continued its policy after the collapse of the Persian mission in May.

Enver arrived in Bagdad in May with a grand suite and, with the German military plenipotentiary, determined details for further active German participation in the operations in Persia.

Colonel von Gleich, the then chief of staff of Halil Pasha, in his reports of May and June, strongly advised against any further participation of Germany in Persia, but he was to know better. He aptly characterized the value of military assistance from Persia in stating:

The number of Persian gendarmes is varying constantly depending on whether battle or pay day impends.

He reported on May 23rd:

I have lost all confidence in any successful ending of the Persian enterprise and consider the expenditure of every penny spent on it an inexcusable waste of money.

and on June 11th:

I believe it my duty to state here that I consider the formation of Persian troops now and in the future, at least during the current year, as impracticable.

In the same report he summarizes his opinion as follows:

I am convinced that we never shall gain sufficient military power in Persia to carry out our plan for her political independence. Moreover, even with German help, Persia could never successfully cope with her internal difficulties.

His view was not accepted.

An attempt was now made to make the Persian gendarmes useful on the lines of communication.

Then, as formerly, there was much divergence of opinion among Germans and Turks as to further measures necessary in Persia, and also a patent lack of mutual trust. Many things were ordered by the commander of the Sixth Army of which the German chief of staff and the German officers were informed later or not at all.

Soon thereafter Colonel von Gleich had to return to Germany because the climate had impaired his health. The Saxon Major Kretschmer of the general staff succeeded him.

There is no doubt that while in Badgad Enver made secret pacts with Nisam es Saltaneh. This Persian field marshal considered it advisable now to make closer connection with the Turks.

Persian military rank should not be taken as seriously as we do in other armies. A German warrant officer by the name of Haase, an otherwise capable and active man, had formerly become a Persian colonel in short order.

The career of another man in Nisam's suite, Masud Chan, was less clear. He held a high post in Nisam's general staff as the only "expert." He had been a pupil at the French non-commissioned officers school and had been clerk in a store in Teheran before the Persian troubles began.

In the conference between Enver and the German military plenipotentiary it had been determined that the German colonel, Duke Adolf Frederick, was to lead the Mosul column into Persia. Halil soon threw difficulties in the way. The Mosul column, which at first was to have the strength of a division, was reduced to an infantry regiment with a cavalry brigade and some machine gun formations, and finally dwindled to a weak Turkish infantry regiment of some 700 rifles. Other conflicts also materialized and the Duke declined his appointment and returned to the European theater of war.

We had had part in the regrettable advance of the Turkish Thirteenth Army Corps into Persia in that we furnished a number of German pioneer officers and men for the Turkish pioneer battalions Nos. 14 and 15. They were used for superintending road construction of the simplest kind on the Bagdad-Kermanshah road. This did not appear to me as a commensurate employment for them and I so reported to Germany and effected the release of a number of the officers. German etape hospitals were established in Suleimanie and Kermanshah, and German auto trucks had been turned over to the line of communication of the Thirteenth Army Corps.

In September I learned from German flying officers and from

other officers returning from the Sixth Army, of the rapid progress of a railroad constructed along the Tigris to the British front, and of the great increase of British transports of all kinds on that river.

I informed Enver and advised him that within a limited space of time Bagdad would be endangered.

A few weeks before I had suggested that the Third, Second and Sixth Armies, i.e., the entire Turkish east front, be placed under one commander, but he could not bring himself to order it.

Unable to do anything in Constantinople for increasing the security of Bagdad I communicated my apprehensions to Adjutant General von Chelius who just then was in Turkey, and made the following report to General Ludendorff. General von Chelius personally handed the report to General Ludendorff in Pless. In consequence I received orders in December to appear in person at the headquarters in Pless for report—of which I shall give an account below.

Report

Constantinople, October 25, 1916

The situation on the Turkish theaters of War at the end of October 1916

East Front: After its retreat the Third Army stands on the approximately due north and south line from Tireboli to Kemah on Kara Lake.

The Russians have pushed the railroad from Sarikamisch to Hassan-kala and to the vicinity of Erzerum, and by this time perhaps to Erzerum.

Between the Third and Second Army lies the Dersim, inhabited by Kurdish robbers, which heretofore has been practically inaccessible for Russians and Turks.

The Second Army stands on the approximate line Temur Bay-Kighi-Ognut-south of Mush-Bitlis.

The offensive taken by this army toward the northeast was soon checked, as the Russians, after driving back the Third Army, had had time to strongly reënforce their left wing, and because the supply of the Second Army had not been properly provided for.

Now that winter has set in, a successful offensive of both armies with a view of driving the Russians from Turkish soil, is hardly practicable in the difficult mountainous terrain.

New units are not available at this time to reënforce the east front.

The Turkish territory occupied by the Russians has a depth of 200–230 kilometers, the principal communications are the railroad mentioned, the road from Erzerum to Ersindjan (Ersingyan), the constructed roads from Trebizond to Erzerum and Ersindjan (Ersingyan), and the old military road from Erzerum to Karakilissa and Bayazid and thence to Persia. The Caucasian coast of the Black Sea is completely dominated by the Russian fleet.

Some small detachments of no decisive importance are operating between the Second and Sixth Army.

Probability points to a Russian advance southeast of Urumia Lake (Suj Bulak, Sakiz, Bijar), because there the Russians have some advantages of communication.

In January 1916 I suggested to Enver Pasha to assemble a strong force at Mosul effective to the north, east or south; the suggestion has not been carried out.

Sixth Army: The situation of the Sixth Army cannot be considered specially hopeful.

The success of Kut-el-Amara has not been utilized to drive the British from Irak. At this time the British there are in a better tactical situation than at the end of April 1916.

It is to be presumed that they will resume operations against Bagdad as soon as the season permits.

In this case their movements will be facilitated by the railroad built during the summer from Busra to Korna and beyond. This railroad, in addition, is of importance in considering the aims of the Bagdad railroad.

It is not believed that the Thirteenth Army Corps of the Sixth Army, which has advanced to Kermanshah and Hamadan, could arrive in time for a decision south of Bagdad, because aside from the distance it will be held fast by the Russians in front, mostly cavalry.

The three Turkish divisions at Fellalieh-Kut are fairly good troops, numbering 120–150 rifles per company. The sick report is high; it generally rises to about 10,000 in summer in Bagdad (malaria, dysentery, etc.). Barring a good German 15-cm. howitzer battery the heavy artillery is poor.

There is no heavy artillery with the smaller Turkish group of Nasrieh. The 6th Turkish Division is about to reach there. (This turned out to be incorrect information.)

All essential preliminary conditions for a successful Turkish offensive in Irak are, in my opinion, lacking.

According to my idea the Sixth Army should have been reënforced long ago, because the center of gravity of the operations now lies on the east front, in Irak. With this in view I suggested two months ago to Enver to give instructions to the Third and Second Army to remain strictly on the defensive and to entrench themselves. In this way troops would have become available for the Sixth Army. Enver Pasha declined, because he believed, that after such an order the Third and Second Army would fail to advance promptly, should the Russians weaken their forces in the Caucasus.

The suggestion was likewise declined of combining the Third, Second and Sixth Armies under one command; it was the only step in my opinion that would establish a basis for effective operations on the east front.

The great distances for troop movements and supply lines must be kept in view. From Constantinople to Bagdad a body of troops requires an average of two months.

Hedjas. The rebellious Arabs have attacked the Turks without success some sixty kilometers southwest of Medina. As the distance from Medina to Mecca is about 350 kilometers on an airline, it shows that the insurrectionary movement has spread considerably and that it is wrong to call it unimportant.

Since that time no information has been received from the Turkish troops in Yemen.

Fourth Army. The first expeditionary corps under Freiherr von Kress cannot think of resuming operations from El Arish with its present strength.

I am unable to form an opinion whether the British are thinking of occupying the Sinai peninsula as might be indicated by an extension of the railroad beyond Katia. It is certain, however, that ever since the spring of 1916 it has been the British endeavor to erect a bulwark east of the canal.

The British, commanding the sea as they do, can easily reënforce their troops in Egypt at any time, while we are limited to the lengthy land roads. Moreover, the British will always receive timely notice of our troop movements from the Arabs.

For this reason, I have ever since the first canal expedition, favored small operations against Egypt for the purpose of containing troops there, and have objected to a large expedition unless much larger forces became available for it and unless the communications were secured on a broader basis.

It is well to view the operations in Irak, Hedjas and east of the canal in their combined entirety.

The harshness of Djemal Pasha prevents the Arabs in Syria from being gained for the Turkish cause. There were serious disturbances this month near Damascus which are being suppressed by the military.

Since the beginning of the campaign the proper authorities have not given due weight to the idea that the only communication, the life nerve, for the four armies leads through the Taurus and Amanus Mountains, and that all available labor should be set to work there in the first place.

Had this been properly appreciated, the railroads from Angora to Sivas, the railroad to Diarbekir, and other great works would not have been begun before the transport ways over the Taurus and Amanus had been securely established for all the requirements of all four armies.

Fifth Army. In the district of the Fifth Army, which extends from Midia on the Black Sea to Alaja on the Mediterranean, the enemy has so far been unable to gain a firm footing.

After detaching the 26th Division, the Fifth Army has the 16th Division in Smyrna, the 24th Division on the Asiatic and the 42d Division on the European side of the Dardanelles. They are the older units; all the others are new formations whose organization is not yet complete, and landsturm troops.

First Army. It consists of two divisions at Constantinople and on the Black Sea. I wish to emphasize that a future operation against the Dardanelles is not precluded while a large enemy army is at Salonika and while the islands along our coast are used and continue to be used as enemy supports.

At any rate I would not advise stripping the Dardanelles of all troops.

The Entente learns of all of our troop movements through a widely extended system of espionage.

When success there appears sure and easy, the Entente will surely consider an operation.

The other sensitive point on the Turkish west coast is the Gulf of Alexandretta and Mersina in the sector of the Fourth Army. Vigorous action here may interrupt the communication to the four armies. Troops from Salonika may be used there, after operations near Salonika have ceased. There is at present no prospect of such an enterprise because so far no base has been prepared in Cyprus.

> Sgd. LIMAN VON SANDERS
> General of Cavalry.

To His Excellency
The Quartermaster General,
General of Infantry
Ludendorff
Pless.

EGYPT

A considerable expedition against the Suez Canal was planned for February 1916. The execution was delayed until summer, because the German and Austrian reënforcements encountered several months' delay on account of great obstructions in railway transportation.

Hearing that the British were beginning to withdraw further troops from Egypt, the German headquarters ordered an attack by a small mixed detachment to rekindle British apprehension for the canal.

The detachment consisted of three battalions, six squadrons, a battery and a machine gun detachment and advanced toward Kantara. At Katia, forty-five kilometers east of the canal, it surprised the camp of a British cavalry regiment and captured a considerable part of it. This accomplished the purpose of the expedition.

The larger expedition followed in July. The arrival of the latest German reënforcements was not awaited, because otherwise there was no telling when the expedition would get started.

The expeditionary corps was composed as follows:

The reënforced 3rd Turkish Division under Colonel Refet Bei

6 machine gun companies	German
1 15-cm. heavy field howitzer battery	German
1 10-cm. long rifle battery	German
1 aviation squadron	German
auto formations	German
2 field hospitals	German
4 anti-aircraft sections	German
1 field howitzer division of two	
batteries of six guns each	Austrian

Instead of being carried out in February the expedition had to be made in the hottest and most unfavorable season of the year.

The participating Turkish troops, in spite of all the labor bestowed on them, were only moderately trained and poorly equipped, and there was a lack of good officers. The German and Austrian units had a high sick report, but were otherwise good.

The old caravan route along the coast from El Arish to Katia and Kantara, used by Napoleon in 1799, was selected for the advance. It offered the best conditions for drinking water and supplies.

The instructions of the expeditionary corps (they came by way of Constantinople, but I do not know who originated them) required an advance so near to the canal that the long range guns could stop the passage of ships.

These instructions I have never understood. The question arises at once how long this interruption by artillery was to last. If it was to be a prolonged one, which alone was of substantial value, it entirely depended on whether the British would tolerate it, or whether the Turko-German troops could enforce it. The former as well as the latter had to be answered in the negative, without question.

The instructions were neither fish nor fowl; they reminded one of washing the hands without wetting the fingers.

There were other circumstances which prevented the execution of the operation.

Colonel Freiherr von Kress had no illusions about the situation. On July 4th, ten days before the advance, he reported:

During the past months the British with an immense expenditure of men, material and money, have erected a complete system of defense to the east of the canal with numerous excellent communications of every kind, and are awaiting us there with a force many times superior to our small expeditionary corps.

Any one who has had the responsibility in a difficult situation knows that in war it is sometimes necessary to carry out hopeless undertakings. The leader is helped over the difficulty by the bitter "must" and by the tiny spark of hope that some miracle will intervene in his favor.

The advance was made in three columns in several echelons to minimize the difficulties of water supply, the obtainable quantity at each place being limited. The laborious march led through undulating dunes in the sand in which the foot sank to the ankle. The marches were restricted to the night on account of the heat, and to escape observation of enemy aviators.

After a march of seven days, the entrenched camp of Romani,

forty kilometers east of the canal, was attacked on the 4th of August. The main attack was to be made against the least fortified west front of the camp.

The Turko-German attack failed completely, because the force used was too small, because its approach was known to the British, and because the expeditionary corps was completely exhausted when it reached the enemy. This time the British had not been playing football.

Instead of turning the enemy's flank, the flank of the expeditionary corps was turned by the skillfully led British cavalry, and by the reënforcements arriving from Kantara by rail. In the end the corps succeeded in breaking away from the enemy, who at first pursued hotly. In the attack and in the retreat to El Arish the corps lost about one-third of its strength.

This was the second and last Turkish enterprise of any consequence against the canal and against Egypt.

The rôles were now exchanged. Heretofore the Turks had been on the offensive and the British on the defensive; now began the strategic offensive of the British in the sense of Lord Cromer's memorandum, heretofore referred to. The execution of the British plan was purposeful, and was carried out without haste and with the help of great experience in colonial wars. The British also gained valuable help by winning the Arabs to their side.

In the summer of 1916 the insurrectionary movements in Palestine and Syria supported by the Entente, gained in extent, and the Emir of Mecca had allied himself with the British and proclaimed his independence. It furnished a firm support for the systematically directed efforts of the Arabs to gain their independence.

The Arabian policy, as represented by Djemal, suffered a complete fiasco.

Enver now decided to organize a Hedjas expedition in order to recover Mecca and install another Emir. The composition and organization of this expedition, in which Christians could not be permitted to participate, was found so difficult by the Turks, that it was dropped in the fall.

While Secretary of State Mr. Chamberlain had telegraphed to the Viceroy of India on October 21st 1915:

The Arabs are hesitating and will probably join the Turks unless we offer them large inducements

the Arabian dice had fallen in favor of the British as early as summer 1916. It was merely necessary to build on the foundations laid. And the British built so successfully, that in the subsequent course of this so called Egyptian campaign they were fighting under conditions as though in their own country, while the Turks in defense of their own country had to fight amongst a population directly hostile.

The British made their rate of progress, in their systematic advance in the Sinai peninsula, entirely dependent on the establishment of secure and efficient communications. It was the opposite of the method adopted by Turkey, which in all plans of operations had underestimated the difficulties of supply.

Though the British controlled the sea and possessed in the old caravan route Kantara-El Arish along the coast, a splendid communication for troop movements according to Turkish notions, they made sure and built a railroad along this route at the average rate of one kilometer per day. It was possible to calculate when this railroad would reach the Turko-Egyptian frontier east of El Arish. It was expected in January 1917.

To meet this slow, but sure advance of the enemy Turkey should have brought up good fresh troops. But there were none to be had, for Turkey was tied up with Galicia, Roumania, Macedonia, with two armies in the Caucasus, in Irak and in Persia, and the Fifth Army, in spite of its important duties, and in spite of all warnings, had been made into an army of depot troops. On account of their lamentable condition and lack of training the forces of the Fourth Army at Adana and Alexandretta could not be considered at all.

The least that could be done was to assemble all available Turkish troops and those scattered through the desert and the hinterland as far as Jerusalem, in the district now menaced by the enemy. That was the region of Gaza. It was still possible to erect there a strong line of defense, provided the situation was clearly understood and appreciated.

Political considerations, however, stood in the way of this simple and obvious military step. The Turks still believed they could make the world and the Arabs look upon the Sinai peninsula as a Turkish pawn. Nor was the desert evacuated in time, so that several reverses were unavoidable and an isolated Turkish mixed detachment at Magdaba south of El Arish was captured by the British. El Arish was finally evacuated. After a reverse at Chan Junis in January 1917 in which a regiment was lost with machine guns and a battery, the Turkish troops were gradually being concentrated in the Gaza-Beersheba region.

OTHER MATTERS

Individual cases of cholera had appeared in various places, particularly along the lines of communications, and had been checked with great difficulty by quarantine, but in the summer of 1916 a severe epidemic broke out in Smyrna and at its beginning exacted many victims from all strata of the population.

Several times Greeks came to me in Smyrna lamenting the impending ruin of Smyrna with tears in their eyes, and begged me to let them depart or to save Smyrna. We endeavored to calm them and promised help. But they were not permitted to leave the place.

The Vali of Smyrna, Rahmi Bei, promptly recognized the danger and in spite of many protests from Turkish doctors gave far reaching powers to staff surgeon Professor Dr. Rodenwaldt to enable him to cope with the epidemic. Through the energy of this eminent and experienced expert in hygiene, and with the effective assistance of other German medical men, particularly Dr. Sauerwaldt and Dr. Zeiss, the epidemic was promptly checked and completely wiped out in a few weeks.

During the year the German medical officers established a policlinic in Smyrna which benefited the Greek population almost exclusively, but was sharply opposed by the Turkish doctors because it interfered with their practice.

Many times the German surgeons were sent into the interior of the Vilayet of Aidin with all available means to combat cholera, spotted typhus and malaria, and make sanitary conditions fairly tolerable. They hardly ever received thanks for their work.

When all Germans, including sanitary officers, had to leave Smyrna after the Armistice, all complained of the immediate change of disposition and the aggressive attitude of the Greek levantines. I myself fared no better.

I had protected the Greeks in Smyrna, and in the entire coast region of Asia Minor, in innumerable cases against Turkish encroachments. My picture was hung as acknowledgment in the large Greek school, and the president of the Greek community in Smyrna had offered me a banquet on behalf of the Greeks. My anteroom was never empty of Greek petitioners, male and female, yet after the Armistice the Greeks overwhelmed me with accusations, pure inventions from beginning to end, of having oppressed the Greeks.

It may be readily understood that we preserved no particular sympathy for these characteristics of the inhabitants of the Turkish levant.

All the warnings from the chancel, and all the means at our disposal, could not stop Greek espionage in the coastal region.

Communication with the islands in the hands of the enemy was not only effected by boat, but technical means of communication were employed. Investigation by a German expert led to such remarkable results, that it had to be stopped in order not to drag in a man in high position.

At the house of a member of one of the first families of
Smyrna a diary was found, in which the military activity of
General Trommer, the general commanding in Smyrna, and
also my own activity in Smyrna, when there, was noted in
correct detail.   It happened that the brother of this gentleman
was an officer on one of the enemy ships stationed on this coast.
During the first half of the year, Greek robber bands, guided
by information from this espionage, came across from the
islands, surprised Turkish villages on the outer coast of Asia
Minor, carried off women, children and herds of cattle, and
burned the villages.   In the second half, however, we instituted
small active operations which greatly limited these predatory
excursions.

Several German officers distinguished themselves in these
small expeditions which had something of a naval character,
particularly Captain Schuler and First Lieutenant Hesselberger, both of the cavalry and without naval experience,
unless it was gained on the Bavarian lakes.

On September 18th First Lieutenant Linsmayer distinguished
himself in a surprise attack on the hostile armed bands from the
Island of Gimnonisi west of Aivalik, where many important
papers were captured some of which gave information of the
espionage.

In a somewhat large expedition of twelve boats and 180 men
under First Lieutenant Hesselberger, the enemy was surprised
on November 3d on the Island of Kekova in the Mediterranean,
east of Meis.   After severe fighting, involving considerable
losses, the enemy fled to Meis.

Many other small expeditions in the Ægean Sea and in the
Mediterranean resulted in a large reduction of the piratical
irruptions into Turkish territory.

While at the Dardanelles at the beginning of December 1916
I received a telegram from General Ludendorff requesting me to
report in person at the German headquarters.   For many
reasons this opportunity was most welcome to me.   In the first

place there was the question of my apprehensions for Bagdad, formerly expressed. Then again all kinds of false rumors starting from Constantinople had spread in Germany about renewed differences between Enver and myself which in this case were devoid of any basis of fact. On November 6, 1916, I had received a communication from the Military Cabinet to exercise far going complaisance toward Enver. On November 18th I had telegraphed to the Chief of the Military Cabinet that the reasons for the communication were unintelligible to me. I added that it was either a case of deliberate Turkish falsification, or of untrue German reports which had been accepted without giving me a hearing. I emphasized that the position of the chief of the military mission became untenable the moment it failed of German support.

There was no doubt that my call to Pless was unwelcome to Enver and to the Turkish headquarters. It came hard on Enver to give his consent which he did after a week in the following words:

> Since Field Marshal von Hindenburg has stated that he merely wished to speak of the German military corps, Your Excellency may depart for Pless.

When I reached Pless on December 18 with Captain Prigge, a telegram had been received from Enver to the effect "that no importance should be attached to any apprehensions that might be expressed by a German officer about the Bagdad situation." There can be no question as to the officer that was meant. Field Marshal von Hindenburg had ordered a becoming reply to Turkish headquarters.

On the 18th and 19th of December I laid my Turkish apprehensions before the field marshal, and on the 26th before General Ludendorff on his return from the front at Verdun.

As a result Enver was advised by telegraph from German headquarters to reënforce the Second Army without delay with three or four divisions. Enver replied that the situation at

Bagdad was considered favorable and that Halil was considering an offensive in Irak as soon as the season permitted. The
suggestion of ample reënforcements for the troops at Bagdad
was not heeded.

Between the two reports in Pless I was ordered to report in
person to H. M. the Emperor in the New Palace in Potsdam.
During this interview I had not much to say, for H. M. the
Emperor spoke of the Gallipoli Campaign and the excellent
conduct of the Turkish troops in Galicia. H. M. was not well
informed about Gallipoli and assumed a much more extensive
participation of the submarines than had been possible under
then existing conditions. After the long explication of H. M.
I stated the limited period within which the submarines had
gained results and furnished the exact dates; the Emperor
seemed displeased at such a correction of former reports. He
ended the conversation briefly, while on all other occasions he
had shown me his good will.

I also had occasion in those days of stating my experiences in
Turkey to the Imperial Chancellor von Bethmann-Hollweg and
stated that too much complaisance toward Enver and too much
emphasis of the value of Turkish help would breed such vanity
among the Turks as would render military influence of the
military mission difficult.

The founding of the German-Turkish Amity House in Constantinople, for which Professor Jaekh had raised large sums, was
bound to be looked upon by the Turks as a courting of their
favor. It was the very last thing for us to do. A certain
reserve was more esteemed and respected by the Turk, and
appeared to me more worthy of the German name.

Temporary visitors, and critics with superficial knowledge,
had spread at home many incorrect opinions culminating for the
most part in exaggerated praise of Turkish cultural progress.

Much to our regret there were Germans in Constantinople,
who within a few weeks after arrival, thought it proper to help
their official work by aping Turkish customs. In the office of

the Grand Vizir I met one day three gentlemen wearing the Turkish fez, who gave me the silent Turkish greeting of the right hand on heart, mouth and forehead. On inquiring for the names of these questionable appearing Turks, I learned that they were honest Germans (the name of one of them was Schmidt) who shortly before had been sent to Turkey on some official duty.

A few days before I had the experience in the anteroom of the Emperor at the New Palace, that the Turkish uniform might bring about errors in nationality. The adjutant on duty had not been informed of the audience set just previously for an early hour, and after eyeing Captain Prigge and myself sus-piciously, opened the conversation with the unusual French words *Le soleil vient deja,* whereupon I informed him in German that I found it rather cold and dispelled the misunderstanding.

To show how incorrectly even German officials estimated the conditions in Turkey, I will state that in 1916 all cars with military freight going from Germany to Turkey had for some time a ticket attached marked "Enverland." The Turkish officers could not see in this word an abbreviation for Turkey; it made bad feelings, the more as even then Enver had many personal enemies in the corps of officers. The practice was stopped.

On December 30 I departed on my return to Constantinople.

CHAPTER 12

EVENTS BEFORE THE JILDERIM

THE MILITARY MISSION

With the arrival of Colonel Von Lenthe, the new chief of staff of the mission, there came an extension of its duties in the winter 1916/17. The organization and division of work were arranged so as to take care of all Germans in Turkey belonging to the German Army.

Up to that time touch with German officers on duty at the outer Turkish fronts, and with the few German formations in Turkey, had been maintained through liaison officers stationed at the principal points on the lines of communication. From that time on, besides handling all personal and juridical matters, the military mission expanded into a great German communication office (*Etappen Behoerde*) ramifying over the whole country. General staff officers were added to the staff, the first one being the careful and industrious Captain Bohnstedt, followed by Tzschirner and others.

The improvement of German sanitary establishments continued. New hospitals and infirmaries were established. Additions were made to the existing medical depots, and to the medical depots on the lines of communication.

Intendance Councilor Burchardi, the experienced intendant of the mission, exhibited great talent of organization in expanding existing establishments for renewal of supplies, enlarging the depots and establishing manufactories and workshops of all kinds in and near Constantinople.

In spite of the amplification of most of these works it became possible to comply with the wish of German headquarters and to return to Germany ninety-three German officers and medical officers from November 1916 to January 1917.

The new organization of the mission was of particular value in view of Enver's patent endeavors to restrict its contractual rights; it received the support of the German authorities. Moreover it proved a salutary lesson for some German officers at Enver's headquarters who had been relying on the Turks alone.

Any stories to the contrary notwithstanding, all must concede that the new organization did not comprise even a breath of political activity.

The supreme German authorities had begun in 1916 to send special representatives to Turkey to supervise the procurement and shipment of ores, and of other products of the country, to Germany. These representatives were not assigned to the military mission, as many erroneously believed in Germany. Separate offices were established for them in the Turkish War Ministry. They corresponded directly with the home authorities or through the ambassador or military plenipotentiary.

These endeavors of an economic character had only limited results. There was constant friction in various directions. There was lack of organization in sending these delegates and commissions, and of proper delimitation of their spheres of activity.

In Turkey they all encountered special difficulties, because the lines of these manifold German endeavors led into the office of the Turkish General Intendant, sometimes without their knowledge, who had seized all economic power. He hampered and delayed the export with the far reaching means at his disposal. He toyed with them and played one against the other, including sometimes the Austrians, and generally pursued his own plans and objectives. Finally he let nothing go out except what he considered proper compensation for other services.

Before briefly describing the course of events in the Turkish theaters of war, it is well to give a brief survey of the distribution of the Turkish Army at the beginning of 1917,

Caucasus:

Third Army. Wehib Pasha

    1. Caucas. A. C. (9th, 10th, 36th Caucas. Div.)

    2. Caucas. A. C. (5th, 11th, 49th Div.)

Second Army. J. V. Mustapha Kemal Pasha.

    2. A. C. (1st, 47th Div.)

    3. A. C. (7th division en route to Constantinople under orders from Turkish headquarters, Genkdo and 14th Div. detached to Sixth Army)

    4. A. C. (11th, 12th Div.)

    16. A. C. (5th, 8th Div.)

 Irak:

Sixth Army. Halil Pasha

    18. A. C. (45th, 51st, 52d Div.)

    13. A. C. in Persia (2d, 6th Div.)

    4. Div. at Mosul.

Syria and Palestine:

Fourth Army. Djemal Pasha

    8. A. C. (27th, 43d Div.)

    12. A. C. (41st Div.)

    1. Expeditionary Corps (3d Div.)

    Adana Corps (23d, 44th Div.)

    22. Div. Hedjas

    53. Div. and 3d Cav. Div. at Aleppo.

Dardanelles and Asia Minor:

Fifth Army. Liman von Sanders.

    14. A. C. (42d Div.)

    19. A. C. (24th, 55th Div.)

    17. A. C. (56th Div.)

    21. A. C. (57th Div.)

Constantinople:

First Army. Essad Pasha

    1. A. C. (54th Div. temp. attached, then to Aleppo)

    16. Div. (reserved by army headquarters, then to Aleppo)

European Theaters of War:

    15. A. C. (19th, 20th Div.)

    6. A. C. (15th, 25th, 26th Div.)

    20. A. C. (46th, 50th Div.)

Yemen:

    7. A. C. (39th, 40th Div.), in Assur 21st Div.

and some other detachments and units not enumerated here.

As previously stated the strength of the units in the Turkish theaters of war was variable and compared with 1915 the quality had been greatly impaired by the constant splitting of units, the deterioration of the human material and the inadequate time for training.

CAUCASUS

After the close of the great operations against the Third Turkish Army, the Russians had greatly improved their communications to the front. The narrow gauge railroads from Sarikamish to Erzerum and from Trebizond to Gümüsh-Khane were completed and in operation. The matter of supplies, heretofore the cause of complaint, was satisfactorily regulated for the entire Russian front, which remained unchanged and included Trebizond, Ersingyan, Mush and Van.

The railroad Igdir-Bayazid-Karakilissa was completed and grading had begun for the extension from Karakilissa to Tutak and Melazgerd, through Armenia. According to available Turkish reports the standard gauge railroad Diulfa-Tabriz was to be extended east of Urumia Lake and a standard gauge railroad from Batum to Trebizond was under construction.

Grand Duke Nikolai meant to provide sufficient bases for his army before resuming operations; his hand was felt everywhere. These far reaching plans were checked by the Russian revolution.

It broke out in April 1917 and up to that time no extensive operations had taken place. During the first months of the year the small skirmishes on the front had no effect except sometimes to change occupants of some unimportant hill top. This did not happen very often, because on these extensive fronts the two hostile positions lay several kilometers from each other. Before the beginning of the revolution the various currents of its movement had permeated the Caucasian Army and damped the offensive spirit. A few officers and some particularly good troops alone retained the will to fight or to attack.

The Turks on the other hand had to restrict themselves to the defensive, because the state of neither the Third nor Second Army permitted of large movements. In both the strength was small, subsistence poor, clothing, equipment and ammunition inadequate, and the means of transportation, so indispensable for any offensive action, was as inadequate in quantity as previously stated.

Turkish headquarters combined the two armies into the "Caucasian Army Group" under Izzet Pasha, but the change of name did not alter conditions. The chief of staff of the army group was the German Major von Falkenhausen. Headquarters was established in Diarbekir and later in Kharput. Mustapha Kemal now had full command of the Second Army.

The Second Army had suffered terribly during this hard winter. The land in which it was stationed was depopulated and desolated by the expulsion of the Armenians. All economic conditions of course were greatly impaired. A large part of the fields remained untilled. There were no mechanics and all establishments requiring technical workmen were standing still. The land could thus furnish neither subsistence nor other assistance to the army. The system of supply was wholly inadequate and, as previously stated, supplied so little that thousands died at the front of starvation or debility. A German surgeon, Dr. Liebert, reported from Assur;

> It is remarkable how little power of resistance these debilitated men have even for slight operations. If we do not operate on them, they die; if we do operate they die also.

On account of defective sanitary arrangements spotted typhus carried off thousands. Fuel was lacking for heating the delousing establishments or the wards in hospitals. There were sufficient medical supplies in Ras-el-Ain, but they could not be brought up on account of lack of means of transportation. Of the German sanitary personnel with the Second Army many sickened and did not see their homes again. In February,

the worst month of spotted typhus, forty-two Turkish surgeons
succumbed to the disease.

It is almost like a nemesis of fate, that the expulsion of the
Armenians had such a repercussion on the Turkish Army.
This is not the place to establish the causes of the persecutions
of the Armenians. With all the condemnation and accusations
rightly heaped upon the Turkish potentates, a just judge will not
overlook that it was not the Turkish potentates that invented
the Turkish-Armenian policy. They themselves had been
raised and had grown up in the idea and believed they rendered
the country a patriotic service for the future, by removing
these elements hostile to the government. The intoxication,
following upon the abrogation of the capitulations, led to the
slogan "Turkey for the Turks," heated the passions, and blinded
judgment. Cause for expulsion was frequently furnished by the
Armenians joining the Russians, and by the many cruelties
against the Mohammedan population proven against them.

In the execution of the expulsions many of the terrible and
damnable cases of ruthlessness may unquestionably be ascribed
to the minor officials whose personal hatred and rapacity gave
to the measures ordered from above, an enhancement of harshness that was not intended. In those regions of the Caucasus
the lower Turkish officials and, above all, the Turkish gendarmery, to whom fell the execution of the expulsion in the first
place, were certainly not alive to the conceptions of European
civilization.

I cannot understand how the levantine calumnies against
German officers of having had part in these persecutions gained
such wide credence. The few present in the staffs and with the
troops in Armenian territory had more than enough to do to
remedy the very difficult situation of supply and training. It
often happened that the German officers were not sufficiently
informed by their Turkish commanders about military events
and measures, and much less, of course, about internal political
matters. It is a totally false conception of their position, to

believe that they were able to exercise any influence other than that pertaining to their rank, the scope of which was jealously guarded by the Turks.

Any one knowing Turkish conditions will understand that these accusations were laid against me also. After the unfortunate end of the war all the levantines simply were bound to ascribe all the fault to the Germans. A glance at the map would have shown at once, that my military activity as army commander in Turkey, was restricted to the extreme western theater of the Osmanic empire and at a distance of more than 1000 kilometers from Armenia. Up to this date I have never set foot on Armenian territory or adjoining lands.

IRAK

The British offensive culminating in the capture of Bagdad began in January 1917.

The only troops available against this British offensive was the Eighteenth Turkish Army Corps. It was at the time on both banks of the Tigris about 170 kilometers on an airline southeast of Bagdad. The river there turns from Kut-el-Amara sharply to the northeast and resumes at Umm el Henna its former direction toward the Persian Gulf. The length of this stretch of the river pointing northeast like an advanced position for the protection of Bagdad is thirty-five kilometers. Kut lies on the Turkish right where the Shat el Hai empties into the Tigris under the name of Gharraff. On the left flank, about four kilometers west of Umm el Henna, a few mud hovels were known by the name of Fellalieh, a frequent name. The Turkish right consisted of the 45th and 52d Divisions, the left of the 51st Division.

From here the Euphrates detachment, consisting of the 156th infantry regiment, three squadrons and two batteries, was echeloned from the right, 150 kilometers down the Euphrates to the vicinity of Nasrieh. A British field railway connecting Busra and Kurna had been extended into that section.

The Thirteenth Army Corps at Hamadan on the Persian plateau was distant from Bagdad 400 kilometers on an airline, separated from the lowland of the Tigris by difficult mountain ranges, and its front held fast by Russian troops, mostly cavalry.

The 14th Division of the Second Army was the only unit coming up in support of the Eighteenth Corps, because Enver and his advisers could see no danger for Bagdad, and had left unheeded the advice, given about Christmas time by Field Marshal General von Hindenburg and by General Ludendorff, to bring forward ample reënforcements.

Hardly ever has an army headquarters, in spite of timely and well founded warnings, acted more imprudently than the Turkish before the fall of Bagdad. The important German advisers of Enver (pronounced step children of the goddess strategy) here, as in so many other cases, closed their ears and stiffly resisted the advice which, if followed, would have rectified their preconceived and erroneous ideas of the proper course of action to be followed by the Turks.

On January 9th an extensive attack against the Turkish position at Imam Mohammed at the curve of the river north of Kut opened the fighting. The Turks report that the attack was made by the 3d Indian Lahore Division. After varying results the Turks had to relinquish their first line. A bombardment of Kut and Imam on January 11th was followed on the 12th by a smaller attack on Imam.

In the secret Turkish report of January 14, 1917, to German headquarters it is stated verbatim:

The situation at Kut is considered perfectly favorable and is so regarded by the army.

From now on the Turkish troops were kept in constant commotion by enemy attacks and step by step pushed out of their positions. They fought bravely, but could not resist forever the systematic advance of the superior British forces with much stronger artillery. On the outer flank the British cavalry advanced, again and again threatening the Turkish flank and rear.

The next attacks took place on the Gharraff and at Imam Mohammed. The advanced position at Imam fell on January 18th. The outer position at Kut had to be vacated on February 3rd. On February 9th the new Turkish positions in rear were taken by the British, the Turks resuming the defense some 1,300 meters in rear.

On that day the 41st Infantry Regiment with mountain artillery, forming the head of the 14th Division, reached Azizie.

On February 15th the Turks, after heavy fighting, had to relinquish their position west of the Gharraff. The remainder of the troops was transferred to the left bank of the Tigris during the night, thus abandoning the west bank to the British.

General Gressmann in Bagdad, who controlled all German officers and formations in the Sixth Army, judged the situation more correctly than Turkish headquarters and telegraphed on February 16th:

Situation on Tigris front serious since superiority of British in men and munitions considerable.

The Turkish left at Fellalieh was heavily bombarded on February 17th, the bombardment being followed by an infantry attack against the 51st Division, in which the enemy, parts of the Indian Mahratta Division, according to Turkish reports, took the two Turkish front lines, and lost them again in a counter attack. A bombardment of four days was followed on the 22d by a heavy infantry attack, which after varying results, caused the Turks to fall back to a position in rear after they had suffered heavy losses.

On February 23d the British successfully transferred troops to the east bank of the Tigris at the bend near Shumran; they entrenched there and could not be dislodged. A bridge was then thrown across the river.

On February 24th a strong infantry attack of troops, that had

crossed the river, broke the center of the 52d Division. The
Turkish 40th Infantry Regiment was almost totally destroyed.
During the night to February 25th the Turks fell back to the
position of Tawil.

The first part of the fighting in the bend of the Tigris at Kut
had ended with the loss of all Turkish positions. The Turkish

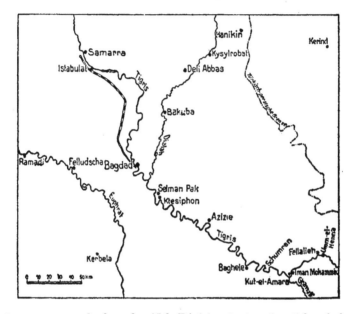

losses were such that the 45th Division had to be disbanded.
Its remnants were distributed among the other divisions.

In view of the danger now threatening Bagdad, the heads of
the Thirteenth Army Corps were set in motion on February
25th from Hamadan in the direction of Kannikin. Russian
cavalry followed at once as was to be expected. On March 1st
the last troops of the army corps finally broke away from
Hamadan. This army corps could not, of course, reach Bagdad
before the decision. Half of the Persian troops deserted at

once upon the departure of the army corps from Hamadan, which was no surprise.

On February 25th a hostile infantry division approached the position of Tawil to within one kilometer. A hostile cavalry regiment turned the Turkish left, attacked the baggage, and trains, and created much confusion. Fighting also took place on the Tigris. Four British gunboats took the steamer *Basra* loaded with Turkish wounded, and the Turkish gunboats *Selman Pak* and *Doghan*.

On the same day the British broke through the position of the Eighteenth Army Corps, which retired with great loss during the night of the 26th to Azizie. An enemy infantry and cavalry division followed toward Azizie.

During the night of the 27th the Eighteenth Army Corps continued its retreat and on the 28th reached the elbow of the river at Selman Pak, where entrenchments were begun at once.

A brief pause now ensued in the enemy's advance. According to Turkish reports the British were entrenching a supporting position at Azizie. We may assume that prior to a final advance on Bagdad they wanted to close up and put their communications in order. The Turkish reports of British movements at the beginning of March read:

Two British infantry and one cavalry division appear to be at Azizie. On the road to Baghele there is what appears to be an Indian brigade in groups. Transport ships with troops are moving to that point. Motor boats are towing pontoons toward Azizie.

The total strength of the Eighteenth Army Corps, inclusive of the 14th Division, was given as 6,200 rifles and eighty machine guns; there were twenty-two field guns, twelve mountain guns and twenty-one howitzers of various models with limited ammunition. Part of the artillery had been lost in the last heavy battles and in the retreat. The evacuation of Bagdad was now begun, and the lightly wounded from the last battles were removed to Samara.

On March 5th the fighting was resumed. A hostile infantry division and a cavalry division advanced. The latter turned the Turkish left. During the night of the 6th of March the Eighteenth Army Corps was withdrawn to the Diala position.

On the morning of March 6th the enemy was moving toward the Diala position. During the night of March 9th the British subjected the Turkish position to heavy artillery fire. Under cover of this fire infantry with machine guns succeeded in crossing to the right bank of the Diala. These advance troops held their ground in spite of heavy attacks of the 44th Infantry of the 51st Division. Protected by this detachment the British threw a bridge and crossed a large force to the northern bank. According to Turkish reports it consisted of fifteen battalions and a cavalry division. The infantry attack opened on the same afternoon, but at first had no results.

During the night of March 10th the enemy forced the 44th Regiment back and renewed the attack. The Turkish troops, enfeebled by continued fighting and the long retreat, were now threatened on both flanks, on both sides of the river, by superior forces. The Diala position had to be relinquished. The 51st and 52d Divisions on the right and the 14th Division on the left bank of the Tigris withdrew in a northern direction.

Bagdad was lost by the Turks during the night of 10/11th March.

During the last few days before the fall of Bagdad supplies of all kinds had been moved north. The large German wireless station, as yet incomplete, was blown up. The rolling stock was taken back to Samara.

The advanced troops of the Thirteenth Army Corps reached Kannikin without much fighting on March 14th, the rear guard at that time being at Kerind. The Russians followed with a cavalry division and a few battalions. The Thirteenth Army Corps continued its march to Kizilrobat.

The so called Euphrates detachment, formerly referred to, reached Feludjah on March 15th in its withdrawal; after being attacked there on March 19th, it withdrew to Romadi.

EGYPT

The English railroad through the desert of El Tih reached Wadi el Arish in January.

Enver, frequently led by political motives, inquired of the Fourth Army whether an offensive against El Arish was not possible; this after the important place had had to be relinquished shortly before by the expeditionary corps under bitter necessity. The leader of the expeditionary corps strongly advised against it. The strength of his troops and their state of training and nourishment prevented such an undertaking, and the number of transport animals was inadequate for any considerable movement. The existing saddle, draft and pack animals were wholly incapable of prolonged exertion, on account of protracted starvation. Enver had to forego the offensive.

Up to March 1917 the British had gradually and constantly reënforced the troops that had crossed the desert. The expeditionary corps also had received some assistance. The 3rd Cavalry Division, consisting of two small regiments, arrived at the front in January, the 16th Division from the Fifth Army in February, and the 53rd Division from Aleppo in March. The Turkish troops were grouped in various positions from Gaza to Beersheba.

At the beginning of March strong British cavalry felt its way to Chan Junis and occupied the place on March 8th. Soon they assembled a considerable force in the region El Arish-Tell Rifah. On March 22d numerous British scouting parties advanced against Wadi Razze, and in the ensuing days the enemy was observed assembling large forces near Chan Junis.

The first Gaza battle began March 26th. At 9 a.m. a division was deployed against the Turkish positions south of Gaza. A strong British force crossed the Wadi Razze at Tell Dschemame. Two brigades with artillery advanced against the section north of Gaza. At 10 a.m. Gaza was surrounded. In the city were the 125th and 79th Infantry Regiments and the 2d Battalion of the 81st Infantry, with machine guns and artillery. After noon they could be communicated with by wireless only.

Height 83 in front of the city was the focus of the action. The British succeeded in taking it in spite of an obstinate defense, and in entering the batteries in rear. A counter attack brought the height back into Turkish hands. It changed occupants three times during the day, toward evening it remained in the hands of the British.

The British entered the city from the north, east and southeast. Every hedge, every house was fought for.

The groups at Dschemame and Tell Scheria had been alarmed at once, but with the customary Turkish delay in starting, the march for the relief of Gaza was delayed into the afternoon hours. The former was to attack the British from the north and east, the latter from the south. Their action did not become effective on the 26th, as both columns were several times checked during the march, and it was 9 a.m. on the 27th of March before they were near enough to Gaza for the relief to become sensible.

The British had to give up their attack from the north and east, and lost height 83 by a bayonet attack of the Turks. By 11 a.m. the relieving troops had established connection with the Gaza group.

The British began to retreat to the west bank of Wadi Razze. They left a rear guard on the east bank, but withdrew it during the night so that by morning of the 28th the east bank of the Wadi was free from the enemy.

The Dschemame group followed the British to the Wadi. The Tell Scheria and Beersheba groups were withdrawn to Tell Scheria on the evening of the 27th.

The Turks buried some 1,500 British dead. Twelve machine guns and twenty automatic rifles were captured by them. Among the Turkish troops the 125th Infantry had specially distinguished itself, and Major Tiller among the German officers.

The results gained by Colonel von Kress by this severe struggle had great value as a serious check inflicted on the British, after their prolonged and systematic advance from the canal.

On the two days of battle there was much friction in the movement of the Turkish troops, explained in part by the condition of the troops, resulting from the constant lack of sufficient food. The disposition of troops in groups required greater mobility and greater offensive strength than the troops had; so a change was made. A continuous line of defense was selected on the Gaza-Tell Scheria front as the one most exposed to the enemy's attack.

The left flank was in the air, and in view of the small strength of the troops the front seemed too extended; but we had to put up with that. About the middle of April the distribution of the Turkish troops was the following:

At Gaza the reënforced 3d Infantry Division.

Between Gaza and Tell Scheria the reënforced 53rd Division.

At Dschemame the 3d Cavalry Division.

At Tell Scheria the 16th Infantry Division.

The 54th Infantry Division was assembling at Beersheba and the 7th was en route.

On the 19th of April the British renewed their attack in the second battle of Gaza. The principal attack was directed against the positions of the 53d Division between Gaza and Tell Scheria, and designed to break the Turkish front.

At 5 a.m. heavy artillery fire opened against the 3d Division at Gaza, supported by the heavy calibers of two cruisers, several torpedo boats and flat-bottomed boats. The fire of the ships was of small effect.

Soon thereafter a heavy artillery fire opened against the 53d Division. At 8 a.m. heavy infantry attacks began in which parts of the advanced positions of the 53d and 3d Divisions were lost. The greater part of them was retaken in the afternoon with the bayonet.

In one attack against the left wing of the 53d Division the British came under flanking fire from the 16th Division, and in an attack on the right of the 53rd under flanking fire from the 3d Division.

The British cavalry had advanced against the left of the 3d and the right of the 16th Division without effect.

An advance of the Turkish 3d Cavalry Division and of the Beersheba detachment south of the Wadi-Tell Scheria caused the British cavalry to withdraw. Toward 7 p.m. the fighting ceased.

On the whole the enemy had been thrown back to his initial positions or had withdrawn to them of his own accord.

On the Gaza front he had made a slight gain of ground, part of which he relinquished on April 21.

A Turkish counter attack against the British right, planned for the morning of March 20, was impracticable on account of lack of ammunition. On the afternoon of the 20th the victorious leader, Colonel Freiherr von Kress, received telegraphic orders from the army leader, Djemal Pasha, not to make the attack.

A landing in rear of the Turks, announced by British wireless before the battle to deceive the Turks, failed to materialize.

After the battle the British entrenched on the line Tell et Tine-Esch Schaluf-El Mansura-Ch. el Maschrafe, particularly protecting their right flank.

The Turkish losses in the battle were 391 killed, 1,336 wounded and 242 missing. They captured six British officers and 266 men. The British losses in the battle were estimated by the Turks as very high, and confirmed as such by the British prisoners.

No notable actions took place on this front during the ensuing months. The constant arrival of British reënforcements decreased the relative strength of the Turks more and more.

The foregoing somewhat detailed account of the spring battles at Gaza is necessary for a proper understanding of the events that took place in this section in the fall.

ASIA MINOR

At the beginning of 1917 one of the operations took place on the coast of Asia Minor which an active defense demanded. It should be kept in mind that the Fifth Army had not a single war vessel at its disposal.

It was the question of a surprise attack on the harbor of the Island of Meis in the Mediterranean. It was occupied by enemy troops, provided with guns, wireless stations, etc., and

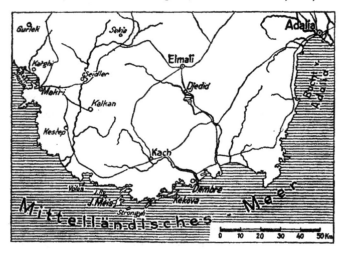

was the point of origin of numerous enterprises against our coast.

After four weeks of severe toil the preparations were completed. A howitzer battery and a mountain battery were moved, from the railroad terminus at Baladis, first on a passable road then through mountains devoid of roads to a rocky promontory opposite the island, and placed in position. Several hundred workmen converted a narrow packtrail into a road three meters wide to get the howitzers to the coast. The pass, by which the mountains were crossed, was 1,500 meters above sea level, the rocky promontory 220 meters.

On January 6th the batteries were in position at a distance of about 5,000 meters from the harbor entrance which was mined. They could lay directly on the fifty-meter opening of the mine field. The ammunition had been brought by about 400 camels. The enemy had not noticed anything.

On January 9th a large war vessel, painted gray, entered the harbor and anchored peacefully close to the entrance. Our artillerists took it for a cruiser, but it turned out to be a mother ship for airplanes.

At 1:30 p.m. the batteries opened fire. After several direct hits the large ship caught on fire. There was no time to use its guns. Subsequently the ammunition exploded and next morning the wreck lay at the anchorage broken through between the two funnels, the forepart almost completely under water.

The torpedo boats in the harbor with steam up, and an armed merchant ship were hit several times but escaped. The wireless stations were destroyed by our batteries.

The Turkish batteries were promptly fired upon by the guns on the island and by the torpedo boats, and were withdrawn for a while.

No further incursions into Turkey territory were undertaken from the Island of Meis.

The success of this laboriously prepared surprise attack is due to the leader of the artillery, Major Schmidt-Kolbow, to Captain Schuler, First Lieutenant Hesselberger and to Captain lttmann. The latter died for the fatherland the following year in Palestine.

These small actions served to keep up the spirit of the Fifth Army which was being completely stripped by Turkish headquarters. After detaching the 16th Division in February three battalions were taken away for the 53d Division of the Fourth Army, and in March every fourth company of every battalion was sent off to the Second Army. Before being detached they had to be brought to full strength from the remaining units.

Through this constant splitting of troops it came about in the end that no commander in the Turkish Army knew his subordinates. The men knew neither their superiors nor their comrades. Had there been a competition in how to ruin an army by continuous wrong measures, the Turkish headquarters would have been sure of first prize.

In April, Enver made the unheard of demand on the Fifth Army to exchange eighteen of its battalions for eighteen Arabian battalions of Djemal's army. As Enver insisted on the exchange in spite of my determined protests, I addressed the following telegram to Ambasssador von Kuhlmann:

23 April 1917

Against my urgent and earnest advice Enver has just ordered the Fifth Army to exchange its own battalions for Arabian battalions to be transferred from the Fourth Army. According to former orders still in force the number of the battalions is eighteen.

I am fully informed by the German officers there that the battalions to be turned over are wholly unfit for use against the enemy. They are neither trained nor disciplined.

Major Niemann knows the military reasons why such an exchange is impossible for the Fifth Army under a German commander. There is the additional political reason that with the wide dispersion of the coast guards along the coast almost exclusively inhabited by Greeks, these wholly undisciplined troops will be useless in preventing espionage and desertion to the nearby islands all of which are held by the enemy. I am therefore obliged to request my relief from command of the Fifth Army.

Request report to His Majesty.

Sgd. LIMAN V. SANDERS.

When General Ludendorff tried to settle the conflict I wrote to him on April 28th:

I am convinced that the military-political situation here will become untenable, when Djemal's wholly undisciplined battalions are placed among the Greeks on the coast of Asia Minor, which is constantly being severely oppressed by the Turks.

In connection with the troops of Venizelos on the islands but a few kilometers distant, and with the British ships along the entire front, this step is bound to have serious consequences on this, the only intact, Turkish front.

On April 28 I received a telegram from the Chief of the Military Cabinet as follows:

His Majesty believes that Your Excellency's relinquishment of command in the present situation would be against the interest of the cause. His Majesty expressed the expectation that ways and means would be found for composing the present conflicts. His majesty believed that means thereto exist.

It was ever so. When I objected to some senseless steps ordered by Turkish headquarters and finally drew the ultimate consequence, I was instructed to be complaisant and had to remain in my position.

On General Ludendorff's suggestion Enver's order was so far rescinded that four battalions only were exchanged.

At that time I had a glance into Turkish administration of justice to which my influence as a German officer did not extend. Moreover it would have been perfectly useless, because neither I, nor my German staff, knew the Turkish criminal law or the written language.

The son of a prominent Greek family had come in conflict with a Turkish officer and had been arrested. I was asked for help. Through an error of the interpreter I was conducted to the building where military prisoners were confined while awaiting trial.

When I entered, the prisoners were lying on wooden bunks along the walls of several large rooms. They all rushed up to me and through the interpreter asked me for help. A large number declared that up to date they had not been informed why they had been arrested. Others had been imprisoned for two years without a hearing. Others stated that they were charged with murder, or theft in places where they had never been. Anyway, it was a cry for help from many a poor devil who felt himself at the mercy of a perfectly arbitrary administration of justice.

I requested the officers of the administration of justice to

come to these rooms and asked them why these men were not
given a hearing. The answer was that the witnesses were
absent in the distant theaters of war and that it was useless
to begin the investigation. When I asked the gentlemen what
they thought would be the further course, if the principal
witnesses had been killed in the meantime, they made no
reply.

I informed Enver at once in writing of these hair raising
conditions, as I could not take other official action.

CHAPTER 13

JILDERIM

After the loss of Erzerum the great offensive of the Second Army against the Russians was initiated, the failure of which has been described.

After the loss of Bagdad, and underestimating the immense difficulties of the plan, Jilderim with open offensive intentions was prepared to retake this prominent and in every way important city from the British.

The term Jilderim was used by the Turks at the time of Napoleon's Egyptian campaign and is well chosen. Jilderim means "lightning."

It is necessary here to go into the details of the Jilderim enterprise, because the principle on which Germany had worked in Turkey, and on which the military mission was based, was completely broken down.

This principle was one of moderate military assistance to Turkey. During peace it comprised the reorganization of the army. During the war it led to a limited augmentation of the German officers, and to the assignment of several German formations for the Sinai front, and of some batteries, flying detachments and auto trucks to other fronts, and to assistance with money and war material.

The Germans were the military instructors and sometimes also the commanders, the latter in collaboration with the Turks. The existing opposition had been bridged over, partly after a severe struggle.

Jilderim was erected on an entirely different basis. At the head of Jilderim there was to be a staff organized like that of a German army group, consisting almost exclusively of German officers, with a German general at the head.

173

The army group was to consist of Turkish armies, to which various German troops and numerous German auxiliary formations were to be attached. For an effective conduct of the war in the Turkish theaters with their enormous difficulties of supply, Jilderim received special German funds, which it was probably not easy to raise, to the amount of £5,000,000 in gold.

General von Falkenhayn was placed at the head of Jilderim; he was a former Prussian Minister of War, then chief of the general staff of the field army, and later leader of an army in Roumania. He arrived in Constantinople on May 7th for a preliminary survey.

The German term for Jilderim was "Army Group F."

Anticipating somewhat, I will here enumerate the German troops and formations assigned to Jilderim as fixed by a decree of the Prussian War ministry of July 2, 1917:

1. Headquarters Army Group F (General von Falkenhayn)
2. Staff Pasha II
3. Three infantry battalion staffs
4. Three infantry battalions, each of three companies No. 701–703
5. Three machine gun companies of six guns each
6. Three platoons of cavalry with two machine guns
7. Three trench mortar troops of four light trench mortars
8. One artillery battalion staff
9. Two batteries of light field howitzers sixteen
10. One battery field guns sixteen
11. One light mortar company
12. One infantry gun platoon with light ammunition column
13. Two mountain howitzer platoons with light ammunition column
14. One antiaircraft gun battery
15. One ammunition auto-truck column for light trench mortars
16. One pioneer section with one platoon of flame throwers
17. One army telephone detachment
18. One division telephone detachment
19. Three heavy wireless stations
20. Five light wireless stations
21. Four aviation sections
22. One sanitary company No. 300
23. Two field hospitals Nos. 218 and 219
24. Auto echelon.

The staff of the Army Group, according to the orders, comprised sixty-five German officers and nine Turkish officers, the latter of low grade, except one major.

Germany assumed a heavy responsibility when she constructed the plan for Army Group F. She was not merely furnishing requested help, but took an active part in the working of the Turkish Army. Any reverse was bound to be charged to the German account.

Had the German centers known the Turkish Army, and the country, and the people, they would have procured the needed help in some other way.

The military mission, with military experience of three and one-half years in Turkey, was not consulted at all, and was confronted with an accomplished fact. It is strange that not even the German officers of the military mission or at Turkish headquarters, who for a long time had been directing the organization of the artillery and train, of communications and sanitary service, and had gathered a wide experience, were consulted in the formulation of such important consequences. These officers were Colonel Schlee, Bischof, Potschernick, and staff surgeon Dr. Jungels with years of experience in colonial wars and a chief of staff of the chief of the Turkish field sanitary service. Nor was Professor Dr. Collin consulted, the meritorious chief of the German sanitary service in Turkey.

According to the ideas of the originators of Jilderim, the enterprise was intended as a complete surprise for the military mission, after the loss of Bagdad.

This disregard of the military mission was not the intention of German headquarters. When I was called to the German headquarters in Kreuznach in November 1917, General Ludendorff told me that he had assumed as a matter of course that all propositions for Jilderim had received my approval, and that the responsible author of the whole plan was the German military plenipotentiary in Constantinople.

The first action of Jilderim was to be the recapture of Bagdad, as stated.   One of the first steps in that direction taken by the Turkish headquarters was the establishment of the "Etape Inspection of the Euphrates" on the 11th of June 1917 with headquarters in Jerablus.

During the same month instructions were given for the reconnaissance of the road from Aleppo to Hit by auto officers— First Lieutenants Kuhner and Herkner—for a convoy of 500 loaded 3-ton trucks.   Other necessary information of the condition of roads and of the availability of drinking water at all seasons, in the districts in which the marching and deployment were to take place, had been neglected.

Subsequent reconnaissances ordered by Army Group F, and other information gathered, caused various doubts as to the practicability of the movement.   They delayed final instructions.

Great difficulties arose for the German staff of Jilderim, composed as it was of officers unfamiliar with the Turkish Army and the country.   That one or the other had done topographic work in Turkey at some time, or had held some post in the Turkish Army, could not alter this condition any more than could the small number of Turkish officers assigned to the German staff.

The German officers of course acted on the experience they had gathered in the theaters of the German fronts, and assumed that here, as in Germany, all orders issued would be carried out. This last named erroneous belief was bound to produce every kind of delay.

In Turkey one can make the most beautiful plans and prepare the execution by drawings and perfect orders, and something entirely different will be done or perhaps nothing at all.

Translation alone caused constant friction, augmented by those who carried out the orders.   It will not be often, that they fully approve of the German instructions; they will feel convinced that this terrible German haste is superfluous, and that many things will turn out differently from what one wants.

"All haste is the devil's" says an Arabian proverb in the Koran. The sacred precepts of this religious book here, as in many other matters, furnish a key to the Turkish character. The highly respected chief of staff of the army group, Colonel von Dommes, heaved many a deep sigh, forced from him by the infinite placidity of the Turks.

The central offices, of course, promised everything the Jilderim asked for, if only for the reason that the Turk considers a direct refusal impolite; but the keeping of the promise was a different matter.

There is no doubt that a certain distrust against Jilderim existed in the Turkish corps of officers from the beginning, because it was looked upon as a German institution. The distrust developed in various places into passive resistance, which was shared in part by the civilian authorities in the provinces.

The military mission had from the beginning taken the only possible position toward Jilderim, that of unreserved coöperation so far as lay within its powers. It was sometimes difficult to withhold it, where Jilderim wanted thorough alterations, which, on account of the peculiar conditions of the country and of the administration, would be left severely alone by one acquainted with the country. This applies particularly to the line of communications.

During the summer an arrangement was made between the military mission and Jilderim for the German administration of the lines of communication; the military mission took the section between Constantinople and Aleppo, Jilderim that south and east of Aleppo, the latter as far as Mosul. Hence the military mission had charge of the organization and management of the transportation of all supplies for Jilderim as far as Aleppo.

Among the new formations organized for Jilderim was the so called Asia Corps, the staff (Pasha II) and portions of which are enumerated in the previously enumerated list of Army Group F. Its basic units were the Infantry Battalions Nos. 701,

702 and 703, composed of sound men suited for tropical service. These battalions were well supplied with light and heavy machine guns and trench mortars, platoons of cavalry, artillery and pioneers were attached to them as might be required by tactical requirements. The Asia Corps was commanded by Colonels v. Frankenberg and Proschlitz.

The extensive personal equipment of the men as well as the scope of the sanitary equipment, covered all requirements for service in a tropical climate in any season. This required more transportation than was customary in Turkey. All requisite horses were to be bought in Turkey, and the numerous train soldiers were to be recruited among the Turkish troops. The completion of this organization required considerable time, and could not be effected without friction.

The completed Asia Corps required for its transport from Constantinople to the front an amount of rolling stock which, in view of the limited capacity of the single track railroad, was extraordinary and quite out of proportion to the modest requirements of the Turkish troops. The uninterrupted supply of the German troops farther on, and the accession of additional formations at the front, were bound to increase the difficulties.

In Germany there probably was no appreciation of how much the German units in Turkey constituted a foreign body, the maintenance of which for service on the extreme frontiers of the Osmanic empire trebled the work of the communications as compared with Turkish formations.

The transport of the manifold supplies for the Asia Corps, and of other German formations attached to Jilderim, called for a considerable augmentation of the German personnel on the lines of communication. Transports of any size had to be escorted and guarded, on account of the great probability that otherwise they would be robbed.

No separate German communication troops had been assigned to Jilderim, so that the additional personnel had to be taken from the troops and formations. It weakened the fighting strength to a most undesirable degree. In the end a far greater part of the German troops was employed on the lines of communication than on the front.

The consequence of it all was that the greater part of the Asia Corps had to wait for weeks and months for its departure for Aleppo, and in November 1917 still lay in the camps of Haidar Pasha.

In the fall of 1917 Jilderim transferred its offensive plans from Bagdad to the Sinai front, as is well known. Since the second battle at Gaza the British were constantly being reënforced on their Palestine front, so that the Turkish situation there was considered serious.

The British, of course, had learned of the plans for the recapture of Bagdad. They selected the most effective means for frustrating it by their decision upon a strong offensive in Palestine. Meanwhile the Turkish headquarters had used the summer to gather up all troops within reach that could be spared, for the operations against Bagdad or in Palestine.

In the spring of 1917 the formation of the Seventh Army was ordered from the Third Army Corps, and from the Fifteenth Army Corps then in Galicia.

Enver gave the command of the Seventh Army at first to Wehib Pasha. Shortly the appointment was rescinded and Mustapha Kemal Pasha was selected for the command. He did not want the command and did not keep it. He was replaced by Fewzi Pasha before the operations began.

The troops to be transported to the south of the Taurus had their ranks filled up before departure from Constantinople. For reasons previously stated, the value of many organizations had deteriorated, and desertions during the long period of transportation tore wide gaps in their ranks.

On June 11 began the departure of the 19th Division from Galicia and on the 20th that of the 50th Division from Macedonia. At the beginning of July the 24th Division was drawn out of the Dardanelles. The departure of the 20th Division from Galicia began August 8th and that of the 59th from Aidin on the 18th, that of the 42d from the Dardanelles in September. All had the preliminary destination of Aleppo.

From the eastward the 48th Division, formerly belonging to the Second Army, and the Caucasian cavalry brigade of the Third Army, were put on march.

The headquarters of Jilderim were transferred to Aleppo at the end of August.

When it was decided to conduct the first urgent operations in Palestine, the following orders were issued from Turkish headquarters which reached the various commands in October:

Gr. Headquarters, operation section.
I 235. Op. secret
To the Fourth Army
and the Army Group Jilderim.

1. Superior Army Command No. 4 ceases.

2. The Lieutenant General and Minister of Marine, Djemal Pasha, is given the title of commander in chief in Syria and West Arabia. He commands the troops in Syria, in Hedjas and in Palestine, as well as the troops in Syria.

3. The Seventh Army pertaining to Jilderim will be transported to the Sinai front. The troops now on the Sinai front will be under the Army Group Jilderim as long as the Seventh Army remains on the Sinai front.

4. The Army Group Jilderim will conduct its operations independently on the Sinai front and in the separate Sanjak of Jerusalem, but Jilderim will keep the commander in chief in Syria and West Arabia informed.

Sgd. ENVER.

This order from Turkish headquarters becomes plain when we add that the troops of the Sinai front under Colonel Freiherr von Kress now came under the orders of Jilderim as the Eighth Army, and that the Seventh Army was ordered to the Sinai front. The sphere of action of the two armies was delimitated in the north by the northern limits of the province of Jerusalem and on the west by the Dead Sea.

The direction of operations in Mesopotamia remained in the hands of Jilderim.

The army command of Syria and West Arabia comprised the Seventh, Eighth and Twelfth Army Corps and the Hedjas Expeditionary Corps.

Assumption of command of the Sinai front by Jilderim (Army Group F) was bound to cause friction with Minister of Marine Djemal Pasha. He had held supreme command there for three years, ever since the fall of 1914. Throughout the country he had assumed a position something like that of Viceroy.

The expedient of giving him command of the country in rear and on one side of the Palestine theater was bound to fail the moment the operations there progressed or regressed.

An arbitrary line of delimitation could not possibly stay the friction which was unavoidable, as the two commands had to coöperate in mány ways and were dependent on each other. Moreover, Djemal had such influence on the civil authorities, that assistance of Army Group F from the resources of the country could materialize only with his consent. Enver's power ceased more or less at the Taurus. Djemal was not willing to coöperate fully, because he felt that he had been thrust from his former position.

In December Djemal had himself relieved as commander in chief of Syria and West Arabia, and devoted himself thereafter to his duties as Minister of Marine in Constantinople. His command was added to that of Jilderim.

At this point we will briefly review the military events that had taken place since spring within the present limits of the command of Jilderim.

IRAK

On the 11th of March the Eighteenth Army Corps had broken away from the enemy and retreated twenty-two kilometers to the north of Bagdad.

The Sixth Army was now operating in two groups, the Eighteenth Army Corps on the Tigris, the Thirteenth Army

Corps on the Djebel Hamrin. The latter corps had the 14th Division at Deli Abbas assigned to it.

On April 9th and 10th the two divisions of the Eighteenth Army Corps, after numerous engagements, reached a prepared position at Istabilat, south of Samara.

The Russians advanced as far as Kizilrobat and gained temporary touch with the British.

After bloody fighting on April 22d, the Eighteenth Army Corps had to be withdrawn beyond Samara, and later as far as Dur, abandoning the terminus of the Bagdad-Samara railroad. The railroad establishments and rolling stock were destroyed.

At that time the Thirteenth Army Corps stood south of Demirkapu. About the middle of May the 14th Division was again assigned to the Eighteenth Army Corps and moved to Tekrit. That was the time when Jilderim made its appearance.

The hot season brought a certain calm. Meanwhile, according to Turkish reports, the British strongly fortified Feludjah and the canal on the left bank of the Euphrates.

On September 28th and 29th the British attacked the Euphrates detachment at Romadi, capturing a large part of the Turkish troops.

The Turkish 46th Division, withdrawn from Macedonia in April, was now approaching the Tigris.

So far as known the First and Third Indian Corps held the British Bagdad front. The 3d, 7th, 13th, 14th and 15th Divisions and a cavalry division were reported there. The British built a field railway from Bagdad to Bakuba and repaired the railroad from Bagdad to Samara for their purposes.

Actual connection between British and Russians no longer existed in the fall.

By a slow but steady advance the British occupied Tekrit on November 6th, a point 150 kilometers north of Bagdad. They still were 200 kilometers from Mosul.

The Eighteenth Army Corps was withdrawn to the Fethie position.

EGYPT

During the summer the British made several strong cavalry reconnaissances and raids against Beersheba. The construction of their railroad to that point proceeded slowly.

In the middle of summer the Turkish troops stood: the 7th and 53rd Divisions south of Gaza and adjoining; on the east toward Tell Scheria the 54th Division; southwest of Scheria the 16th Division; at Beersheba the 27th Division and 3d Cavalry Division; the 3d Division in reserve at Hudsch; the 26th Division withdrawn from Roumania in the spring was assembling at Ramleh and for the present reserved by headquarters though later assigned to Twentieth Army Corps.

In September the British pushed their left wing closer to the Turkish positions. Their total strength at that time was estimated at eight divisions.

Of further Turkish reënforcements: the 24th Division was assembling at Ramleh; the 19th Division was to follow there; the 59th Division, without artillery, was at Aleppo; the departure of the 20th Division from Haidar Pasha began September 12.

The amount of troops transported by the Anatolian railroad to Syria in 1917, in spite of all obstacles, is astonishing, while from March 1st to the fall of 1918 not one single complete division could be gotten through from Constantinople to the front.

The 48th Division, detached from the Second Army, and stationed in the Damascus-Deraa region, was assigned to the Eighth Army Corps, and was thus under the orders of the commander in chief of Syria and West Arabia.

The 1st Division, likewise coming from the Second Army, had reached Damascus by the end of November, and the 11th Division, which formerly belonged to the Second Army, was ordered to move to Aleppo. Both were meant for the Palestine front.

I abstain from sketching the events on the Palestine front
from November 19, 1917, to March 1, 1918, because they took
place under German command, and because details are not
accessible to me.   It should be mentioned, however, as important
for the events in their entirety, that Akaba, the sea gate to the
East Jordan country, was taken from the Turks in June 1917
and that soon thereafter Scherif Faisal made his formal entry
there.

Important for Army Group F was the explosion of the great
ammunition depot at the railroad station of Haidar Pasha on
September 6th, which destroyed a large part of the harbor and
railway establishments, warehouses, subsistence depots, etc.
The ammunition had been transported through half of
Europe and certainly was not so sensitive as to explode from
the dropping of an ammunition box, as was stated.   Hence it
was very probable that the explosion was intentional to impair
the Turkish conduct of the war.

CHAPTER 14

THE WAR IN TURKEY OUTSIDE OF JILDERIM

From spring to the end of 1917 no important events took place in the other Turkish theaters of war.

CAUCASUS

In front of the Second Army the Russians began, toward the end of April, to evacuate some villages and withdraw some of their troops. On May 1st the Turks reoccupied Mush without fighting.

The Third Army was active in scouting and there was some artillery firing.

The inactivity within the radius of these two armies continued through the summer. The withdrawal of Russian troops continued until winter.

In November there was little fighting for the Third Army; Turkish ports like Espije, Kerason, Termeh and Sinub were sometimes bombarded by Russian ships, until the Armistice of December 7 stopped further hostilities.

ASIA MINOR

The beautifully drawn organization sketches, sent from Turkish headquarters to German headquarters, were apt to create wrong ideas of the condition of the Fifth Army. General Ludendorff had been informed by Turkish headquarters in July 1917, that two divisions of the Fifth Army would become effective at the end of July and two other divisions at the end of August. I corrected that statement by a telegram which I give here verbatim:

20. July 1917

The information communicated to Your Excellency, that two divisions become effective at the end of July and two more at the end of August, is not entirely correct.

At the end of July there is

a) the 60th Division. Today, July 20th, it is lacking five of its six field batteries. The prescribed nine machine gun platoons and many other things are also lacking.

b) the 61st Division. It lacks four field batteries, the nine machine gun platoons and many other things.

At the end of August

c) the 47th Division. One infantry regiment has been formed, but is only half strength. Otherwise the division consists of cadres totalling some 600 men, without guns, machine guns and horses;

d) the 49th Division. It consists exclusively of cadres, about 600 men, without guns, machine guns and horses.

The men required to fill up the four divisions can be gotten only gradually and in small detachments, as the filling up of the ranks has become exceedingly difficult.

Sgd. LIMAN V. SANDERS.

Had it been permitted to fill the ranks with deserters, it would have been easy to fill them beyond the prescribed strength. Those in my district, where there was still a fair degree of order, were estimated at 16,000; everywhere they made the country insecure and laid it under contribution. Our headquarters guard was turned out several times for the protection of the vicinity of Panderma, and lost five men killed in one of the actions against these deserters.

Active defense of the coast with a few long range guns, which moved about the country and changed their positions, brought many small successes. Tenedos was several times successfully bombarded and the wireless station there destroyed. A harbor on the east coast of Imbros also was bombarded.

On July 21 a motor boat, forty paces long and loaded with depth bombs, was captured near Conidie (near Cheshme west of Smyrna).

On August 17th the lighthouse on the Island of Kalolimni was destroyed by a party shipped on three motor boats made in Smyrna.

On December 13 an auxiliary cruiser of the enemy was sunk near Ava south of Adalia, and the crew of fifty-two men captured.

Numerous other small enterprises against the islands off
the coast were successfully carried out.

OTHER MATTERS

In the fall of 1917 it again appeared as though the military
mission was destined to cease its function. The German
military plenipotentiary in Constantinople, in collaboration
with German authorities, formulated a German-Turkish military convention early in the summer of 1917, which was to take
the place of the contract of the military mission. It meant a
return to the former system of German reformers working
individually, except that the local senior officer had some
supervision.

Complete equality of German and Turkish officers was provided. A number of the latter were to be sent to Germany for
instruction. The organization of the Turkish division was to
be the same as that of the German division, so that in case of
war an exchange could be made.

The complete transformation of the Turkish corps of officers
was wholly overlooked, which was the first requisite for raising
them to a degree of efficiency sufficient to enable them to train
their own army. I considered the whole idea of the military
convention a great mistake, and the time for this proposal a still
greater mistake. However, as no term was set when the military convention was to become effective, I assumed that this
question would not be taken up until completion of the World
War. Any discussion prior thereto I considered valueless, and
I had little to say when the convention was referred to me.

In the negotiations the method of transition from the military
mission to the military convention was left untouched. In
my opinion it could be effected only on demobilization, as the
entire communication (*etappen*) service of the military mission,
with its numerous fixed establishments, would have to be disposed of. The contract of the military mission ended December
14, 1918. It will astound any soldier that the German military

plenipotentiary formulated these propositions in conjunction
with the German home authorities, without imparting the least
knowledge of the plan to the military mission. But a still
greater surprise was in store.

In October 1917 I was informed that H. M. the Emperor was
coming to Turkey to view the battlefields of the Dardanelles
Campaign. At the same time I was told that on the occasion
of the Emperor's visit the military convention would be signed
by the two War Ministers and become at once effective upon
their signature.

I wired at once to the Prussian Minister of War, von Stein,
that the only practical way by which the transition from the
military mission to the military convention could be accomplished without injury to the officers concerned was by the
abrogation of all contracts and by my recall. The basic
stipulations of the contract had been completely overlooked
so far.

I now entertained the hope of getting away from a situation
which had become intolerable to me. In reply I was informed
that the paragraph relating to the time when the military convention was to take effect had been altered, and that the
convention would not become effective until after the conclusion of peace.

On the occasion of the Emperor's visit the military convention was duly signed by War Minister von Stein and by Enver.

His Majesty the Emperor visited the battlefields of the
Dardanelles on the 17th of October. I delivered a brief dis-
course on Suvla Bay in the presence of a great suite, in which
there were several high naval officers, explaining the limited
activity of the U-boat war in the Dardanelles and the reasons
for it, without His Majesty appearing in the least displeased.

In November I was called to the headquarters in Kreuznach,
where I stated the grounds for my worries about the constant
errors of Turkish headquarters. Ten days later the English
papers reported that I had been called to headquarters for an

important conference about the situation in Turkey and had a long audience with the Emperor. It appears that the enemy's connections extended to Kreuznach.

In December Enver received a new chief of the general staff in the person of Major General von Seekt, who had rendered valuable service in the war on the German and Austrian fronts. He had only a theoretical knowledge of Turkey.

To give him timely information I sent him on December 13 the following brief statement of conditions in the Turkish Army at that time, sending at the same time a copy to German headquarters in care of the chief of the operation section "Orient."

Panderma 13th December 1917

Condition of the Turkish Army today.

Through a series of errors the numerical strength of the combatant troops of the Turkish Army and their fighting efficiency has sunk to a level so low that it cannot be overlooked. The causes of both defects must be clearly understood in order to devise a remedy.

Any remedial measures must expect to encounter many difficulties from the unsatisfactory condition of transport roads and transport means.

I. Numerical Strength:

In the unavoidable battles in the various theaters of war, the Turkish Army has suffered severe losses, which it could not escape. But it suffered further great losses which with some care might have been avoided, and which should be instructive for the future. In the latter class are:

a) The first Caucasus campaign in December 1914 and January 1915. The Third Army (leader, Enver Pasha, chief of the general staff, Major General von Bronsart) numbered about 90,000 good troops at the beginning of December 1914.

It held a favorable defensive position in the mountains near Hassan Kala, near the frontier; the opposing Russians were not superior in numbers.

An offensive against Sarikamisch-Kars was decided upon, against my urgent advice, although in case the army succeeded in forcing a passage through and out of the mountains, it would be unable to take Kars because the Turks had no siege artillery.

The advance by the left with two army corps on snow-covered mountain roads and trails, with inadequate provision for supplies, led to the separate defeat of each corps while the third corps fought without result on the front. According to official reports barely 12,000 men returned, and these in a miserable condition. All the rest were killed, died of hunger or cold, or were captured.

The history of war will never find grounds on which to justify this offensive.

b) The offensive of the Third Army undertaken with insufficient forces against the Russians in the early summer of 1916.

On the retreat a considerable part of the army dispersed.

c) The concentration and fruitless offensive of the Second Army in the summer of 1916, which started from the line Lake Van-Mush-Kighi in the general direction of Erzerum, and collapsed at its beginning.

The contemplated operations against the enemy's flank and rear were quite impracticable, because there were no practicable roads to the front, or usable communications to the rear, and because the trains necessary for mobile war were non-existent.

According to the lowest statements this army lost 60,000 men from hunger and disease, and later from cold, the loss from enemy effect being the smallest.

d) The advance of the Thirteenth Army Corps into Persia in the summer of 1916 and winter of 1916/17, which from a military point of view was a great mistake. This advance should not have begun until the British in Irak were driven back to Gurna, if not to Basra. The loss of Bagdad was an immediate consequence; the corps was absent from the decision in March 1917.

I refer here to my report of October 25th or 26th, 1916, handed by General von Chelius to H. E. General of Infantry Ludendorff and to my personal report at the headquarters in Pless in December 1916.

e) The hopeless advance of the expeditionary corps against the Suez Canal in August 1916 with an eye to the conquest of Egypt.

This advance of only 18,000 fighting men was condemned to failure from the beginning, and it caused the British to follow through the desert of El Tih, though originally they merely meant to defend the canal. Their progress today in Palestine was initiated through this mistaken measure.

Here also I refer to my report to H. E. General von Ludendorff of October 1916.

I am perfectly aware that one cannot invariably succeed in war, and that even the best are not spared reverses, but I am also aware that one should not sacrifice valuable troops where there is no hope of success, simply because one does not know whether to take the offensive or to remain on the defensive.

f) The desertions from the Turkish Army which exceed all bounds.

The Turkish Army today has more than 300,000 desertions. They are not men that go over to the enemy, but for the most part return to the country in rear where they rob and plunder and make the country insecure. Everywhere detachments had to be formed for the pursuit of these deserters. The reasons for this desertion en masse are stated in part II.

Only those familiar with the events can understand the low combatant strength of the Turks.

The First Army has divisions temporarily attached only, besides the replacements in and near Constantinople, and the labor formations, which are mere paper formations and of no military value.

The Second and Third Army (Caucasus group), Izzet Pasha, commander of the group told me a few days ago has an effective strength of some 20,000 rifles.

The Fifth Army, charged with the protection of the coast from the Bulgarian frontier to Alaja on the Mediterranean (approximately 2,000 kilometers) has slightly over 26,000 rifles.

The Sixth Army, according to a statement of a few months ago by Major Kretzschmer, the then chief of staff, had about 31,000 rifles.

Of the fighting strength of the armies in Palestine and Syria I have no knowledge at this time.   '

II. Deterioration of Fighting Efficiency.

The Turkish soldier, particularly the Anatolian, is excellent fighting material.

Well looked after, sufficiently nourished, properly trained and calmly led these men will accomplish the highest aims.

A large part of the Arabs may be made into good usable soldiers, if from the very beginning of their service they are treated with strictness and justice.

The diminution of the efficiency of many parts of the army is chiefly due to the mistake of Turkish headquarters.

For about two years now a great part of the troops have not been granted sufficient time for training. They have been torn apart, before the small and large units have been properly cemented together.   ⌐

Companies, battalions, machine gun companies, garrisons of batteries have been detached and sent elsewhere. The strength of the departing troops has been complemented at the last moment by slightly trained or wholly untrained troops, or the men were taken from units that had just become effective, and they in turn had to be detached before recovering their efficiency.

When sent to the railroad station, the men for the most part did not know each other or their superiors. They only knew that they were being sent to some bad place. Hence they ran away whenever they could, and risked being shot while running. They jumped from the cars in motion, from the marching column in covered terrain, or from the bivouac, or from their billets.

There is hardly a division that has not lost thousands of men while en route by rail or march to the theaters east or south of the Taurus.

The Turkish soldier needs a certain amount of care, and a certain firmness in his treatment.   When he has learned confidence in his superiors, they can accomplish anything with him.

The present phase of inordinate desertion is not a hereditary defect of the Turkish Army.   Izzet Pasha, the leader of the Caucasus Group and a wholly reliable man, has told me that this kind of desertion was formerly unknown.

There is no doubt that the unsatisfactory condition of the roads, of the means of transportation, and of subsistence contributes its share.

The present condition of the Turkish Army shows that the road followed is a wrong one, and that another must be taken to gain success.   It should not be forgotten that it has become difficult to get replacements.

Sgd. LIMAN VON SANDERS.

CHAPTER 15

EVENTS UP TO MARCH 1, 1918

During the last third of January 1918 I was ordered temporarily for information to the German west front, and to the Fourth Army under the command of General Sixt v. Arnim.

On the day before my departure I went on board the steamer *General* in the Golden Horn, on which the German naval headquarters was established, to ask for a few non-commissioned officers to give special instruction to a detachment which was to take part in an enterprise against one of the large islands.

While there I offered to the chief of the naval staff the loan of a map of the mine fields outside the Dardanelles, that we had found on a small steamer sunk in the upper Xeros Gulf; he urgently requested me to give him the map at once. The *Goeben* and *Breslau* were to leave the Bosporus at that hour and sail out of the Dardanelles next morning. I at once sent for the map; it reached the *Goeben* before her departure. But I called the attention of the chief of staff to the fact that I should have been confidentially informed, since the troops on the outer coast of the Gallipoli peninsula and on the Asiatic side of the Dardanelles were under my command. It was necessary that they all be at their posts when the ships passed out.

No one need know the cause of the alarm, but the artillery on the outer coast must be standing by their guns, and the aviators must be ready to mount their machines. I ordered this by telegraph and the necessity of the precaution was proven by the well known ending of this advance.

Being without any information the Turkish batteries might otherwise make a mistake in the dawn and fire on our own ships.

When the *Goeben* lay fast at Nagara, I ordered the aviators from Smyrna up for her protection.

On the evening of January 22d I departed, and traversed Europe from Constantinople to Thielt in Belgium.

I saw the naval front on the coast of Flanders, part of the battlefields of Wytschaete, and later visited the information school in Namur and the general staff school in Sedan.

In addition to Major Prigge 1 had been permitted to bring along Colonel Kiazim Bei, chief of the general staff of the Fifth Army, who had been my faithful assistant since fall of 1914, and had cleared away many a difficulty for me. Still difficulties were not entirely spared to the German general in Turkey.

On my return journey at the beginning of February I touched at headquarters at Kreuznach. There I learned to my surprise that the new chief of the Turkish general staff, General von Seekt, would shortly take over all establishments erected and administered by the military mission on the lines of communication. The Turkish headquarters thus was to exercise a direct and uniform influence on the entire supply of all armies.

Those on the outside and unfamiliar with Turkish conditions will find this proposition justified, since everything was placed in one directing hand. But among those who had an insight into the interior administration of the Turkish Army during more than four years of work, it was bound to raise much doubt.

The position of the chief of the Turkish general staff was in many ways dependent upon Vicegeneralissimo Enver; that of the chief of the German military mission was more or less independent, insofar as, in spite of friction, the stipulations of the contract had been enforced. It was this kind of independence that made the mission so disliked by Enver.

The collaboration of the military mission with the Turkish authorities on the lines of communications was not an ideal one, but much had been accomplished and many improvements had been made. The conflict necessarily preceding any improvement in Turkey would, in my opinion, be much harder for a chief of staff of Enver if just arrived from Europe, and restricted by strange conditions and certain unavoidable considerations for the person of the Vicegeneralissimo, than for the military mission with its experience of years.

The condition of the railroads and of the coal supply showed that the German organs at Turkish headquarters were frequently unable to gain their point or to exert decisive influence the moment Turkish and German interests clashed. Neither the railroad section nor the coal section had been able, so far, to remedy the grossest defects in these two departments. There was shameful traffic in the letting of cars, by which they became unavailable for transport of subsistence for the army and for the civilian population. Things had gone so far that in Smyrna, Adana, Aleppo and Damascus as much as 1,000 pounds were paid for the letting of a car to private persons for commercial purposes. The money went into the pockets of the Turkish officials who had the disposal of the cars. In the delivery of coal which came weekly from Germany, or was mined in the Turkish mines at Songuldak, Soma, Solia, etc., other than military considerations frequently prevailed and caused complaint on the part of the army. In both directions headquarters was unable to bring about improvements. And now this office which had to admit that the Turkish troops on the front were half starved, or starved to death, and dressed in rags, was to be charged with the additional duty of effecting the supply for the Germans. With the loose Turkish methods this could only have a bad ending. In my judgment the incorporation of a German mission in Turkish headquarters meant an impairment of German interests.

Being confronted with an accomplished fact, according to the chief of the operation section "Orient," I requested this chief to lay before General Ludendorff, who happened to be absent, my request for immediate recall from Turkey, and reported so in person to Field Marshal General von Hindenburg. I now felt sure of my early recall to Germany and awaited the decision after my return journey.

On February 19th Enver asked me to see him at the War Ministry. We did not discuss my recall to Germany I was wishing for. Enver asked me whether I was willing to take command of Army Group F in Palestine. I stated my willingness provided H. M. the Emperor and German headquarters approved. I told Enver that I considered the situation on that front as very unfavorable, and could not hope to hold the present positions, unless unreservedly supplied by Turkish headquarters with troops and everything I should ask for. This was the basic condition, I said, for the possibility of successful resistance in the future. Enver promised this unreserved support.

According to my wish the Sixth Army in Irak was separated from the command of Jilderim, because in view of the great distance I believed I would be unable to influence operations in that quarter.

I further asked for authority to take with me my chief of the general staff, Colonel Kiazim Bei, and a number of Turkish officers from the headquarters of the Fifth Army who had worked under me since fall of 1914. This too was granted.

I must state specifically, that Enver said not a word, that headquarters was preparing new and extensive operations through Azerbaijan. Had I known that, I would have insisted unconditionally on my recall from Turkey which I had requested while in Germany. I knew the Turkish Army too well not to understand that the present personnel and material resources of Turkey were sufficient only for a vigorous campaign on *one* front. This is sufficiently evidenced by my opinion of the Turkish Army expressed December 13, 1917, and hereinbefore quoted in full. As soon as I knew that there were to be new Turkish operations on another uttermost frontier of the empire, I also knew that Enver would not keep his promise for the Palestine front. Thus I accepted the command with good faith in the promises made in this conference for the unreserved support of the Army Group.

I had to defer my departure for several days because the Cabinet orders had not arrived from German headquarters. Finally I was permitted to start and receipt of the order was reported to me by telegraph during the journey.

I left Constantinople on the evening of February 24. Somebody evidently objected to this journey as undertaken with the usual German haste, for I found attached to the special train for myself and staff a large number of cars holding the headquarters squadron of Turkish headquarters. I was informed that headquarters had decided at the last minute to go to Aleppo, I knew nothing of it. This overloading of the train caused us to be five hours behind schedule next morning (one hour of it was consumed by the watering of the horses from some well along the railroad), so at the station of Ekischehir I simply ordered the uncoupling of the cars of the squadron. Neither it nor headquarters ever went to Aleppo. The squadron was peacefully taken back to Constantinople.

After numerous changes of trains caused by the incomplete state of the Taurus tunnel and by differences of gauge south of the Taurus, I reached Samach on Lake Tiberias at noon on March 1st.

CHAPTER 16

THE MONTH OF MARCH 1918 ON THE PALESTINE FRONT

I shall give a description of this last part of the Palestine campaign in monthly installments according to the data in the military journal. Some of the data have been added to. The non-essential details are omitted.

It seems necessary here to go more into military details because deceptive news has been spread in Germany by persons who have never been on the front with those troops, or had an insight into the actual situations and battles.

A more detailed account is deemed necessary for the additional reason, that English reports in German translation have produced the wholly erroneous idea that the last half year of this campaign was a triumphal march. The account which follows will show that up to September 19, 1918, there was no such march.

It will also be explained why the Turkish Armies on the Palestine front no longer held their own against greatly superior forces in the fall, and why many Turkish troops were demoralized during the retreat.

For an understanding of the events which caused the loss of the northernmost part of Palestine, and that of Syria, on the part of Turkey, it is necessary to quote verbatim the most essential parts of the correspondence. They will be an indisputable source of information for a future description of the campaign.

Every one can form his own opinion from them.

At the station of Samach I met Major von Falkenhausen, chief of staff of the Seventh Army, with a considerable number of officers of his staff. They were on the point of going via Deraa to Amman on the Hedjas railroad, whither army headquarters had been transferred from Nablus. According to the statement of the chief of staff, Fewzi Pasha, commander of the

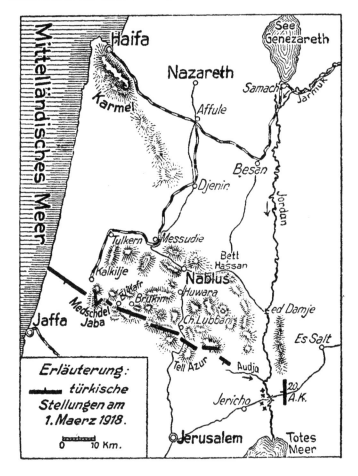

army, was preceding them to Amman through the East Jordan country.

I requested the gentlemen not to go any further, because

after taking over the command of the Army Group I would immediately return the headquarters of the Seventh Army to Nablus. Major von Falkenhausen, a highly efficient chief of staff, informed me that the British were so superior along the entire front, that they could pierce the front at any time and place they might select. That did not alter my decision.

At 3 p.m. we arrived at Affule, the railway station for Nazareth. From there it was three kilometers of bottomless road before our car reached the road winding in sharp curves up to the height of Nazareth. Thanks to the uncoupling of the headquarters squadron we had covered the journey from Constantinople to Nazareth in not quite five days; ordinarily ten days are counted for the journey.

In Nazareth the transfer of the supreme command was effected without delay; the headquarters of the Army Group had been established in the old pilgrim house of Casanova. General von Falkenhayn was under orders to proceed to some German front and assume command of an army.

The same night I had to go to Nablus, because the massing of heavy British forces was reported on the Nablus road in front of the Third Army Corps.

The situation of the Army Group on March 1st was as follows: After protracted fighting in retreat following upon the loss of Jerusalem and Jaffa, Jericho had to be given up on February 20th. It was occupied by the British on February 21st.

The Eighth and Seventh Armies held a front, the extreme right of which comprised the hilly sandy country between the foot of the mountains and the sea, about abreast of the railway station of Kalkilje. The width of this entirely open strip of coast was about fourteen kilometers. It was adjoined by mountainous country of exceedingly rugged form with numerous, mostly bald, peaks and slopes, and was strewn with millions of boulders. These mountains extended to the Jordan.

From the western foot of this mountainous country the Turkish positions followed the heights, first in a southern, then southeastern direction across the Nablus road and the Tell Azur to the Jordan, abreast of the Audja. The length of the Turkish position in an airline was seventy-five kilometers.

The front then passed to the east side of the Jordan, because after withdrawing from Jericho, the Twentieth Army Corps of the Seventh Army had crossed to that side, leaving on the western bank of the river a mixed detachment in the bridge head on the Jericho-Tell Nimrin road. The old Jordan bridge was prepared for destruction. The lower course of the Jordan to the Dead Sea was watched by a few camel riders.

Hence there were two battle districts: the land west of the Jordan, where by far the greater part of the British Army in Palestine confronted us, and the land east of the Jordan, where the Arabs were making war against us, led by the British and assisted with every kind of war material.

The West Jordan land and the East Jordan land are separated by the depression extending north and south, through which the Jordan runs from the southern foot of the Hermon range to the Dead Sea. This cleft in the ground, the bottom of which lies 200–400 meters below sea level, has an average width of seven to ten kilometers. It is lined by steep walls perforated by a few wild ravines. Through this depression with its torrid summer heat the Jordan runs with innumerable windings and with considerable fall. Fords are the natural passages; the water is breast high even in summer. The information given me by many "experts of the country," that in summer the Jordan hardly carried any water and ceased to be an obstacle, proved erroneous like much other information. The river is then fed by the melting snows of the Lebanon and Anti-Lebanon.

The wide treeless plains and steppes of the East Jordan land pass eastward into the immense Syrian desert.

The guards of the Hedjas railroad, belonging to the Fourth Army, were the only troops in the farther East Jordan land in March. In addition parts of the Eighth Army Corps, the only large unit of this army, and assisted by a battalion of the Asia

Corps, were operating against the insurgent Arabs who had occupied Tafileh situated in the rich grain country southeast of the Dead Sea.

The Seventh and Eighth Armies were under my full command, the Fourth Army with headquarters in Damascus I controlled only for purposes of supply. This army was also charged with the supply of the Sixth Army on the Mosul front, which was directly under Turkish headquarters.

The Second Army with headquarters at Aleppo was directly under Turkish headquarters. It guarded the coast from halfway between Haifa and Beirut to the Gulf of Alexandretta and Mersina. This separation of the Second Army from the Army Group, stationed as it was in the rear of the Army Group, was not a sound arrangement.

On the morning of March 2d I reached Nablus, the former Sichem. This considerable city, inhabited mostly by Arabs, lies between the mountains at the mouth of the defile between the Jordan and the Mediterranean. Here I met Djevad Pasha, commander of the Eighth Army, whom I knew from the Dardanelles Campaign. He had just taken command of the troops between the sea and the Jordan, and had come there to inform himself. Fewzi Pasha at Amman on the Hedjas railroad was to take command of all troops east of the Jordan.

After a lengthy conference I requested Djevad Pasha to return to Tulkern and resume command of the Eighth Army alone, and ordered Fewzi Pasha with his staff by telegraph to return to Nablus.

In Nablus all military telephones, telegraphs, etc., had been taken down and had to be put up anew. The highest military person present was a major of cavalry in charge of some line of communication detachments.

I rode to the front of the Third Army Corps to get information from its commander, Colonel Ismet Bei. The ride to Jerusalem presented unpleasant aspects. After the protracted rains the road and the country on either side were a sea of mud. On the short stretch to Huwara alone I counted seventeen German trucks stuck in the mud up to the axles. With our feeble lifeless horses it took us nearly five hours to reach Chan Lubban where the road to Jerusalem winds up another steep ridge. There I met Ismet Bei, one of the most capable of the higher Turkish commanders. There was no question, the situation was serious. The two divisions of the Third Army Corps, 1st and 24th, both under German commanders, Lieutenant Colonel Guhr and Colonel Boehme, were good and in good positions, but they were weak in numbers, like all Turkish units. There were no reserves. The left flank of the corps was in the air, the interval of twenty kilometers between the main position and the Jordan being guarded only by a few small detachments.

I therefore telephoned orders from Chan Lubban to the Twentieth Army Corps to recross to the west bank of the Jordan by crossings farther up the river and to take post between the Third Army Corps and the Jordan.

To deceive the enemy a small widely extended detachment was to remain in the Jordan bridge head and, if necessary, to retire to the east bank after blowing up the bridge.

The night march of the Twentieth Army Corps and the subsequent crossing of the river by the detachment were skillfully carried out.

On the morning of March 3d I returned to Nazareth. At the time of my arrival there on March 1st a large part of the Army Group had departed under orders for Damascus where the headquarters were to be established. They were now ordered back to Nazareth.

All effective troops within the control of the Army Group, including the headquarters' guard, were ordered immediately to move to the front of the Third Army Corps as reënforcements.

The 11th Division in Damascus was ordered to expedite its march from Damascus to Nablus via Nazareth. Meanwhile the British were massing more troops on the Nablus front without as yet attacking.

On March 5th I inspected with Djevad Pasha the coast sector and the second and third positions there under construction by Arabs. This coast section did not offer good natural positions. On this side the next good line of defense was the ridge of the Carmel.

I could not move the right wing so far back, because it was already somewhat farther back than the rest of the front. It would have been necessary to withdraw the rest of the front to the heights of Djenin-Besan.

In that way we would have abandoned a large part of Palestine, the northern part of which I had explicit orders from Enver to defend. It would also have opened for the British direct communication via Es Salt-Amman with the Arabs in the East Jordan country.

On the occasion of this ride I discussed with this army leader all measures necessary in case of retreat. The retreat of the Eighth Army was to be straight to the rear from section to section, for which the great north and south road via Jenin was available.

I felt certain that the superior British forces could break through at any point, if massed at *one* point.

The Turkish battalions, which I saw at the front, numbered 120 to 150 rifles. According to a written report the Eighth Army had 3,902 rifles available for the defense of the left sector with a front of twenty-eight kilometers. And thus it was everywhere.

When I returned to the front of the Third Army Corps on March 8th, the last parts of the Twentieth Army Corps had just reached the front assigned to it, and the small reënforcements ordered to the Third Army Corps had also arrived.

On March 9th the British began the heavy attack on the Nablus road which had been expected ever since March 1st. The Turks call it the battle of Turmus Aya.

From March 9th to 11th there was heavy fighting for three days in which both sides lost heavily. The height of the Tell

Azur was taken and retaken five times and finally remained in the hands of the British. The village of Turmus Aya, another contested point on the second and third day, remained in the hands of the Turks. The Turkish front was slightly pushed back on both sides of the Nablus road, but remained intact.

As the heavy fighting took place east of the Nablus road, the movement of the Twentieth Army Corps into the space between the Third Army Corps and the Jordan proved of decisive importance. The front of the Third Army Corps was considerably shortened and received active support from the 26th Division on the right of the Twentieth Army Corps. Instead of meeting one army corps, the enemy had encountered two.

From orders found on the persons of British dead it was learned that the British intended to take Nablus. They did not get there until six and one-half months later.

The small detachment of the Twentieth Army Corps on the Jordan fully performed its duty of deceiving the enemy. Its small strength and the withdrawal of the Twentieth Army Corps to the west bank were not discovered clearly by the British. During the battle they left a large force in front of the bridge head.

The spirit of the Turkish troops after the three day battle was full of confidence.

The 24th Division, commanded by Colonel Boehme, had borne the burden of the attack and lost heavily. It was fortunate that the heads of the 11th Division were coming up to take over the positions of the 24th Division on the Nablus road. The 24th Division was withdrawn to Kubalan behind the front to await replacements.

This was the only division of the Army Group which was sometimes available as a reserve during the ensuing months.

The Army Group was now ordered to expedite the construction of the road Nablus-Bett Hassan-Beisan with all available means, because it was to be the main line of retreat of the right and center of the Seventh Army, in case the present position had to be given up.

The construction of the road was very difficult. Following an old pack trail it had to be dug out of the steep slopes; it wound in sharp curves along vertical walls of ravines until at Bett Hassan it forked to Besan and Ed Damje. Except an old Arabian water mill in the low ground the road touched only upon the lone dilapidated mud hovel called Bett Hassan. No village was anywhere near. Eagles were soaring above the steep bald rocky walls which limited the view. They were the only sign of life in this apparently lifeless section.

An European can hardly conceive an idea of this road which became one of our most important communications.

The road from Bett Hassan to the crossing of the Jordan at Ed Damje was made practicable for wagons. New ferries were built at Ed Damje because there was no material for the construction of a bridge that would stand up against high water.

Ali Risa Pasha was given command in the East Jordan section with Lieutenant Colonel v. Hagen as chief of the general staff. The troops under Ali Risa Pasha were small until the return of those of the Tafileh expedition.

The situation east of the Jordan was not without misgivings, since the organization of the insurgent Arabs was steadily becoming more extensive and stronger. British officers, machine guns, field guns, airplanes and armored cars were attached to them, and since the capture of Akaba the sea route was open for any kind of effective British assistance. The Hedjas railroad was again and again interrupted by the Arabian troops of Sherif Faisal, to whom British pioneers with explosives were attached, and the weak Turkish forces along the long line, running for the most part through the desert, were unable to prevent the interruptions.

I knew Sherif Faisal well from the summer of 1914 in Constantinople. He was the type of an Arabian grand seignior. He had an European education and spoke good English. Mutual interest in sport had brought us together there in various places, and we had visited each other at our homes. The harsh Arabian policy of the Turkish government made him its bitter enemy.

The Hedjas railroad was the only communication with Medina which was successfully held by the corps of Fachreddin Pasha, after Mecca had fallen into the hands of the rebels, as the Turks called the rival caliph and the hostile Arabs. The protection of the Hedjas railroad under existing conditions was an almost impossible military task. In connection with its defense within insurgent territory it should be kept in mind that the length of the road from Deraa to Medina was 1,220 kilometers. Nothing but political and religious interests of Turkey caused Enver to call attention again and again to the great importance of Medina and of the only communication with the city. The railroad had been built with money contributed by the entire Islamic world, and the troops along the railroad as far as Medina were the only support of the Turks in this large Arabian section. They were the only connecting link of the Osmanic empire with the holy cities of Islam, as navigation on the Red Sea had been stopped long ago.

Had military grounds been the only ones, the Turkish line of defense in the East Jordan section should have been drawn back long ago to the section Kalat el Hesa, abreast of the southern shore of the Dead Sea. It was unnatural and impracticable to continue indefinitely the defense as far as Medina, after the country to the west and southwest of the Dead Sea had fallen into the enemy's hands.

It should have been enough to hold the section of Kalat el Hesa and to save for the Turks the resources of the rich grain country east of the Dead Sea.

The Turkish troops now scattered along the length of the Hedjas railroad could then have been assembled at some one point.

During March and April I made several attempts through my

Turkish chief of the general staff to have the foregoing views accepted, but invariably met with an inflexible resistance which can be explained only by the Turkish national point of view.

The defense of the East Jordan section had become much more difficult since the British had taken Jericho and were in position to break into the East Jordan section by crossing the river.

No troops were on the east bank of the lower course of the Jordan, except the small posts referred to, with a small reserve at Tell Nimrin. This weakness had resulted from the withdrawal of the Twentieth Army Corps to the west bank. It was unavoidable, however, as otherwise the front of the Army Group could not have been held.

During the first few weeks I used various expedients to gain time by deceiving the British. Several times portable wireless stations were sent to a flank or to the rear to report from there the approach of reënforcements of the Army Group. These reports were made in cipher which we knew could be read by the British, just as we often deciphered their wireless messages in spite of their frequent changes of the cipher key. The airplane reconnaissances regularly following such messages proved that our messages were understood by the British. In order to deceive the aviators also, active movements of mounted men, trains and long stretching columns were brought forward in the terrain concerned. Several times we read in British papers of the considerable reënforcements we received.

In the present situation it was advisable to concentrate all the cavalry on the open flank on the Jordan for employment in the East Jordan section. This cavalry was at the time on the opposite flank of the Eighth Army. The Caucasian cavalry brigade was Djevad Pasha's reserve and posted in the extreme west on the coast. The other large cavalry unit, the 3d Cavalry Division of two lancer regiments and a horse battery, was in the front line of the Eighth Army. Its withdrawal, and the changes of position incident thereto, had to be carried out slowly, because the Army Group had no reserve to give to the Eighth Army in exchange.

Colonel Kiazim, the chief of the general staff, assisted by the very active Major Muzzafer of the Turkish general staff, sometimes discovered quite extraordinary formations. In Damascus he discovered a company which gradually had recruited itself to a strength of 1,200 by attracting all sorts of men. In the organization tables of Turkish headquarters such troops were of course not enumerated. In our country such a formation would be detected at once on asking for pay. However, that did not happen here because there was no pay anyway. The company simply requested the necessary subsistence from the nearest depot and received it regularly. It was assumed that some higher officer was extending his powerful hand over this formation. Of course, the company had rendered no service for months.

In some places artillery units were found without guns, and in others guns without men and horses. At the railway station of Affuleh alone we gained 700 men in this manner, who had gradually assembled there. A German could never have discovered all these troops. But Major Muzzafer found them. All of them were brought forward to reënforce the front. They had had ample rest.

Many changes were made in the staff of the Army Group, as the accession of many Turkish officers did away with the necessity of using a large number of German officers. In my opinion it was impossible to lead Turkish armies consisting nine-tenths of Turkish troops, with a predominantly German staff.

Though many such changes in the staff had been made, Enver would still communicate with army leaders direct over the head of the Army Group. He always did it when it seemed proper to him, that the Germans should not be informed, or informed too late, of some steps taken. Thus he ordered about March 20 the immediate removal of all Jews of the Seventh and Eighth Armies to the Caucasian front. When I accidentally heard of it, I forbade the execution.

After a few weeks I received a request from Enver for an

expression of my operative intentions. In my opinion operative intentions were out of the question, and the best we could do was to hold our front. Upon receipt of the request I thought of the drowning man who is asked by some one on shore whether he would take part next day in a swimming competition. I declined to say anything about operative intentions.

In the second half of March the British attempted a partial attack against the advanced portions of the 7th Division near Medschdel Jaba, that part of our front being annoying to them, as it was on a ridge projecting to the south and flanking part of the enemy's coast sector. They gained a few advanced positions without special value, the position proper remained in our hands.

The expedition to Tafile became engaged in several heavy, but successful actions, and on March 20th began its return march to the Hedjas railway.

THE FIRST JORDAN BATTLE

On March 26th the British suddenly crossed the lower Jordan on quickly thrown pontoon bridges and over a ford, with a strong force of cavalry and camel riders, followed by infantry and artillery, and advanced eastward. They surprised the Turkish detachments on the eastern bank and their reserve at Tell Nimrin. The main force, of which the Australian cavalry division, an infantry brigade, artillery and trains were first observed, took the direction of Es Salt-Suvela toward Amman on the Hedjas railroad, while a smaller part turned in a southeasterly direction. Other cavalry with armored cars turned directly north on the east bank of the Jordan, and engaged our cavalry detachments pushed out from Ed Damije. The latter attack was merely meant as protection for the flank of the main attack.

In Amman were three small Turkish companies, a German flying detachment, automobile columns, and small German formations of the line of communications.

As soon as the enemy's attack was recognized as an attempt to break through at Amman, the Army Group at once ordered that all troops and replacements in Damascus, or en route south of the Taurus, should be sent to Amman with all possible expedition. The expedition returning from Tafileh was directed to use every means afforded by the railroad to come up to Amman via el Katrane. The transportation of all these detachments encountered many delays, because the railroad between Deraa and Amman, and south of Amman, was simultaneously interrupted in various places by enemy cavalry patrols and Arabs, and the troop trains were fired on several times.

The repair of the railroad cost precious hours, but the obstacles were at last overcome and the troops came up, partly on foot.

On the 28th of March the advance guards of the British encountered the garrison of Amman, which had occupied the heights three kilometers west of the town. Every man, no matter to what organization he belonged, was drafted, the fire action became stationary and Turkish reënforcements were coming up.

In severe fighting they repeatedly checked the attacks of the enemy who had been reënforced, on the heights of Amman.

In their advance, the British had encountered unexpected obstacles. Several days of rain softened the tough clayey soil and the advancing reënforcements were impeded on the dirt roads beyond Es Salt. The march of the artillery and of the trains was particularly delayed. Even camels could barely get over this ground on which they were constantly slipping. We intercepted a British wireless message complaining of this condition.

The long British communication line from the Jordan to Amman was endangered in other ways. The Army Group had instructed the Seventh Army to press with all available means upon the enemy's rearward communications, the weak point

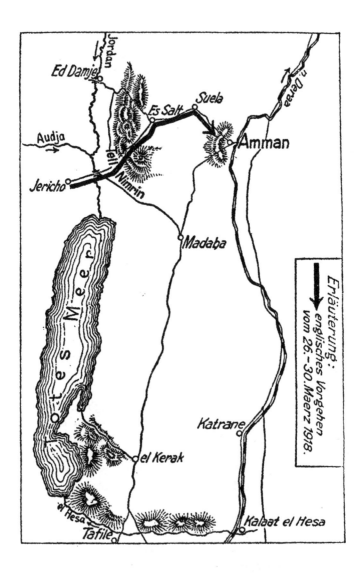

of the whole enterprise. Under this order the brave leader of the 3rd Cavalry Division, Colonel Essad Bei, advanced in the most effective direction against Es Salt. He had only a few squadrons (the greater part of his cavalry was still with the Eighth Army), two companies of the 145th Infantry Regiment and two mountain guns. With these troops be mounted the height of Es Salt over steep and difficult trails, which sometimes led over stone steps. After driving away some weak British scouting parties, he opened fire on the road in the low ground near Es Salt. The British were compelled to transfer their communications to the south of Es Salt where the roads were still worse.

At Amman the fighting became very severe. The Turkish right had to be extended several times northward to meet the enemy's repeated attempts to turn that flank. Under the repeated attacks of the enemy the Turkish positions had to be drawn back in some places, but remained on the heights west of Amman and facing west.

On the afternoon of March 30 the Turkish leader became doubtful whether the position could be further held, because a retreat to the north or northeast seemed dangerous. I then gave orders for resistance to the last, regardless.

On the evening of March 30th the Turkish right, with the German Infantry Battalion No. 703, under Captain Grassmann, made a counter attack and drove the enemy back. Captain Sydow who distinguished himself in this attack, died a hero's death later in September.

As the British had failed to realize the immediate tactical results they had expected, as their lines of communication became more difficult, as our troops were gaining in strength and as their left had been thrown back by our counter attack, they withdrew on the night of March 31, Easter, along the whole front.

During all this fighting they were unable to reach the town or railroad station of Amman. The enemy had suffered heavy losses in his attacks. During the latter part of the fighting Djemal Pasha, commander of the Fourth Army, had been brought up from Damascus and had taken command. He is not related to the Minister of Marine Djemal, former commander in chief in Syria and Palestine, as might be inferred by the Germans from the name. There are an infinite number of Djemals in the Turkish Army. This one knew the country of Arabia and the Arabs well from years of service in these provinces. The inhabitants trusted him, because he was considered wise and just. Several times he acted as their representative to lay their wishes before the government. He was beyond question a wise general who could be counted upon.

During the night the Turkish troops received orders to pursue the enemy in order to complete the success. However, since on the Turkish side there was no cavalry beyond a few patrols, they could merely follow, but not pursue the enemy. The British rear guards several times faced about, perhaps to restore order in the retreat. The brief rear guard engagements were without importance.

The enemy's columns, passing south of Es Salt, retreated directly across the Jordan. The Turkish troops followed until abreast of the hill of Tell Nimrin, where a new front toward the Jordan was prepared.

The foregoing actions had stopped the British in their first attempt to gain a firm footing in the East Jordan section with regular troops. Had they succeeded, the expeditionary corps of Tafileh and all troops farther south would have been cut off, and the only railroad connection of the Army Group through the Yarmuk valley to Deraa and Damascus would have been seriously threatened.

It should be stated that in these days of battle the Syrian and the Hedjas railroads did splendid work.

CHAPTER 17

THE MONTH OF APRIL 1918

After their unsuccessful attempt to break through our front into the East Jordan section, the British withdrew their troops to positions of rest. In their retreat they had taken along a number of Arab inhabitants who had acted as guides, or who had compromised themselves by assisting the British, or taking part in the attack against our troops. It was said soon afterward that these inhabitants had been promised that the British would conduct them back at an early date to their homes in the East Jordan section.

The Army Group inferred from this, and from new enemy preparations on the lower Jordan, that the British would soon renew their attempt to break through our front into the East Jordan section. The Army Group took the following steps to meet this new attempt:

All Turkish troops that fought at Amman were brought forward under command of Colonel Ali Fuad Bei to the strong position at Tell Nimrin. As the greater part belonged to the Eighth Army Corps, they received that designation. The army corps was divided into two divisions as soon as anywhere near enough troops for that purpose were at hand. The position was immediately entrenched.

The Eighth Army Corps was reënforced, though not in great numbers, by German and Austrian artillery, and by the 4th Company of the German Infantry Regiment No. 146 which reached Es Salt on April 5th. Other Turkish troops were assigned to them, and replacements as fast as they arrived.

The headquarters of the Fourth Army, of which Major von Papen had become chief of the general staff, was established in Es Salt, this citadel of Arabian influence in the northern part of the East Jordan section.

215

At Mafid Dschozele, south of Ed Damije, means of crossing the Jordan were placed in readiness and hidden among the willows.

The transfer of the 3rd Cavalry Division and of the Caucasian Cavalry Brigade to the Jordan was completed during April. The main body of this cavalry under Colonel Essad Bei remained assembled on the west bank of the Jordan abreast of Mafid Dschozele, a small part was transferred to the east bank for reconnaissance and observation and to maintain connection with the Eighth Army Corps. A combined German machine gun detachment, and the German Pioneer Company No. 205, were added to the command.

When I hunted for the first time for the camp of Essad Bei on the Roman road in the valley of the Jordan, I found it with difficulty. Nowhere was there a place looking like a camp. Scattered over the country were some individual tents and brush huts, such as the Bedouins use. No horses were in sight. On close inspection it turned out that the stables had been put underground wherever pits or ditches were not available. All were surrounded with oblique standing branches which also gave protection against the sun. No flier would here suspect a cavalry camp.

The Twentieth Army Corps, posted at Medschdel Beni Fadil where the headquarters of the army was, received instructions to push light artillery forward to the edge of the ridge which commands the valley of the Jordan from the western bank. These were all the preparations it was possible to make against a second British attempt.

The 703rd Infantry Battalion, on returning from the Tafileh expedition, was turned over to the Eighth Army to reënforce the Asia Corps.

The fighting along the front of the Army Group was generally slight during April, but on April 10th a heavy attack was made against the left group of the Eighth Army, commanded by Colonel von Frankenberg, which developed into a three-day battle. The focus of this very severe fighting was the villages of El Kafr and Berukin. On the whole the attack was repulsed, and the British gained but little ground, in spite of their heavy losses. The brunt of the attacks fell on the Asia Corps and the 16th Division. Under instructions from the Army Group, the Seventh Army had placed reënforcements in readiness on the left of the troops under Colonel von Frankenberg. The conduct of the Turkish battalions in these battles was unequal; some fought very well, others showed mediocre bravery and endurance.

According to British orders found on the dead, the attack was to be carried forward until abreast of the railroad station of Kalkilje. It would have meant a gain of ground fourteen kilometers in depth; in fact, however, the attack advanced only at a few points more than one kilometer. It may be assumed that in case of success a British attack in the coast section would have ensued. Numerous British cavalry stood assembled there in rear, perhaps to complete the results of an attack carried forward as far as Kilkilije.

In the second half of April British cavalry several times advanced in force against the new Jordan front of the Fourth Army on the heights of Tell Nimrin, and in a northeasterly direction; each attack ended with the early withdrawal of the British cavalry. They were probably made to reconnoiter the strength and preparedness of the troops there.

Meanwhile the British had constructed a broad bridge head on the Jordan on both sides of the road to Tell Nimrin, and covered it with obstacles. Artillery also was placed in position there. We also observed the construction of an extensive bridge head farther north at the Mendesse ford over the Jordan. Our fliers reported several pontoon bridges, and foot bridges, within these bridge heads; they were several times changed and rebuilt.

On the coast of Palestine there were two naval posts of a few men each to observe the movement of hostile vessels. I wanted to augment the post at Haifa sufficiently to enable them to fight, because it was the point where a hostile landing might first be

expected to endanger our present position. The harbor of
Haifa was closed by mines, but a landing was quite possible
outside the harbor. Before my departure from Constantinople,
I had been informed that about thirty officers and 500 men of the
navy were employed in the district of the Army Group. It was
found, however, that with the exception of two officers and fifty
men, they were chiefly employed on the Euphrates River etape
in the district of the Sixth Army. On being informed that they
could not be spared, I had to give up hope of coöperation of the
navy in Palestine.

The 17th Depot Regiment brought forward to Nazareth could
be given Arabian replacements only, barring a small number of
Turks accidentally found, or discharged from the hospital.
The troops disliked to receive Arab soldiers though they might
be well trained, because they no longer trusted them, since the
Arab movement in favor of the British was steadily progressing.
The replacements from Constantinople were just sufficient to
make good the battle losses, and to give some reënforcement to
the Fourth Army on the Jordan front, and along the Hedjas
railroad.

The request for replacements brought on a collision with
Enver, within a few weeks. In a telegram of April 11th signed
by him he made reflections on the Army Group, based on
complete ignorance of the circumstances. He stated that if I
delayed the transport of the German troops assigned to the
Army Group (it was Infantry Regiment No. 146) in favor of
Turkish troops, the former would be used elsewhere. Paragraph 9 reads verbatim:

We cannot afford to leave these troops standing idle. The situation
demands that these troops be again placed at the disposal of the supreme
command.

I replied on April 13th:

Referring to paragraph 9 I request that the report of Major Beckert be
heard. I strongly deny the charge that I desired to delay the transportation
of German troops in favor of Turkish replacements. As the Army Group
has ten times more Turkish than German troops, Your Excellency will

acknowledge that in view of the recent battles we are in need of Turkish replacements. From the first day, when I took command here I have urged that the transport of the German troops be expedited.

At the conclusion of my letter I requested Enver to submit to the Sultan my request to be relieved from the command of Jilderim. After these wholly unfounded charges, there was no doubt that other difficulties would be thrown in my way. I was unwilling to have them added to the difficulties of my thankless task.

When I went to Palestine, I presumed that Turkish headquarters would show some appreciation of my accepting a command that offered so little hope of a satisfactory solution. I saw that I was badly mistaken.

No one can long ward off attacks from the enemy in front, and assaults from the rear.

Enver refused to submit my request to the Sultan and made half apologetic and half elusive statements.

Nor did the conflicts about the military mission come to a stop, as I had hoped. The chief of staff of the military mission, General von Lenthe, informed me that a commission had convened in Constantinople to confer about the transition of the military mission into the ways fixed by the military convention, and that the German military plenipotentiary, a representative of German headquarters, one of the Prussian War Ministry, and General von Lenthe were members of the commission.

On April 14th I received a telegram from General von Lenthe, where it is stated verbatim:

According to confidential statements by the representatives from home, the present chief of the general staff of the Turkish Army is to be considered as the senior officer provided in the military convention, whose future position is to be prepared by giving him now certain functions, etc.

On April 15th I addressed the following telegram to General Ludendorff:

Thankful for the confidence ever shown me by Your Excellency, I address to Your Excellency the respectful and urgent request that, in case that army headquarters has disposed of the functions specified in the contract and its annex and appointed my successor, I receive direct information, before the matter is submitted to officers in Constantinople who are subordinate to me.

Your Excellency may rest assured that I am ready at any time to ask H. M. the Emperor and King, for my recall, when my person is an impediment to the supreme command. As the situation now is, and is handled in Constantinople, I am placed in a position which is difficult and unbecoming the senior Prussian general here in the eyes of the Turks, against whom I have maintained my position for four years and four months, with much strife.

The annexed stipulations of November 13, 1917, state:

All troops named, formations and members of the army, are under the chief of the military mission as regards all interior and economic matters, as disciplinary punishment, administration of military justice, replacements in German formations, subsistence, clothing, pay, postal matter, care of the sick, etc.

On April 17th I received the following reply from General Ludendorff:

I know nothing of a plan of investing the present chief of the general staff of the Turkish army with certain functions as a preliminary to his future position as senior German officer. As long as the military mission exists, the functions conferred on Your Excellency will be respected.

The conferences ceased and the outsiders took their departure. I mention these things without comment.

The Army Group was contemplating a surprise attack against the Msallabe in the first few days of May; the hill was held by small British advanced detachments. This small sharply detached hill was the most advanced post of the British north of the Audja, and very inconvenient to us. The 24th Division was brought to Dome to undertake this night enterprise in conjunction with the 3rd Cavalry Division.

But in the early morning of April 30th began the great British advance against the East Jordan section, which brought on the five-day fighting of the second Jordan battle.

CHAPTER 18

THE SECOND BATTLE OF THE JORDAN

In the first Jordan battle the British had made a direct attack on Amman which failed on account of our tenacious resistance and on account of the long and insufficient lines of communication; this second great operation contemplated the quick capture of Es Salt by surprise, and its use as a base for further advances.

If the British drove back the Eighth Army Corps and permanently occupied the position on the heights near Es Salt, the Seventh and Eighth Armies would be compelled to withdraw as far as the Yarmuk valley, because the British troops on the heights of Es Salt would have been in rear of the left wing of the Seventh Army, and would have menaced the railroads Biesan-Deraa and Deraa-Amman. As supplies from Damascus were coming via Deraa, it would be impossible to keep the army supplied.

The preparations for the attack were made secretly, and so skilfully, that their largest and last part was not discovered by our fliers, or by observation from the ground.

About 4.30 a.m. on April 30 a strong force of British cavalry with artillery and armored cars crossed the Jordan on six bridges from the road Jericho-Tell Nimrin, and at Mendesse. One cavalry division turned north, the other northeast toward Es Salt via Aere.

Immediately thereafter a reënforced infantry division deployed for a frontal attack against the weak Eighth Army Corps, under the protection of a heavy artillery fire from the large bridge heads.

A little later an attack of British troops developed on the west bank of the Jordan starting from the lower Auja, against the left wing of the Seventh Army, the 53rd Turkish Division.

The enemy's artillery fire grew in intensity, along the entire front of the Army Group from the sea to the Jordan.

The cavalry division, which had turned northward, quickly drove back the Turkish mounted men in the eastern part of the

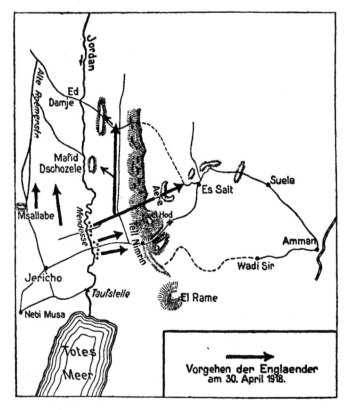

Vorgehen der Englaender
am 30. April 1918.

Jordan valley, and its main portion followed the road along the foot of the mountains until opposite Ed Damije. Its remaining parts, estimated as a brigade, took the direction of the flat hill opposite Mafid Dschozele. The retreating Turkish cavalry regiment had withdrawn to this point, to which the commㅜnder of the 3rd Cavalry Division now sent the German machine gun detachment, and the German pioneer company which occupied a position resembling a bridge head.

The repeated attacks of this detached cavalry, supported by artillery and numerous machine guns and made concentrically against the small height, failed to break the resistance there. The height remained in our hands.

The main part of the cavalry division advancing in a northerly direction, arrived opposite Ed Damije soon after 7 a.m. The division here did not occupy the crossing of the Jordan, but took post facing west along the slopes in rear. Judging by the subsequent situation it may be assumed that this cavalry meant to cover the flank and rear of the cavalry division advancing via Aere toward Es Salt, and to prevent the Turks from crossing at Ed Damije. A small plateau separated this cavalry from the rugged and craggy hills which parallel the Jordan at a distance of about one and one-half kilometers. Soon thereafter the British horse artillery opened fire against the ridge west of Ed Damije.

Meanwhile the British attack against the Eighth Army Corps at Tell Nimrin was strongly pushed, with the help of constantly arriving reënforcements. On the left about fifteen squadrons threatened to turn the left flank, while the right and rear seemed threatened by the cavalry that advanced toward the northeast.

The army corps under Colonel Ali Fuad Bei fought with determination and held its ground.

The command of the Army Group at Nazareth did not hear of this great enemy action on the Jordan until 7.30 a.m. There were difficulties of communication which were increased by Arabs cutting telegraph and telephone wires. The chief of the general staff, General Kiazim, had flown early in the morning to Amman to confer with the commander of the Fourth Army and to proceed by automobile from Amman to Es Salt.

On learning of the development of the situation at 8.30 a.m. I telephoned to the commander of the Eighth Army to start the 24th Division at Ed Damije at once toward the Jordan with the objective of either Ed Damije or Mafid Dschozele depending on the state of the battle.

I further ordered the 3rd Cavalry Division to be assembled at one of these crossings. Both divisions were then to cross the Jordan and attack.

The railroad guards in the Yarmuk valley were alarmed and reënforced by the Army Group. The railway authorities in Damascus were directed by telegraph to push to Deraa all troops en route north of Damascus, with further instructions to follow.

Soon after 10 a.m. the advanced parts of the cavalry division moving via Aere appeared on the ridge in front of Es Salt. They had gained the ascent to Es Salt by trails unknown to us along the creek of Abu Tara under the guidance of Arabs.

It should be stated here that the British cavalry made extraordinary marches on the first day of the attack.

The few Turkish companies remaining in Es Salt for the protection of the headquarters of the Fourth Army were hurriedly gotten together, and placed in position against the leading squadrons, which were deploying to fight on foot. The small body of Turks was reënforced by the men of the German telephone and chauffeur detachments.

The advance of the 24th Division and of the 3rd Cavalry Division, ordered to the Jordan by the Army Group, met with delays. The leader of the 24th Division, Colonel Boehme, with part of his officers had ridden forward early in the morning for reconnaissance in connection with the attack planned against the Msallabe and did not return until near noon. The division did not get underway until 1.30 p.m. on its march to the Jordan. On account of the steep and very difficult descent into the Jordan valley, the march to the bank of the river required five hours.

The 3rd Cavalry Division had sent several squadrons to the foremost line on the western bank; these had to be relieved by the 145th Infantry Regiment, before the cavalry could be assembled.

The march of the 24th Division came near taking a direction that would have been fatal to the decision, and the 3rd Cavalry Division also was delayed.

Fewzi Pasha, the commander of the Seventh Army, whose chief of staff Major von Falkenhausen had hurried to the Jordan early in the morning, became apprehensive for his left flank west of the Jordan, the 53rd Division. The British attack at that point appeared to him to indicate the British intention to break through there. He therefore requested the Army Group to change the orders given by me, so that the 3rd Cavalry Division would remain in its position west of the Jordan, and that the 24th Division also be left there at his disposal. I entertained a different view of the attack, believing it to be merely an enemy attempt to contain our troops west of the Jordan. I therefore ordered the commander of the Seventh Army to carry out the original orders with the utmost expedition. Neither division could be assembled on the Jordan before dark.

At Es Salt a decision took place about 4 p.m. Strong British forces had advanced and taken the town. The headquarters of the Fourth Army escaped by a road to the north and withdrew in that direction, accompanied by a few small detachments; others withdrew toward Suela. Soon after 4 p.m. communication between the Army Group and Es Salt was interrupted. The last telephonic report stated that the British were entering the town.

I at once ordered all railway and etape officers to expedite the transport to Amman of all troops en route by rail, and of any other troops that could be gotten hold of.

Toward evening the 24th Division under Colonel Boehme, and the 3d Cavalry Division under Essad Bei, were assembled near the ferry of Ed Damije. The 1st and 2d Company of the German Infantry Regiment No. 146 just then arrived via Beisan, and were placed under the orders of the 24th Division. After dark both divisions began to cross over to the eastern bank of the Jordan. As the effective strength was small, and as for the present combatant troops only were crossing, our means were adequate to effect the passage to the other bank. The 3rd Cavalry Division at once sent advanced posts toward the rugged hills east of the Jordan and pushed back the enemy's detachments.

Late in the evening the Eighth Army Corps reported that all attacks of the enemy against the right wing had been repulsed with little loss of ground, and that the morale was good.

At daybreak of May 1st I joined the headquarters of the Seventh Army at Nablus, where communication with the headquarters of the Fourth Army was regained by cutting in on some wire. The headquarters of the Fourth Army was instructed to reach as soon as possible the road from Amman to Es Salt in the vicinity of Suela, and to collect there all troops coming from Amman for a later attack on Es Salt.

The crossing of the 24th Division and of the 3rd Cavalry Division at Ed Damije, during the night preceding May 1st, had not been noticed by the enemy. At daybreak the divisions advanced, the 24th Division southeastward, the 3rd Cavalry Division due east, to attack the British cavalry division still in its position of yesterday along the slopes in rear. The horse battery of the 3rd Cavalry Division reached the top of the rugged hills with the leading Turkish troopers, and immediately opened an effective fire against the enemy's horse batteries. Meanwhile the foremost skirmish lines of the 24th Division and the horsemen of Essad Bei were traversing the small plateau in front of the enemy.

The attack was a complete surprise for the enemy. Before the Turkish horsemen and running skirmish lines could reach them, the British cavalry avoided the attack and galloped away to the south in disorder. One cavalry regiment turned away to the north.

The enemy's artillery attempted to escape partly to the south and partly into the eastern rifts of the mountains.

One of the batteries going south was captured by Turkish infantry. Several other guns, stalled on the mountain slopes, were also taken, so that in the course of the morning nine undamaged guns of the cavalry division and one gun belonging to another unit were captured. A number of prisoners, numerous horses, artillery ammunition, camel columns with medical supplies and food, an armored car, etc., fell into Turkish hands.

After the 3rd Cavalry Division had been assembled, it began at once the ascent of the heights west of Es Salt by a narrow mountain trail. Prior thereto it had exchanged its horse battery for a mountain battery of the 24th Division.

The enemy attack on the 53d Division on the west bank of the Jordan had died out on April 30th; on May 1st Ali Fuad Pasha, commanding the Twentieth Army Corps, took command of the troops that had crossed at Ed Damije.

The 24th Division was sent south in the Jordan valley to disencumber the right of the Eighth Army Corps. It was joined by the troops that had become available on the height opposite Mafid Dschozele.

The vigorous attacks against the Eighth Turkish Army Corps on the heights of Tell Nimrin were constant. The Army Corps held its ground. Its right division lost some ground on the slopes of the El Hod mountain without, however, any impairment of the situation.

The 24th Division in its advance in the Jordan valley southward soon encountered serious resistance, and gained only a few kilometers of ground until evening.

The 3rd Cavalry Division on the heights west of Es Salt became engaged with the skirmishers of the British cavalry division, which according to Turkish reports, was reënforced by infantry and pioneers.

The staff of the Fourth Army reached Suela and took charge of the Turkish troops so far assembled there, and was joined by an Arab tribe under Miskal Pasha.

About a brigade of the British cavalry from Es Salt, advancing toward Amman, encountered these Turkish troops near Suela. A standing fire fight ensued.

The Eighth Army Corps, now menaced from three directions, reported in the evening that its artillery ammunition and food were running low. It received these supplies during the ensuing night by camel columns, by trails, via Wadi Es Sir, without being discovered by the British squadrons pushed southward from Es Salt.

On May 2d I went to the Jordan valley and to the heights of Ed Damije. No effect of the Turkish advance from Suela was as yet noticeable. Unfortunately the brave leader of the division, Colonel Essad Bei, was seriously wounded in the course of the morning, and had to turn over the command to his chief of staff, Lieutenant Colonel Machmud Bei, according to Turkish custom.

The troops of the 24th Division, who had fought until late that night and were exhausted, rested during the morning in their positions; in the afternoon I ordered them to renew their attack southward.

The assaults of the enemy on the Eighth Army Corps were renewed with great severity on this third day of the battle. The right of the Army Corps lost some ground, but the corps held its ground. The seriousness of its position was increased during the day, because portions of the cavalry pushed out from Es Salt to the south were advancing and finally stood ten kilometers in rear of the Army Corps. Ali Fuad Bei formed a covering detachment against this cavalry. When the Austrian battery, fighting in the front line of the Army Corps, had expended its ammunition, the gunners, armed with carbines, formed the covering detachment.

The Turkish troops at Suela were slowly increased by the reënforcements disembarked at Amman, among them a German howitzer battery. In the course of the day the Suela group, under Djemal Pasha, pushed back the opposing cavalry and advanced nearer to Es Salt.

The 24th Division, advancing with its left along the slopes descending from Es Salt to the Jordan, encountered strong resistance, and gained little ground toward the Eighth Army Corps. Here I ordered renewal of the attack in the early morning hours of May 3rd.

During my return to Nablus in the afternoon, in the vicinity of Bett Hassan, my chauffeur suddenly exclaimed "strong British cavalry in front of us." We saw a long column in khaki with tropical helmets coming down the winding road at Bett Hassan. It turned out to be the staff and pack train of the 1st Battalion of the German 146th Regiment. The tropical helmets, with which the 146th Regiment was equipped, were bound to cause mistakes, and the battalion commander told me that on his way from Biesan his column had several times been fired on from the mountains by Turks. I now forbade the use of this head dress by German troops.

There was no essential change in the situation up to the morning of May 3rd. The strength of the 24th Division unfortunately was so small, and its losses were so high, that I could not carry out my intention of advancing to the Wadi Er Retem and cutting the British communications with Es Salt.

I felt certain that a decision at Es Salt had to be brought about within twenty-four hours if the fighting was to result in our favor. The troops were on their fourth day of heavy fighting, and approaching the limit of their endurance. Neither the Army Group nor the Seventh Army had a reserve. Es Salt must be taken by the troops from Suela and by the 3d Cavalry Division, no matter at what sacrifice.

The Suela group had reached by evening the height just east of Es Salt. The German howitzer battery and the Turkish artillery were bombarding the town. The 3rd Cavalry Division on the west also had gained ground.

In the evening I gave instructions to the commanders of the Fourth Army and of the 3d Cavalry Division to force the town by a night attack from the north, employing all available men regardless. The direction from the north was selected, because the ground there facilitated the advance, but also to enable the British to withdraw from Es Salt toward the southwest. From the desk at army group headquarters in Nazareth I received a telephonic request to order the attack from the south in order to cut off the British in Es Salt. But I was certain that our weak and exhausted troops were unequal to a desperate battle which was bound to ensue when the British saw their line of retreat threatened. It would have resulted in our defeat. Hence I did not change my instructions.

The attack began about 10 p.m. Some companies on the extreme right of the Suela group lost their way and were captured, but the remainder of the group, the 3rd Cavalry Division and the Arab tribe of Miskal succeeded, after heavy fighting, in entering the town from the north toward midnight.

The British began at once to evacuate Es Salt and to withdraw toward the southwest via Aere.

Es Salt had been retaken!

The Suela group and the 3rd Cavalry Division followed during the night toward Aere.

The 24th Infantry encountered fresh British infantry brought up in automobiles, which carried wire obstacles for strengthening its front.

On the morning of May 4th the attacks on the Eighth Army Corps became weaker.

In the forenoon as soon as the first retrograde movements of the enemy to the west bank of the Jordan were noticed, the Eighth Army Corps was ordered to advance toward the Jordan. The 53d Division on the west bank of the Jordan also was ordered to attack. Unfortunately the troops no longer had enough strength left to complete the success.

The withdrawal of the enemy across the Jordan lasted all afternoon and evening as well as the ensuing night.

The Turkish cavalry advanced on the same evening toward Neby Musa, crossing the lower Jordan at the Place of Baptism.

Later superior forces drove it back to the east bank.

The fliers had attacked the retreating columns with all means at their command.

The second battle of the Jordan was won all along the line. The non-existence of reserves prevented us from fully profiting by the success, and taking the heights on the west bank of the Jordan. This would have been of decisive import for the situation in Palestine. Only by bringing the Eighth Army Corps over to the west bank would it be possible to shorten the overextended line of the Seventh and Eighth Armies, so that the position would possess some degree of security.

At any rate, we had succeeded once more in preventing the enemy from gaining a footing in the East Jordan section.

There is no doubt that this success (even the *Times* called it a British reverse) had a certain repercussion on the disposition of the Arabs. No great importance, however, should be attached to that. The differences between Turks and Arabs were such that a temporary success over the far superior enemy could by no means remove them.

A few days after the battle the Arabs renewed their attacks against Maan and the stations on the Hedjas railroad farther south. They were repulsed in many places, but could not be stopped at all places. The continued blowing up of bridges and rails was sensibly felt because repair material was becoming scarce.

However, a temporary interruption of the Hedjas railroad could not bring about the fall of Medina. The troops of Fachreddin Pasha were strong enough to hold their ground, and he had several sources of his own for the subsistence of his troops. He repeatedly telegraphed to the Army Group that he and his men were condemned to starvation, but that was only the customary Turkish exaggeration. The end proved that he was able to hold out in Medina beyond the Armistice.

The reports of Turkish headquarters on these battles of the Jordan, as sent by wireless in German from the great station of

Osmanie, caused me to seriously object to this kind of reporting news.

The report of the first battle read verbatim:

Palestine front.   West of the river Esh Sheriah and on the river renewed fighting.

On the morning of April 30th strong British infantry and cavalry forces sought to penetrate our lines west of Esh Sheriah, but the attacking troops melted away under the fire of our heroic soldiers.   Our positions remained completely in our possession.   North of Esh Sheriah a cavalry patrol sought to advance.   It was likewise driven back by our fire.

To point out the misstatements of facts it is only necessary to indicate that in each case the words east and west were wrongly used, that on that day Es Salt had been taken by the British, that a reënforced cavalry division, not a patrol, had advanced northward, and that the Esh Sheriah (Jordan) flows from north to south so that "north of the Jordan" would mean the district of its sources which lay 180 kilometers from the battle field.

The army report of May 5th stated verbatim:

The British attacked on the east side of the Esh Sheriah, but were repulsed.   They had made strong preparations to capture the lines of communication of the Esh Sheriah.   For this they had assembled many military forces.   On the morning of April 30th the soldiers and the artillery on the heights crossed the Esh Sheriah.

The British, after gaining some ground at Jericho and Es Salt, attacked with cavalry, artillery and machine guns along the Esh Sheriah to take us in rear, etc.

A glance at the map shows that the report is complete nonsense.

When I made representations to the Turkish headquarters that these reports, which were everywhere publicly posted, were likely to have dangerous consequences, the chief of the Turkish general staff replied that he could not admit the obscurity and untruth of the report.

On May 7th he telegraphed that it must be that the army

report of May 5th was improperly translated by us. That was quite impossible since the army reports were sent by wireless from Osmanie in the German language.

Finally it turned out that in spite of repeated requests of Captain Schlee, chief of the Osmanie station, Turkish head-quarters continued to send him the reports in Turkish. They had to be translated at the wireless station and it was stated that the errors in the translation were made there. It is to be noted that the personnel of almost all wireless stations in the country and on the frontiers, was predominantly, and sometimes exclusively, German, and that it was therefore advisable to furnish them with a German version of the reports. I mention the circumstance to make it clear why so many reports of Turkish actions as published were wrong.

Immediately after the battles the Fourth Army was ordered to fortify the heights of Es Salt with field works. At Aere a connecting group between the Eighth Army Corps and the left of the Seventh Army was formed. A new battle unit was formed at Tell er Rame, some distance from the left of the Eighth Army Corps, to meet any new advance of the enemy cavalry. It consisted of two cavalry regiments and a German machine gun detachment. The group was commanded at first by Lieutenant Colonel Kemal Bei of the Turkish general staff, and later by Colonel von Schierstaedt. Its task was activity against the enemy cavalry on the lower Jordan. It was not impossible that a third enemy attempt to break through our lines and into the East Jordan section was contemplated in order to make direct connection with the Arabs fighting there.

In the course of the month of May further parts of the German Infantry Regiment No. 146 were sent to Es Salt where they successively arrived by rail. The 146th Infantry Regiment was to be followed to Palestine by the 11th Reserve Rifle Battalion. Both were being withdrawn from the Macedonian front.

A few hours after the severe fighting of the second Jordan battle, I was informed on May 6th by the chief of the Turkish

general staff, that the German headquarters left it to us to post
the German troops during the hot season in regions with more
salubrious climate. I could not understand this message from
Spaa, since there was a German commander in chief on the spot
to care for these troops, since in the summer of 1916 and 1917
German troops had fought much farther south in the desert of
El Tih, at Kut-el Amara and between Mosul and Bagdad in the
hottest parts of Turkey, and some of them were still there.

Neither did I know how to evaluate the authorization, because
the German troops had been specifically selected and equipped
for use in a southern climate, and because the greater part of
them were only beginning to reach the front. There was a
further gap in my course of reasoning because all the auxiliary
formations of Jilderim which was organized on German ideas,
the aviation, information and railway troops, truck columns,
sanitary formations, etc., had to be withdrawn. But they had
been created and were employed not only for the German troops,
but also for the Turks.

I replied that the Asia Corps was in the mountains and that
the other German troops would be used in a manner compatible
with their health, and that I considered the withdrawal of the
German troops inadvisable for political reasons and because
the troops were engaged with the enemy.

I thought this reply had settled matters, but learned better a
few weeks later. About May 10th I was confidentially informed
that the Turkish government intended to confer on me the
internal political power in Syria.

It is proper here to cast a glance at the inner political conditions of Syria, as otherwise it is unintelligible why the Turkish
government contemplated this step which was contrary to all
of their previous principles.

The interior situation must be characterized as completely
hopeless. An orderly and reliable civil administration was a
prerequisite for effective influence on the population.

Maladministration of centuries, the corruption of high and

low officials (with a few exceptions) and the total lack of discipline of the Turkish gendarmery had brought about a state of general dissatisfaction.

The poor inhabitants, no matter of what religion, were exposed to any license and spoliation, which were increased under wartime conditions. This people, living in an ancient civilization and which had laid down its just demands in the fifteen articles of the Beirut reform program, enjoyed fewer rights during the war than ever.

How was an orderly administration of justice possible in a country where not even the judges understood Arabic, the local language!

Among the mixed population of Syrians, in which the Semitic elements predominate, there is a good deal of pure Arabic stock.

The real Syrian is a shrewd trader and an enterprising merchant. The Christian Syrian as a rule represents the wholesale business, the Mohammedan the retail trade. The development of commerce and industry, instead of being favored and fostered by the government, was at the mercy of the intrigues of Turkish officials unless they were bribed.

It is not surprising that by far the greater part of the people longed for orderly conditions regulated by law, such as were possible only under the protection of some European power since no Turkish promise had ever been kept. The differences between Syrians and Turks are perhaps best characterized by the Syrian adage: "Wherever a Turk sets his foot, there the earth becomes unproductive for a century."

The Turkish government in Constantinople was unwilling to meet the just demands of the people. The government declined to give assurances of an administration that would give the desired degree of local autonomy. It did not want to bind itself for the future.

The credit of the government throughout the country was poor, as many army contracts of the preceding year still remained unpaid. Existing conditions could not improve the credit. In spite of repeated and urgent requests the Army Group failed to receive the money necessary to make its purchases of supplies or to make even partial payments.

Had the money been available, all requirements of the Army Group, and large additional supplies, could have been purchased from the Arabs. As the money was not forthcoming, a large part of the harvest of the Arabian grain lands and thousands of camel loads from Huarun, inhabited by Druses, went to the British who paid in gold.

Though informed of all this, the government in Constantinople closed its ears to any kind of advice, and instituted a tax on grain which was impossible for Syrian and Arabic conditions. The three most influential Valis, those of Damascus, Beirut and Aleppo, who knew the country well, remonstrated against this step and were promptly dismissed.

Of course, I declined the offer of the government, transmitted to me through Enver, in no uncertain way, claiming that my military duties required every minute of my time.

In the face of the existing Turkish administration I would have been unable to improve conditions, but the responsibility for the continuance of these hopeless conditions would nevertheless have fallen on me.

After the second Jordan battle the 24th Division, with its ranks replenished after the heavy losses, was withdrawn to the vicinity of Mafid Dschozele. When I saw Infantry Regiment No. 2 of this division after the battle, it numbered about 150 men. The 3rd Cavalry Division also had had severe losses; it was withdrawn to the vicinity of Ed Damije.

Up to the end of May we had only the ordinary small enterprises of the enemy against the Seventh and Eighth Armies, which almost invariably remained without result. It was only during the night of the 29th and also of the 30th of May that the action in the coast section was somewhat more extensive. On the 29th five Indian battalions advanced west of the road Haikar Bridge-Miske. In the first assault they overran some of the heights of the main position. The heights were retaken by counter attack. In the next night the attack in the same terrain was repeated and repulsed with considerable loss to the enemy.

Anglo-Arabian action soon became lively along the Hedjas railroad. It was evidently the intention to wipe out the reverses of the battles by minor successes.

On the 8th of May the station of Katraneh, lying abreast of the southern shore of the Dead Sea, was attacked by strong bands of Bedouins. The attack was repulsed, but a Turkish company was captured. On the 9th the attack was renewed without result. A third attack, for which the enemy had brought up more artillery, was repulsed on May 12th. On the 15th the station of El Hasa was surprised by Arabs and taken. Various railway material was destroyed by them. A detachment of the Fourth Army, approaching from the north, soon retook the station. The enemy withdrew southward after heavy losses. The destruction of twenty-five bridges of the Hedjas railroad from May 1st to 19th shows how difficult it was to maintain the Hedjas railroad in operation.

On May 30th the Arabs surrounded El Fifre. The garrison broke through the enemy's lines during the night and cut its way out to Katraneh. El Fifre was subsequently retaken by us.

On May 26th Enver informed me, that in agreement with German headquarters he would not renew the contract of the military mission, which expired on December 14th, 1918. He offered me a personal contract to remain in the Turkish Army thereafter. I replied to him on the 27th of May that my further stay in the Turkish Army and a personal contract were out of the question.

CHAPTER 19

THE MONTH OF JUNE 1918

On June 4 the last part of Rifle Battalion No. 11 reached the station of Messudie, the intersection of the railroad to Tul Keram with the road to Nablus. The transportation of this battalion in numerous sections had been expedited ahead of other urgent replacements and war material, in order that the Army Group for once might have a reserve.

The Turkish battalions and replacements from Constantinople, insofar as we did not have to use them immediately in the Fourth Army, had only sufficed to balance the losses in the Seventh and Eighth Armies. The Turkish battalions sent to us had hardly any efficient officers, and were devoid of training, so that the army commanders preferred to distribute them as replacements.

The German Rifle Battalion No. 11 was an elite body of troops. With its strength of 800 men and numerous machine guns, and on account of its splendid training, it was of high battle value on the Palestine front. It was posted in the valley between Messudie and Nablus near Der Scharaf so as to be available as reserve for the Eighth Army as well as for the Seventh.

Major von Menges, its commander, on my request undertook to improve the training of the Turkish officers sent to him in installments.

On the part of the British there was, this spring, a partial change of troops. The army of General Allenby had received numerous Indian reënforcements which were particularly suitable for service in the Jordan section during the hot season. An Indian cavalry division had been brought from France to the Palestine front. The Indian infantry divisions contained some British battalions and all the higher posts were in the hands of

British officers. The machine gun formations of the infantry and cavalry were entirely, or predominantly, British, so far as leadership and the service of the guns was concerned. Supernumerary troops were made into new formations by the British, as we were informed by prisoners and agents.

In comparison it was doubly regrettable that the Turkish units received wholly insufficient replacements.

In the first week of June the British artillery fire in the coast section several times increased to a high degree of intensity. Our fliers reported an augmentation of troops there. Numerous British reconnaissances were repulsed. As an attack seemed to be in preparation, I sent the rifle battalion there.

On June 9th a strong force of the enemy's infantry advanced west of the Haikar Bridge-Miske road. Our advanced troops were driven back in the main position. The attack was repulsed after bitter fighting with bayonet and hand grenades, the dunes frequently changing occupants. Battalions advancing directly on the coast at Arsuf and Sch. el Muntar were repulsed. About eight British battalions took part in the attack. The British made progress only in the foreground of our positions. Their losses were considerable.

Detachments of the Rifle Battalion distinguished themselves by bold reconnaissance attacks into the very trenches of the enemy, gaining their first laurels in the Palestine theater of war.

As previously stated the last parts of Rifle Battalion No. 11 had arrived June 4th.

On June 10th I received the following telegram from Enver:

Upon the orders of the German headquarters the 11th Rifle Battalion will be sent by rail to Constantinople.

Vicegeneralissimo.

I answered at once:

Further information relative to the Rifle Battalion is requested if any importance is attached to success in this theater.

Sgd. LIMAN V. SANDERS.

I did not receive an immediate reply.

A telegram from General von Lenthe of June 11th, based on information from the quartermaster general of the Turkish general staff, informed me that it was probable that the battalion would be sent to Batum on the Black Sea.

On June 13th the chief of the Turkish general staff telegraphed:

Chief of staff German field army renews instructions to withdraw German troops from Jordan valley and post them in mountains. Cause is that in addition to Rifle Battalion 703, the 146th Infantry is posted in the Jordan valley. German headquarters deems posting of battalion in mountains of East Jordan section practicable in spite of imminent British attack.

Sgd. v. SEECKT.

My military reasoning refused to work in those days. I could not understand why headquarters in Spaa 4,000 kilometers distant wanted to fix the position of a single battalion on a battle front where tactical considerations prevail.

I replied:

As early as June 7th, when it became very hot, I had withdrawn the German troop in the Jordan valley: 1st Battalion 146th, 703 and Pioneer Company 205 to the mountains east and west of the Jordan.

I am compelled in the following account to repeat the wording of the telegrams exchanged so that there may be no mistake in judging the events.

On June 15th Enver telegraphed:

In view of the general situation the German headquarters is considering the withdrawal of all German troops from Palestine, and has ordered the departure of the rifle battalion. No details as yet known of further withdrawals of German troops.

I shall ask for Your Excellency's view when the negotiations with German headquarters have cleared the situation.

Sgd. ENVER Turkish Hq. No. 1210 Secr. Op.

The foregoing telegram reached me at Nablus at 12 o'clock

noon on June 16th. My immediate reply to Enver was as follows:

Nablus, 2 p.m. 16/6/18 via Nazareth.

Receipt of your telegram No. 1210 secr. op. I have the honor to acknowledge. If the German headquarters deems it necessary to withdraw the German troops to the German west front, where the decision of the whole war lies, it will have to be done of course, however unfavorable may be the consequences in this theater.

But if the German troops here are withdrawn for use in the Caucasus, or in another Turkish theater of war, that is contrary to the conditions under which I accepted the command of the Army Group from Your Excellency.

In that case I am compelled, at once and irrevocably, to lay down the command of the Army Group, as the orders in question must certainly be based on completely incorrect reports of the situation on the Palestine front, and will be followed by incalculable consequences.

In that case I shall hold myself in no way responsible for the retreat which at the next great British attack will become an absolute necessity, and for the step by step defense of Palestine and Syria.

Conditions here are such that the German troops have become the backbone of all further operations.

It was only with the help of the German troops that we repulsed the great attacks of April 10th and 12th at Rafal and Berukin, and won both Jordan battles.

At the last great attack in the coast section June 7th to 9th, the rifle battalion was the sole reserve of the Army Group and had to be thrown into the fight at the last.

After the continuous hard fighting of the last three months and the heavy losses, the strongest Turkish regiments average 350–400 rifles in addition to machine guns, and many Turkish regiments are weaker.

On the side of the enemy the partial exchange of troops for Indian battalions 800–1000 strong has increased his numbers, and the Indian troops so far engaged have fought well. In infantry the enemy is three to four times superior to us, and in artillery he is far superior.

The hostile Arabs in the trans-Jordan section maintain more and more regular organizations under British organization.

These are the real conditions.

The moral impression of the withdrawal of the German troops upon our Turkish troops, with whom they are fighting shoulder to shoulder, is incalculable, and it would be much greater upon the attitude of the Arabs who at present have great respect for German officers and troops.

Such consequences can be justified only by the use of the German troops on the decisive German west front which will decide everything, including the fate of Turkey, but never by their use in another Turkish theater."

Sgd. LIMAN V. SANDERS.

After receipt of Enver's telegram of June 15th I naturally assumed that my reply would be awaited before a decision was made. That was not the case. At 5.10 p.m. of June 16th the following telegram of the chief of the Turkish general staff was sent me from Constantinople before my reply had been received:

Constantinople 5.10 p.m. June 16.

There is no doubt that the German headquarters has resolved upon the gradual withdrawal of all German troops from Palestine. The departure of the 146th Infantry Regiment is to follow upon that of the 11th Rifle Battalion, etc.

The further text stated that upon representation it might be possible that special troops and formations needed by the Army Group might perhaps not be withdrawn. Some prospect was held out of a division being sent to the Army Group from the Caucasus, and another from Smyrna.

I knew beyond a doubt that it would be months before these divisions would materialize.

My telegram to Enver furnished a reply to this despatch. The important decision had been made of withdrawing the German combatant troops without giving me a hearing.

On the forenoon of June 20th I addressed the following telegram to the German Ambassador, Count Bernstorff, which was receipted for at the German Embassy at noon on the 20th:

20. June 18.

Ambassador Count Bernstorff

Constantinople.

I am compelled to inform Your Excellency, as the representative of His Majesty, that the military and political interests of Germany are being seriously impaired by the way in which decisive questions concerning the German troops of Army Group F are handled by Turkish headquarters. Without hearing me as the responsible commander in chief of the Army

Group F, which is based on German foundations and without hearing me as chief of the German mission accountable in the first line for the care of the German troops in Turkey, the Turkish headquarters has given orders for the withdrawal of all German troops and formations from Palestine. This step will be shortly followed by a collapse of the Palestine front and the political consequences will be Germany's responsibility. The preservation of a large part of Palestine and of all of Syria to our ally has been possible only by supporting the Turks with German military strength and German prestige which alone can give the Arabs guaranties for the future.

With the removal of these bases the Arabs will no longer resist British influence and British gold.

Every German officer of my command who knows the conditions is of exactly the same opinion.

The Turkish troops here cannot hold the front by themselves. Other events have sufficiently demonstrated what will happen when Turkish troops are retreating. Moreover the troops today are undernourished, very poorly clothed and wretchedly shod.

All these things will happen shortly, if the steps referred to are carried out.

The responsible office informs me that the traffic changes of the railroad with its very limited equipment, incident to the transport of the German troops, would make it impossible to supply the remaining troops with war material and subsistence.

By the rights with which I am invested by the contract of the military mission as chief of that mission and by the specific right of the *"influence effective"* conveyed to me by the treaty of alliance of August 2, 1914, it becomes my duty to state that the present state of the Turkish Army does in no way permit of far reaching offensive operations, such as I am informed are being planned in Trans-Caucasia.

The number of Turkish deserters is higher today than that of the men under arms. A guaranty for the subsistence of the troops can never be given by the Turks. The promises are made and broken.

The clothing of my army is so bad that many officers are wearing ragged uniforms and even battalion commanders have to wear tschariks in lieu of boots. We, on the part of the Germans and Austrians, help as much as we can, but it is small help in great need.

According to reports of German officers of the Sixth Army from Irak, which are on file in the Prussian War Ministry, 17,000 men of that army have died of hunger and its consequences, up to April 1918.

Far reaching enterprises should not be based on such Turkish conditions. Any one understanding the Turkish Army knows that they must fail.

Through the advance into Persia, against which I urgently warned, the

Turks have lost Bagdad, through the initiation of the Jilderim enterprise planned against Bagdad, the Turks have lost Jerusalem, and now through the bottomless advance into Trans-Caucasia they are going to lose all of Arabia, Palestine and Syria.

The responsibility for it will some day be placed on the shoulders of Germany.

What the Turkish state needs, and what the Turkish Army needs, is internal consolidation, not far reaching plans of conquest.

This is my conviction based on accurate knowledge of the Turkish Army after four and a half years of service with it.

Should the German troops and formations be withdrawn from here for the purpose of other Turkish enterprises, against my protests, I shall at once lay down the command of the Army Group, in order that the name of a Prussian general may not be made responsible for wholly untenable Turkish conditions which are going to cost the Turks several provinces.

Your Excellency is requested to inform His Majesty the Emperor and King to whom I shall at once report the case by telegraph.

Sgd. LIMAN VON SANDERS.

Enver telegraphed at 3.10 p.m. June 20th that he had not in mind to send the German troops from Palestine to another Turkish theater. He requested to know how I came to have that idea.

As above stated I knew from the military mission since June 11th, that it was intended to send the Rifle Battalion to Georgia. On June 21st Count Bernstorff telegraphed me that the Rifle Battalion was to be sent to Georgia. The telegram is as follows:

21 June 18.

Liman von Sanders, Excellency
Headquarters Army Group F.

I thank Your Excellency most sincerely for the confidence shown me; I believe however that there is some mistake as to the facts.

Only one rifle battalion has been reserved by order of German headquarters to be sent to Georgia.

It is not a question of Turkish wishes, but in order to bring about order in the Caucasus so that the Turkish Army now there may march to Mesopotamia via Urumia and Tabriz.

I shall be glad at any time to collaborate with Your Excellency in the questions nearest our hearts.

Sgd. BERNSTORFF.

My immediate reply was:

Ambassador Count Bernstorff, Constantinople
21 June 18.

Thanking Your Excellency I desire to state that Your Excellency is quite incorrectly informed of the events.　It is a question here of the serious fact that upon orders from Turkish headquarters all German troops on the Palestine front, among them the Rifle Battalion, are to be transported back to Constantinople.

As Palestine cannot be held without German troops, and as a collapse will be the consequence, I explained the situation to Your Excellency in my telegram of yesterday.　As no change has been made in spite of my decided objection and my reference to the consequences, I have today informed Enver Pasha that I am laying down the command of the Army Group.

Sgd. LIMAN VON SANDERS.

At 5 p.m. June 21st General Ludendorff telegraphed that it was intended to use the Rifle Battalion in Trans-Caucasia. It seems hard to believe that Enver was the only one who knew nothing of the use of the Rifle Battalion in the Caucasus. In the following telegram I informed Enver that I was laying down the command:

21. 6. 18.

Enver Pasha, Constantinople.

To Your Excellency I beg to reply as follows:

Before details were arranged for the withdrawal of German troops from the Palestine front, as has been done in part by No. 1213 secr. op., I, as responsible commander in chief of Army Group F, should have been consulted about the possibility and method of such withdrawal.

Likewise I should have been heard as chief of the German military mission charged with the care of the German troops in Turkey.

The first attempt to withdraw German troops from the Palestine front was made at the beginning of May on the ground of sanitary reasons.

I strongly objected to that step, the necessity of which I alone could judge here on the front.　That it is the intention to use the 11th Reserve Rifle Battalion in Trans-Caucasia, I had learned from a reliable source in Constantinople, and the information was confirmed by telegram from German headquarters No. 8758 secr. op.

So far as I know the transport of the German troops that are to be withdrawn was not contemplated by German headquarters, either on the

16th, or 20th of June. The subject was the difficulty of finding replacements for the German troops here.

Had I been listened to, the question of replacements would never have caused the transport of the German troops to Constantinople.

There is no doubt, unfortunately, that the news service of Turkish headquarters was entirely wrong. From among the many proofs in my possession I will quote the following only (relative to the Jordan battle).

It is due to my decided protests that some improvement has been made. Since accepting the command of the Palestine front I have had constant obstacles thrown in my way by Your Excellency's headquarters. Their official adjustment is reserved to the proper German authorities. What has now been done exceeds all bounds.

Without giving me a hearing, orders are issued for the withdrawal of my most valuable troops, without which the front cannot be held, and the withdrawal of the remaining German formations, without which the war cannot be continued by Turkey, is to be expected according to 1213 secr. op.

My protests receive no consideration whatever.

I am therefore compelled to lay down the command of the Army Group.

I request Your Excellency to so inform His Majesty the Sultan, and I further request immediate instructions to whom to turn over the command. General Djevad Pasha is the senior of the three army leaders. Report of my resignation I have caused to be forwarded to His Majesty the Emperor and King.

Sgd. LIMAN v. SANDERS.

On the forenoon of June 22d I reported to His Majesty the Emperor, through the chief of the military cabinet, that I was compelled to lay down the command of the Army Group.

On the evening of that day a telegram came from Enver quite improper as to contents and tone; I had better omit it.

On the following day, June 23rd, I received the following order from German headquarters:

His Majesty the Emperor and King cannot concur in your resignation and requests that you remain at your post until further orders.

By command of His Majesty
The Chief of the Military Cabinet
Sgd. FRHR. v. LYNCKER.

In a communication from the cabinet of July 7th this decision was repeated and explained.

I was compelled to remain at my post.

The transport of the Rifle Battalion in small sections began during the ensuing days. Other German reënforcements en route to the Palestine front, particularly artillery, were stopped on the railroad after their heads had gotten to Damascus. They were transported back to Constantinople.

I will add that I have recently been informed by the commander of the Rifle Battalion, that it found no further employment at the front during this war. It was withdrawn at first to Vranja in Serbia, and later to upper Silesia. The equipment of the Rifle Battalion for a campaign in a tropical climate had cost many hundred thousand marks.

The transport of the 146th Infantry Regiment still awaited the decision of the German headquarters.

During the same month General Freiherr von Kress and many German officers and officials were sent to Tiflis, followed soon thereafter by various German troops. This German group was also equipped with armored trains. Army Group F had not one of them, though they were urgently needed.

The Army Group had to help itself as best it could. In the month of June the 13th Depot Regiment at Baalbek, under Major Würth von Würthenau, was brought forward to Nazareth. After its trained portions had been sent to the front, it could be given none but Arab replacements. The 17th Depot Regiment, under Major Blell, was transferred from Nazareth to Haifa, with the idea of forming a complete replacement division there, in the course of the summer, in rear of the right wing of the Army Group.

No further warlike events occurred in this month on the Palestine front; on the other hand, the activity of the Arab troops, under Scherif Faisal, in the East Jordan section, continued to increase.

The position of General von Lenthe as my representative of the military mission in Constantinople was so regulated in June by communication from the cabinet, that as chief of the mission I retained only the decision of general principles. It was quite according to my wishes. The distance between my present post in Nazareth and Constantinople was so great, that details could not be transacted. General von Lenthe was given a chief of staff in the person of Colonel Dove.

The German military persons with the Sixth Army were now also placed under the military mission, after General von Gressmann had been recalled to Germany for other employment.

CHAPTER 20

The Month of July 1918

The over-extension of the front of the Seventh and Eighth Armies became more and more felt during the hot season, as there could be no relief of divisions. In many parts of this loose line the artillery fire and action of airplanes gave the troops no rest. Moreover, at the height of the summer, water had to be brought up frequently many kilometers, because it was impossible to organize the few troops in rear so that they could provide water for the troops in front in the requisite amount. Saddle and draft animals suffered exceedingly from the lack of water, and often had to traverse great distances for watering them once a day. The various German formations for drilling for water worked with indefatigable industry with very limited results in this arid country.

A shortening of the front of the Seventh and Eighth Armies was possible only by the Fourth Army taking over the positions of the Seventh Army on the west bank of the river. As the Fourth Army had no reserve, it could be done only by utilizing the troops in the deep rearward bend at Aere and southwest of it.

This in turn could not be done without first driving the advanced posts of the enemy, on the Msallabe and on either side of this hill, back to the lower Auja.

Success here, at the same time, would make a third attack for gaining the East Jordan section improbable, because it made the space too narrow for the British deployment.

An enterprise against the front on the Msallabe had to be a complete surprise. The timely arrival of numerous British reënforcements was to be prevented. Command of this enterprise was given to Ali Fuad Pasha, commanding general of the Twentieth Army Corps. The German Infantry Battalions

702 and 703 were assigned to him, as was the only remaining company of the Rifle Battalion. The Turkish troops assigned for the attack were the 53d Division now in that section, and the 24th Division now again numbering some 1,000 rifles whose successful leader, Colonel Boehme, unfortunately was sick, and the two weak regiments of the 3d Cavalry Division.

The Army Group had ordered the attack to be made in the night of the 13/14 of June. The main attack was to be made against the Msallabe and on either side of it, and a secondary attack in the narrow delta between Wadi Mellaha and Jordan was to drive back the British troops there. For the latter attack the Fourth Army was to furnish two companies of the 146th German Infantry Regiment and two Turkish battalions; it was also to make lively demonstrations on the lower Jordan to attract the enemy's attention to that point.

In spite of the superiority of enemy fliers, the concentration and preparation of troops for the attack remained concealed from the enemy.

Ali Fuad placed the Rifle Company and the two German battalions in the center, on their right the two Turkish Regiments Nos. 58 and 163, on their left the Turkish Regiment No. 32, and Regiment No. 2 in rear of the center.

During the night the troops were brought up closer to the enemy without detection, and were ordered to begin the advance at 3 a.m. At the exact hour the German infantry advanced, overran the first position of the completely surprised enemy with insignificant losses, broke into his second position and in part advanced beyond into the scattered British camps north of the Auja. The enemy's barrage came too late.

Unfortunately the German troops were left in the lurch as the Turkish infantry failed completely. The 58th Infantry Regiment had advanced about 300 meters when a weak fire came from the foremost British lines. The regiment halted at once and made no further attempt to advance. On its right the 163d Regiment advanced about three kilometers without meeting notable resistance, and came to a stop because the 58th Regiment was not on its left.

The 32d Infantry Regiment advancing on the left of the German troops, permitted itself to be held by the fire of the small garrison on the Msallabe, though it was directed only against the center which in its first advance had gotten half way up the hill.

Instead of pushing forward its wings, as had been specifically ordered, they halted when the center halted. When the enemy opened with artillery, the center withdrew to the foot of the hill, and the wings at once joined in the rearward movement.

Infantry Regiment No. 2 was to follow in rear of the center, but Ali Fuad Pasha, fearing a reverse, held it four kilometers in rear.

When day broke the German companies were alone fighting in part in the second British line, in part in the British camps in which only a few British groups made serious resistance. Had the Turkish troops simply advanced alongside the Germans, the Msallabe and adjoining British lines would have been overrun, with small loss.

British reënforcements were soon hurrying up from every direction, mostly Australians. The British communication service functioned faultlessly. The German companies had captured an infantry gun and several machine guns, and put up a desperate resistance. Not receiving any kind of support, they had to withdraw.

Even now the Turkish infantry did nothing to support them so that in the retreat they received a heavy fire from the rear and from both flanks. Their losses were high. Many officers, non-commissioned officers and men were killed or wounded. The excellent commander of the 703d Infantry Battalion, Captain Gressmann, died a hero's death here. The brave Rifle Company was almost completely destroyed. The Turks, of course, hardly had any losses at all. The German troops were withdrawn in rear of their initial position.

The half hearted secondary attack between Wadi Mellaha and Jordan was soon checked when Australian cavalry threatened to turn the right flank. The 3rd Cavalry Division was absent because the commanding general of the Twentieth Army Corps had held it back to seek connection with the main attack in the

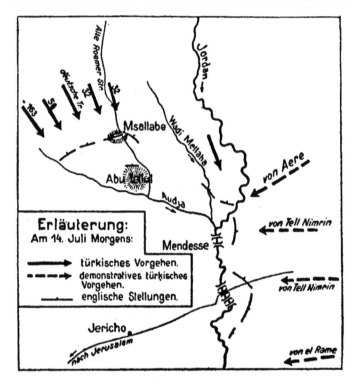

rear instead of in front. The advance ended with a slight gain of ground.

After receiving the most contradictory and incorrect reports at my post of command, I realized that the original objective could no longer be realized on account of the continued arrival of British reënforcements, which I could plainly see. I therefore declined the suggestion of Ali Pasha to renew the attack with all the troops in the middle of the day. It was bound to end in a reverse as the Turkish troops had completely failed in the morning when success would have been easy.

Results were more favorable with the Fourth Army because some vigor of action was shown there. The artillery of the Eighth Army Corps took an effective part in the action. Small infantry detachments along the entire front advanced beyond the line of outposts and engaged the enemy. The cavalry brigade of Colonel von Schierstaedt, with the machine gun detachment commanded by Captain von Sydow, and with the German pioneer company, advanced to the Place of Baptism. Toward noon a strong enemy mounted force with armored cars deployed against Schierstaedt's brigade. The cool German leader let them come close and received them with a destructive fire. The cavalry flooded back with great loss.

A greater reverse was soon thereafter incurred by the Indian cavalry division which, advancing from the bridge head, deployed against the southern part of the front of the Eighth Army Corps, the Lutfi Division. It was shot to pieces at close range. The remnants of the squadrons galloped back in disorder to the bridge over the Jordan. Many horses were captured by the Turks.

The terrible heat inhibited further action on that day. The thermometer indicated plus 131 degrees Fahrenheit. No British counter attacks were made until evening. An attempt of the enemy late in the evening to cut off Schierstaedt's brigade miscarried, except that parts of the 11th Turkish Cavalry Regiment missed their connection with the brigade in the darkness and were captured, with them the regimental commander.

Nothing proved better the deterioration of the efficiency of Turkish troops than these events of July 14th. The things which happened here would have been impossible with any of my troops in former years. The utmost that could be expected, from the present condition of the deteriorated regiments, was that they might hold their ground against attack. I therefore gave up the idea of retaking some sand dunes in the foreground of the coast sector with a battalion of the 146th Infantry Regiment.

Of considerable influence on the conduct of the Turkish troops was the departure of many Turkish officers from the army under my command for service in the East Caucasus. A decree of Enver promised to officers volunterring for service in the East Caucasus advantages of promotion and double pay. The departure of numerous such volunteers was natural, because in the Army Group they received no pay and lived in anxiety about their families. It will ever remain unique in military history that promotion and increased pay were offered to officers for transfer from a severe battle front to service in a much more pleasant theater, where no fighting was in prospect for a long time. The lack of officers increased after the great fire in Stambul, to which place many officers were furloughed because their families had been made homeless. According to Turkish custom such a furlough may not be denied. The ominous part of it was that their return could not be expected for months.

Further actions on the front during July were nowhere of decisive character. The Battalions 702 and 703 were withdrawn into the valley west of Nablus. The last Rifle Company, after being restored to a strength of about 120 men, was shipped to Constantinople.

The hostile Arab troops continued their enterprises in the East Jordan section. During the month of July Menzil, Anese, Wadi esch Schar were attacked by them with varying success. On July 20th and 21st they made a more extensive attack against Maan which was repulsed. On July 21st and 22d the Arabs, with 2,000 regular troops, 600 Bedouins, twelve guns and numerous machine guns, tried to take the station of Djardun, but were repulsed, and left twenty-four officers and about 200 men dead before Djardun.

CHAPTER 21

THE MONTH OF AUGUST 1918

On August 1st I gave the following written instructions to Major Ludloff, the quartermaster general of the Army Group, for his report at German headquarters in Spaa where he had been ordered. It was sent to him through the official channel of the military mission and explained how the headquarters of the Army Group viewed the situation.

1. August 1918

For Colonel Dove to Major Ludloff, Berlin.

As was to be foreseen, Constantinople made promises which were of no effect for the supply of our army (concerns Vali Tachsin Bei as director of supply).

The real reason of the impossibility to hold our front for any length of time, according to my view and that of Kiazim, is that available resources no longer permit Turkey to conduct simultaneous operations in two theaters so eccentric as here and in the East Caucasus. Many things that should be supplied to this theater, we lose to the East Caucasus. With a supply of coal, communications with the Army Group might be maintained, but this coal is used on the Black Sea. On the 26th and 30th of July no trains could be run on the line Aleppo-Rajak.

Please inform the German headquarters and the Prussian War Ministry plainly of my views. I am unwilling to share in the responsibility for false measures which continue to be taken in Constantinople.

It is my firm conviction that the operations in East Caucasus with their indefinite objectives will and must fail. All such Turkish projects since the beginning of the war have failed, but I have never been listened to, and shall not be listened to in this case, until too late. German headquarters is greatly overestimating the slim material resources of Turkey.

The 146th Infantry Regiment will have to remain here, if it is desired that this front be held. The Indian prisoners and deserters of the last few days already say that the German troops are being withdrawn, and that they had been told that British troops would be used against such German troops as were still present and that the Indian troops would make quick work of the weak and ineffective Turks. Please make unreserved use of the foregoing.

Sgd. LIMAN VON SANDERS.

Postscript for Colonel Dove. Please inform German Ambassador of my foregoing views, because decisive measures must be taken and half measures must stop.

On June 24th the German headquarters had approved the assignment of a German chief of the general staff and of general staff officers to the Turkish army group in the East Caucasus. For the former place Major von Kiessling was designated who had rendered good service under Field Marshal General Frhr. v. d. Goltz and later on the Palestine front. He declined with my full concurrence, and the post was now offered to Major von Falkenhausen, the chief of the general staff of the Seventh Army. He also declined, and the chief of staff of Halil Pasha, Major Paraquin, was designated. General staff officers for the East Caucasus were taken from the German west front, where they were urgently needed.

I will endeavor to explain briefly, how the Turkish political aims with a very real eye on pecuniary gains in the Caucasus, and the detaching of numerous Turkish troops to Trans-Caucasia and Azerbaijan influenced the situation on the Palestine front.

In the middle of the summer of 1918 six strong Turkish divisions were in Trans-Caucasia or in Azerbaijan, or were en route there. The strength of some of these divisions was 9,000 men and over. The transport of these troops, of the replacements, of war material and subsistence to that theater, was for months consuming the coal which would have made the transport of numerous troops from Constantinople to Aleppo possible. The distance from Constantinople to Batum by way of the Black Sea is about 1,100 kilometers, and the railroad communication from Batum to Tiflis and Tapriz about 850 kilometers more.

I will not discuss the question whether through the army group of East Caucasus pan-islamitic plans alone were pursued, or whether a new British front was to be evoked in northern Persia, or, as telegraphed by Count Bernstorff on June 21st, the ulterior aim was to march these troops to Mesopotamia.

According to my view we already had too many fronts. It will hardly ever be advisable for one inferior in numbers to force a much superior opponent to form some new front.

The urgent need of troops on the hard pushed battle front of Palestine should have disposed of this idea.

At any rate it stands beyond doubt that, on account of the operations referred to, sufficient troops were not ordered by Turkish headquarters to Palestine.

It stands equally beyond a doubt that, on account of these same operations, sufficient replacements were not assigned to Army Group F.

Furthermore the requisite war material could not be sent to Palestine, because it was being used in another direction of no influence whatever on the decision of the war. The funds necessary for the purchase of subsistence for the Army Group in Syria and Arabia, were expended for other purposes.

To refute forever the statement that even with sufficient coal the railroad could not have carried many more troops, or much more material to Aleppo, I point to the fact of the transport of six Turkish divisions from Constantinople and Aidin to Aleppo in summer of 1917. I quote the following data which irrefutably show the conditions.

In those days fourteen coal trains came weekly from Germany to Constantinople. Seven train loads were used for the water supply, illumination and traffic arrangements of Constantinople. The remainder was turned over to the Anatolian railway, barring some 2,500 tons turned over monthly for the navigation of the Black Sea, largely for purposes of the East Caucasus operation. The coal mined in Turkey (in Soma the daily production was raised from 300 to 500 tons per day) went for the most part for industrial purposes or for railroads or ships, based on Constantinople or Smyrna. In 1917 some of this coal was used for the transport of troops to Aleppo.

From Aleppo the divisions allotted to the Palestine front might have been marched to the front, as was frequently done, or by granting but a small part of the coal a large part of them might have been transported by railroad. The Etra Aleppo and Damascus in the summer of 1918 contain in the weekly reports the invariable remark: no coal.

A brief comparison of what the railroads in Syria and Palestine were capable, in the spring of 1918, when they used their last reserves of coal in order to get the troops and material accumulated south of the Taurus to the front, with what they were capable of doing in the middle of the summer, when they had no coal at all, furnishes irrefutable proof.

The work of the railroads on the stretch from Deraa to Damascus during three weeks in May 1918 is compared in the following table with that of three weeks in August:

Average daily work

8–14 May 627, 1 t.	14–20 August 231, 4 t.
15–21 May 697, 5 t.	21–27 August 236, 4 t.
22–28 May 670, 7 t.	28 Aug.-2 Sept. 239, 1 t.

The procurement of wood for the railroad in Syria and Palestine became more and more difficult, because during the past few years the supplies anywhere near the railroad had been used up, and because the means of transportation for bringing the wood from a distance were scarce. When the Army Group detailed numerous detachments from the depot regiments for the procurement of wood, the greater part of the men deserted within a week, frequently assisted by the rebellious civil population. Toward the last it became necessary to cut down the olive plantations in Palestine and even use the vines to feed the locomotives. It is well known of course that wood is a poor substitute for coal.

The influence of the unfavorable transport situation on the Palestine front was felt in many ways in August. In that month, beginning with August 12th, the first reënforcements from the 47th and 37th Caucasian Divisions, promised in a communication from Turkish headquarters of June 16th, began to arrive in small detachments and so slowly that frequently but one battalion was shipped in a week. The transport of artillery ammunition was so delayed that the prescribed supply was nowhere on hand, and a strict control had to be kept of every round fired by the artillery. The supply of subsistence was so defective that frequently the troops did not have enough food on hand for the next day.

In consequence of the insufficiency of the food, the desertions to the rear became exceedingly numerous in August. To check them to a certain extent, the Eighth Army provided that only the troops in first lines got anywhere near enough to eat, while toward the rear the rations became smaller and smaller. Any soldier will admit that such steps are lamentable measures.

On August 10th Major Ludloff reported from Berlin, that he had induced German headquarters to leave the 146th Infantry in Turkey for the present. He added that the Prussian War Ministry was opposed to the withdrawal of the German troops, and that Count Bernstorff had urgently asked for a reënforcement of three to four battalions, but without success.

On August 4th a small British attack was made in the coast section, which was repulsed without much loss.

At 10 p.m. on August 12th, after a long and heavy bombardment, the British attacked the Turkish positions on both sides of the Jerusalem-Nablus road. The fighting was severe and bloody, and lasted until 4 a.m. East of the road the enemy's attack was repulsed before it reached the Turkish positions. West of the road the enemy penetrated a part of the Turkish position, but was driven out by counter attacks in bitter hand to hand fighting. The attack east of the road was made by three, west of the road by seven British and Indian battalions. The action took place abreast of Turmus Aya. The entire position remained in our hands without any loss of ground.

The Turkish soldiers regarded with jealous eyes the felt soles of the boots of British dead and prisoners, which were nailed on to deaden the sound of marching on rocky ground. Their own feet were often wrapped in rags, or at best they wore tschariks, i.e., animals skins tied with strings. Many officers had no other foot gear.

In the 19th Division in the coast sector, which on account of much malaria had been exchanged in August for the 7th Division in the western hills, the infantry patrols frequently returned with bleeding feet and without accomplishing anything, because with their miserable foot gear they could not march on the stony slopes, though in the coast sector their foot gear had sufficed after a fashion.

From August 19th to 20th a stronger British attack took place after extensive preparation by artillery, in the dune terrain of the coast, the left being directed against Birket Atife. The 7th Division posted there under its brave leader, Nashui Bei, repulsed the attack after several bloody hand to hand actions. At the beginning of the war Nashui Bei became a Russian prisoner of war. After many adventures he found his way back to Turkey via China. It appears that the British had learned of the exchange of the divisions from their spies and wanted to test the efficiency of the new troops in the open coast terrain.

When I learned that the Taurus tunnel would be closed for all traffic during the last third of the month of September, pending the completion of its last section, I addressed the following telegram to Enver Pasha on August 17th, sending a copy to the German Ambassador with request to pass it on to the German headquarters:

17. August. 18

Enver Pasha, Constantinople.

The Taurus tunnel is to be closed for ten days from September 21st, as you know.

As their spies keep the British well informed of everything that goes on in the front and rear of our army, it may be taken for granted that they already know of the closing of the tunnel, the only communication with the Army Group, and are planning to turn it to their advantage.

While we probably may expect a great attack in the coast section, as reported to you in another message, there is the probability that other heavy attacks may follow on the closing of the tunnel.

In that case we shall be short of ammunition and the other necessary replacement of troops and material, unless we bend every effort now to the accumulation of large reserves of every kind south of the Taurus.

Instead of taking this into account and satisfying the urgent needs of the Army Group, the contrary has been ordered from the headquarters of Your Excellency.

Instead of running nine Taurus trains, as requested by us, their number has been reduced to four, in spite of our protests.

I request Your Excellency, in the interest of the three armies which have been fighting here so bravely, to see that the absolute needs of the Army Group be satisfied.

The check in the transport from Aleppo on account of lack of wood, was temporary and we have taken measures to remedy it.

This check, in my opinion, should never be a reason for not furnishing the replacements, which five weeks from now will be of decisive importance.

Sgd. LIMAN VON SANDERS.
D. A. 113 secr.

On August 19th I received a personal letter from General Ludendorff of August 3rd, in which, in view of many contradictory reports, he requested my personal view of the military, political and economic conditions in Syria and Palestine. I explained the situation in my report of August 22d. I spoke also of the deleterious effect of the East Caucasus operations on the Palestine front and described the lamentable political and economic conditions of the country.

My military fears for the front I expressed in an enclosed personal letter, stating that we could hold out for a limited period only, and that the campaign could no longer be carried on with half measures.

It was clear that we had to expect a big attack in the coast sector. In view of past experiences I was in hopes that we might weather it, though the front might be pushed back at some points. But the situation of the Army Group would become critical, if we were beaten on the Jordan, or east of the Jordan. Retreat to the base (the communications via Deraa and Damascus) would be impossible as this base was too far to the east. The constantly increasing force of the hostile Arabs held the shortest line to these communications.

In the second half of August I was informed by Djemal Pasha, commander of the Fourth Army, that Sherif Faisal was willing to take over the Jordan front of the Fourth Army with his troops, provided he received definite guarantees from the Turkish government that an Arabian state would be formed; that according to the statements of Faisal a great British attack was in preparation in the coast district, and that in this case the troops of the Fourth Army would become available to reënforce the front between the sea and the Jordan. Through General Kiazim, my Turkish chief of the general staff, I instructed General Djemal Pasha to open negotiations to that effect. In the same way I requested Enver to give the desired guarantees.

Neither from Enver nor from Djemal did I ever receive information, or a reply, concerning this matter. I am therefore unable to judge of the sincerity or of the scope of Faisal's offer. From the report of my Turkish chief I gained the impression that the Turks distrusted the offer and considered it merely a trick to put our Jordan positions into the hands of the Arabs, while the British main attack took place in the coast sector, or between the sea and the Jordan.

To give an idea of the extent of British relations with the hinterland of the Army Group, I quote the following extracts from two reports of the German Consul General in Damascus, which he had made to his superiors and communicated to me. He reported on August 19th:

For about two months an organized caravan traffic has existed from Akaba across the Huarun, the Druse mountains. Sugar, coffee and cotton goods are imported, and apricot paste is exported, together with great quantities of grain from the Huarun.

The arrival of caravans from Akaba is known here weeks in advance, and is publicly discussed. The goods are sold by the caravan leaders for gold, and are not consigned to any particular recipient. The leaders also buy here British notes which, like other securities of the enemy, come here from Constantinople in great quantities.

Sgd. DR. BRODE.

Also on August 22d:

As stated in my previous reports to Your Excellency a regular and daily more open traffic of persons and goods has been going on for months between Damascus and Akaba, with the Huarun as intermediate station.

In the Huarun are about 30,000 well armed warriors and at least an equal number of armed bands that have joined them in the last few years, mostly deserters.

Since the departure of Vali Tachsin Bei there is complete anarchy in the administration here, with increase of highway robbery, as one of the consequences. The authorities look on with folded arms at the traffic with the enemy. A number of officials probably are making large profits.

The population of Syria is friendly toward the Entente, and therefore inclined to assist the enemy. It will gladly avail itself of the occasion to do so when it involves no more danger than now. I know of numerous cases of persons travelling safely from here to Jerusalem. There are regular agencies for such travel with fixed tariffs. The journey to Cairo is offered for fifty pounds gold, that to Akaba for eight pounds. There is a great demand for English banknotes, etc.

In view of their character, and in view of the progress of British propaganda and of the embarrassments of the Turkish government, the Druses seem to consider themselves the tongue of the scales; I cannot risk a statement whether it is still possible to bring them back under effective Turkish control. In view of the preparations the British are making for a great attack in the fall (the establishment of great depots at Akaba is reported) the importance of the question is so great that I could not omit to inform Your Excellency.

Sgd. DR. BRODE.

The Huarun range, known for ages for its fertility, and situated east of the upper Jordan, flanked our Deraa-Damascus railroad. As the entire Druse population of the Huarun is estimated at no more than 80,000 to 90,000, the number of warriors reported by the consul general is probably too high. The Druses are one of the sects of Islam condemned as heretics. They do not take Mohammed for the last prophet, but Hakim, the founder of their sect. The Druses are a warlike people and have maintained themselves in semi-independence.

It was plain that in case of a retreat the Turkish Army, though fighting in Palestine for the defense of their own country, would meet with friends nowhere, and with enemies in many places.

The commander in chief of the Seventh Army, Fewzi Pasha, who had been sick and confined to his house for some time, left on August 1st on an extended furlough. Nehad Pasha, the commander of the Second Army, temporarily took his place, until Mustapha Kemal Pasha took definite command of the Seventh Army before the end of August.

This splendid general, whom I knew from the Dardanelles Campaign, was greatly disappointed on his arrival by the small number and exhausted condition of his troops, the more as Enver had put the situation in a far too favorable light and had given him incorrect figures.

The German chief of the general staff of the Seventh Army, Major von Falkenhausen, had to render tribute to the climate and he as well as Major von Papen of the Fourth Army had to be sent to Germany on furlough.

Colonel von Frankenberg, chief of the Asia Corps and commander of the left group of the Eighth Army, was recalled to Germany for a command, and replaced by Colonel von Oppen.

Mustapha Kemal posted the two battalions of the 109th Infantry Regiment, the leading troops of the 37th Caucasian Division, which began to arrive August 12th, in rear of his wholly unsupported front line.

It is characteristic of the kind of support given to Palestine, that before departure from Constantinople the commander and staff of this regiment were transferred for service in the East Caucasus, and were not replaced.

The 3d Battalion of this regiment deserted *in toto* on arrival at Affuleh on September 3d. After a hunt of several days the greater part of the men were rounded up in the various towns east of the Jenin-Messudie road. They had been induced to flee before reaching the front by numerous agents in Turkish uniform who distributed handbills at the station of Affuleh, in which the Turkish situation was described as hopeless.

The British very skillfully used all imaginable means to influence the disposition of the Turkish soldier. They used gold freely. The Arabs were their willing intermediaries. Propaganda was also made openly. Among many other kinds of papers the British airplanes dropped wagon loads of the most beautifully illustrated pamphlets showing the physical comforts the Turkish soldier enjoyed in British captivity. The effect of such means on men that never got enough to eat and in many ways received no care of any kind should not be underestimated. Exaggerated news about the unfavorable situation on the German west front were constantly being distributed among Turks and Arabs by means of leaflets.

Subsequent reports of German officers from various sectors of the front showed that the disposition of the Turkish soldiers was unreliable in some parts of the front. I quote below the statements of two officers who had been proved in war and may be accepted as calm observers and trustworthy witnesses. Both reports originated from the coast sector and refer to the end of August and September. Lieutenant Heiden writes:

The Turks were tired of war and unwilling to fight, as evidenced by the mass desertions of the Turkish soldiers. These deserters took with them not only their rifles and hand grenades, but also machine guns. The headquarters of the Eighth Army took energetic steps by guarding the country in rear, but trucks with armed infantry had to be sent after these deserters, with whom sometimes regular actions took place, as at Anabeta. I was told several times that unless peace was made before Bairam, the soldiers would go over to the enemy or desert, and that they would fight no longer.

The last day of Bairam this year was September 18th. Lieutenant Ricks writes:

Through my contact with Turkish units I, as well as probably all others, knew that the Turks did not intend to stand at the great British attack that was expected. I therefore returned to the intermediate depot of Jenin, as much of the well drilling apparatus as was no longer needed.

Malaria and dysentery exacted many victims during this hot summer. All hospitals and convalescent homes far to the rear were over-crowded.

In the valley of the Jordan, where the heat frequently rose to 131–133 degrees Fahrenheit, troop movements between 8 a.m. and late afternoon were impossible.

The Turkish soldiers had no summer clothes, but wore their cloth uniforms which might better be called rags. They suffered the more as fully three-fourths of them had not had underclothing for a long time, and wore their clothes next to the body. That, after the many futile attacks, the British or Indian dead left before the Turkish front were promptly robbed and found naked is not to be looked upon as intentional cruelty. It appeared to the Turkish soldiers the only means of procuring clothing, linen or boots. All orders against the spoliation of the dead were in vain. European drill at such times does not hold the men, the loosely donned garment of culture is quickly thrown aside by the Turkish soldier.

When I inspected the 3rd Cavalry Division, after hearing that they had received new uniforms, I found them in the hot valley of the Jordan in the thick cloth uniforms of the 1st Prussian Guard Uhlans. They were the uniforms for the Selamlik in Constantinople, and had probably been seized upon by the poor intendant general as a last expedient.

As it was perfectly clear to me that the ultimate decisive events were approaching, I returned to commanding officers all troops which had been detached from them from necessity and had been used elsewhere. The 702d and 703d Battalions were returned to the Asia Corps at Azzun from the coast sector. The 2d Battalion of the 146th Infantry Regiment was taken from the coast sector, where it was posted in reserve at Muchalid, and started to join its regiment by marching; the two battalions of the Turkish Infantry Regiment No. 191, which had been detached to the Fourth Army, were returned to the Eighth Army.

The 24th Division was inserted between the 53d Division (left flank division of the Seventh Army), and the west bank of the Jordan, in order to shorten the front of the latter, which up to that time had been guarding a front of fifteen kilometers with 1,300 rifles.

The 24th Division and the 3d Cavalry Division were placed under the orders of the Fourth Army to make them available for its support in case of an attack on the west bank. This army was ordered to expedite the construction of further crossings over the Jordan within its area, and to use every means for the improvement of the roads from Aere and Es Salt to the ferry at Ed Damije.

Anticipating somewhat I will state here that in the subsequent retreat this arrangement of the 24th Division did not prove useful. But there was no other arrangement by which we could gain what was denied to us in the battle of July 14th. It was an error of judgment on my part.

Enemy agents let it be known that two Jewish battalions and some French and Italian troops had arrived at the Palestine front.

CHAPTER 22

THE MONTH OF SEPTEMBER 1918

TO THE GREAT ATTACK OF SEPTEMBER 19TH

At the beginning of September I learned from the military mission in Constantinople, that the Turkish press was severely criticizing a Russo-German pact about Baku and demanded the erection of Azerbaijan into an independent buffer state through the mediation of Germany.

I also heard that in view of the Turkish pan-Islamic plans the pursuit of trade policies in Trans-Caucasia by Germany was causing Turko-German friction. The Turkish government based its far reaching demands in Trans-Caucasia, which exceeded the stipulations of the Brest-Litovsk treaty, on a communication of 1914, from the Ambassador, Freiherr von Wangenheim, the genuineness of which is doubted. The government claimed that as reward for its entry into the war it had been promised Batum, Kars and Ardahan, and drew the conclusion that it was now entitled to additional compensation after the collapse of Russia.

These claims may be politically intelligible, but they should have been denied military support, until the two Turkish battle fronts, on which the existence of the Osmanic empire was at stake, were sufficiently strengthened.

No hostile attack menaced Turkey either in Trans-Caucasia or in Azerbaijan. It was not the time merely to bring a new British battle front into existence in northern Persia, which at some time perhaps might serve to disencumber the secondary Turkish front between Mosul and Bagdad.

The British operations in Palestine and Mesopotamia were both based on excellent lines of communication, and were on converging lines. In view of the limited Turkish resources a

decisive effect could not be obtained within a reasonable time
by operations based on an exterior line of communications, of
interminable length, through the inhospitable sections of the
Caucasus and of Persia.   Such an operation was condemned to
failure from the beginning.

Political aims should not have been permitted to determine
the military decisions of Turkey, until military successes had
restored freedom of action to the Turkish Army.

The situation on the front of Army Group F was steadily
growing more serious.   Bad news came from all sides about the
complete exhaustion of the troops and the gradual failing of draft
and pack animals.   The latter was a very serious consideration,
because the mobility of the army depended on it.   These
animals for several months had been receiving the very insufficient ration of one to one and one-half kilograms of barley
(when any was to be had) and had suffered from lack of water,
and now died by the hundreds in all three armies, because the
torrid heat since May had destroyed all nutritious pasture.
The nightly change of position of batteries or guns to alternate
positions a few hundred paces distant became exceedingly
difficult, because the major part of the draft animals was no
longer able to pull the guns uphill or over cut up ground.

In the face of these conditions it made a queer impression on
the army commanders and on myself to receive the letter of
Enver of September 4th which contained tactical advice for
the defense of the Palestine front.   Neither he nor any of his
officers had ever seen infantry positions on our front.

I replied September 7th that the advice had been followed
for months and that, as I had informed him before, the Army
Group had far too few troops, particularly infantry.

On September 11th Enver promised all kinds of help for the
Army Group, but none came in time.

To give an idea of the conditions under which the British
made their great and decisive attack on the Turkish front on

September 19th, I am giving a statement of the positions of the troops between the sea and the Jordan for the 15th of March, and again six months later on September 15th.

The statement shows that eight of the ten infantry divisions present had been on the front line for six months without any relief, not to mention their sufferings from the climate of Palestine. It further shows that, with the exception of the 46th Division of the Eighth Army, numbering some 1,100 rifles, neither the armies nor the Army Group had a division available for reserve.

Each Turkish division averaged about 1,300 rifles. The strength of the battalion, of which each division had nine, averaged 130–150 rifles. Some battalions had reached a strength of 180, others had been reduced to 100 by sickness and other losses.

The number of desertions had increased alarmingly during the last few weeks. In the Eighth Army they amounted to 1,100 between August 15th and September 14th. The invariable excuse of the men when captured was that they did not get enough to eat, that they had no linen or foot gear, and that their clothing was in rags.

The cavalry regiments altogether numbered about 1,200 men. Their horses were in a tolerable condition as compared with the draft and pack animals.

The artillery on the whole was good, but the state of the draft animals, as previously stated, was such that it was incapable of extended movement.

The state of the Fourth Army, whose Jordan front had not been attacked since May 4th, was slightly better. Its front along the Hedjas railroad was harassed by the attacks of the Arabs, so that the first two battalions of the 12th Infantry Regiment (47th Division, Fourth Army) were sent to Maan immediately after their arrival.

Turkish Troops between the Sea and the Jordan

Arranged according to the divisional numbers

15th March 1918

1st Div. west of Nablus road	46th Div. south of Bidja, four bat-
7th Div. at Medschdel Jaba	talions strong
11th Div. on Nablus road	53d Div. south of Ch. Fasail
16th Div. South of Serta	3d Cav. Div. between the infantry
19th Div. Coast sector	in left sector in front line
20th Div. Coast sector	Cauc. Cav. Brig., in coast sector as
24th Div. as reserve at Kubalan	reserve
26th Div. east of Nablus road	Reserve: see 24th Div. and Cauc.
	Cav. Brig.

15th September 1918

1st Div. no change	26th Div. no change
7th Div. in coast sector	46th Div. at Felamie, reserve of
11th Div. no change	Eighth Army
16th Div. no change	53d Div. no change
19th Div. changed with 7th Div.	3d Cav. Div. in valley of the Jordan
20th Div. no change	Cauc. Cav. Brig., on east bank of
24th Div. west bank, Jordan	Jordan
valley	Reserve: see 46th Division

The 1st, 7th, 11th, 16th, 19th, 20th, 26th and 53d Divisions had been in the front line without relief for more than six months.

New accessions during the six months: no division.

Four battalions of the 37th Caucasian Division arrived by September 15th; the division had been assigned on June 16th to the Seventh Army as reënforcement.

REMARKS

1). Between March 15th and September 15th the following German combatant troops arrived: 146th Infantry Regiment, joined Fourth Army; 205th Pioneer Company, joined Fourth Army.

The Reserve Rifle Battalion No. 11, the reserve of the Army Group, was returned to Constantinople soon after its arrival at the front.

Two German batteries also had arrived, and the artillery of
the Asia Corps; the horses for the latter had to be procured in
the hinterland.

On March 15th the 703d Infantry Battalion was with the
Tafileh expedition east of the Jordan, and afterward rejoined
the Asia Corps, headquarters at Azzun.

2). On September 15th one group of the Fourth Army was on
the Jordan front, the other along the Hedjas railroad. This
army was not attacked on September 19th. Up to that time it
had been joined by four battalions of the 47th Division which
were sent to the Fourth Army as reënforcements.

3). Replacements to the number of 3,559 arrived from Constantinople between April 1st and August 31st. The remaining
replacements of 6,160 came from battalions which on arrival
were broken up and used as replacements, from formations
discovered in the hinterland, and from Arabs.

The six German battalions with the Army Group, three of the
Asia Corps and three of the 146th Infantry Regiment, had
received no replacements since spring of 1918, owing to the
urgent need of men on the German west front. Battle losses
and sickness had reduced their numbers considerably.

The German aviators on the Palestine front had a very hard
time against the British during the summer. The German
machines were greatly inferior to the modern British types in
speed and climbing ability. In two shipments of replacement
machines almost all were found useless. Further replacements
could not be furnished on account of their urgent need on the
German west front. From spring to fall this excellent body
of fliers had lost fifty-nine pilots and observers. Air reconnaissance against the enemy ceased almost completely in
September. As soon as a German machine appeared, it was
attacked by such superior British air forces that reconnaissance
became impossible.

Colonel von Oppen, chief of the left group of the Eighth
Army, asked me in Azzun on September 3rd to stop air recon-

naissance on his front, as the sight of the now invariably luckless air fighting was calculated to further reduce the low morale of his troops. On September 19th the chief of the flying corps reported but five machines of the Army Group fit for use against the enemy.

At that time it was the intention of the headquarters of the Eighth Army, in case of an attack in the coast sector, to send the 16th Division there which had but two infantry regiments. The division was holding a front of seven kilometers and was to be replaced by the Asia Corps. Colonel von Oppen declared it quite impossible to defend this part of the line with his small force and, moreover, it was to be expected that the division would arrive much too late. Even if placed in readiness at Serta before the beginning of the attack, the division had to make a march of sixteen kilometers to the edge of the coast sector at Kal Kiliyas.

Reserves from neighboring sectors, when called on for help, could be gotten only by still further weakening the overextended divisional fronts, and by leaving their defense largely to machine guns. This method had heretofore been used with good results. It was the only method practicable for establishing supports.

At the beginning of September, I pondered the idea of a voluntary retirement to a position with the right abreast the Lake of Tiberias, center and left in the Yarmuk valley. Aside from Enver's instructions to hold Palestine, I gave up the idea, because we would have had to relinquish the Hedjas railroad and the East Jordan section, and because we no longer could have stopped the progress of the Arab insurrection in rear of our army. On account of the limited marching capacity of the Turkish soldiers and of the very low mobility of all draft animals, I considered that the holding of our positions to the last gave us more favorable prospects than a long retreat with Turkish troops with impaired morale. The lack of sufficient troops to establish rearward positions of support was fraught with danger for the retreat; it also was the cause of the collapse of the front. In my reckonings I made the mistake that while considering possible a step by step retreat of units, I had not calculated upon the collapse of whole divisions. During the entire campaign I had observed such failure of Turkish troops under my command but once, in the attack on July 14th, but never in defense.

On September 17th a deserter, a sergeant of an Indian company, came to the right group in the coast sector and stated that a heavy attack on that part was in contemplation for September 19th, which he wanted to escape.

On the same day reports came that hostile Arabs were menacing the railroad north and south of Deraa, and that the line had been blown up in various places.

I realized at once that these attacks on our only line of communications were the beginning of serious fighting. I ordered two companies of Blell's depot regiment, which were reserved for emergencies and numbered 300 men, to be alarmed and sent by rail that evening to Deraa. The Fourth Army received orders to collect all available German officers and men in Damascus and send them at once to Deraa. Major Willmer, who had just joined the Army Group, was placed in command.

During the ensuing days the interruptions of the railroad in the vicinity of Deraa could not be entirely prevented, as the numerous and mobile Arabs were equipped with armored cars and British airplanes, and suddenly appeared in unexpected places to blow up the railroad; still traffic was promptly resumed thanks to the indefatigable work of the German railway troops. Meanwhile Major Willmer maintained order in Deraa, after driving back the Arabs at Mezeirib and between Mezeirib and Deraa.

On the 18th of September the Eighth Army ordered its only available division, the 46th, to Et Tire to a prepared position in the first line, and placed its few reserves in readiness. Just prior thereto I had attached to this army an Arab infantry battalion of about 500 men, which had been held back during the summer for the local protection of Haifa.

THE BRITISH ATTACK ON SEPTEMBER 19TH

On the night of September 18/19 the heavy battle opened on the front of the Seventh Army.

At 3.30 in the morning of September 19th began a tremendous drum fire against the whole front of the right wing of the Eighth Army from the coast to the mountains.

Shortly after daybreak squadrons of British fliers appeared over the houses of headquarters of the Seventh and Eighth Armies, over the tent camps of the various corps headquarters, and over the central telephone office of the Army Group in Affuleh; flying low, they threw bombs on them and destroyed part of our wires. In the entire section between coast and Jordan we had but the two anti-aircraft guns of the Eighth Army, so that the task of the enemy fliers was an easy one.

Numerous wires of our land lines had been cut in the early morning hours by the Arabs.

Telephonic and telegraphic communication between Tul Keram and Nazareth ceased about 7 a.m. The wireless station of headquarters of the Eighth Army also ceased to respond when called.

Between 9 and 10 a.m. headquarters of the Seventh Army wired from Nablus that Colonel von Oppen had reported that the front of the right flank group in the coast sector had been broken through, and that strong cavalry forces were advancing northward along the coast.

I at once sent orders to Colonel von Oppen, through head-quarters of the Seventh Army, to advance toward the railroad and road at Kal Kiliyas, toward the coast sector. Colonel von Oppen had anticipated the order and reported that he had put three battalions and two squadrons in march toward Kal Kiliyas and Felamie.

We did not learn until later that the British had broken

through in the western part of the coast sector before 7 a.m. without meeting with resistance. At that time they also occupied the height west of Et Tire and armed it with numerous machine guns. At Et Tire the weak 46th Division under Major Tiller made an effective resistance and checked the

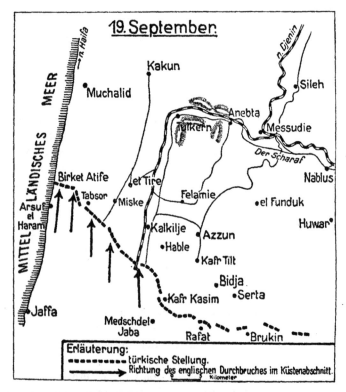

hostile advance for a time. The greater part of the division was soon destroyed. Its only German regimental commander, Major Pfeiffer, here died the hero's death.

Up to this day no exhaustive account has appeared of the complete and sudden collapse of the 7th Division in the western part of the coast sector, and of the adjoining two regiments of the 20th Division. Though the force was very small for such a large sector, it had stood up well in prior battles. After two hours of drum fire they had completely disappeared on September 19th, before a hostile infantry attack had been launched. Nor did I ever during the retreat see officers or small parts of this division.

After the transmission of the above orders to Colonel von Oppen the telegraph and telephone communications between Army Group headquarters and Nablus were interrupted for two hours, so that the scope of the above events could not be discerned there. It was assumed that the 7th, 20th and 46th Divisions were falling back to the prepared positions in rear.

The commanding officer at Haifa was instructed to alarm his troops, as enemy cavalry was advancing along the coast.

The events I am about to describe now became known to me later, piece by piece.

The 19th Division of the left group stationed at Kafr Kasim, adjoining the coast sector, could observe the irruption of the enemy; its troops quickly lost their morale. The 57th and 77th Infantry Regiments in the front line left their position of their own accord without having been attacked and without orders. Colonel von Oppen promptly sent them orders to face about, but in the disorderly retreat, part of the men had already left their organizations.

By 10 a.m. British cavalry with armored cars had broken through the front at Hable and Kal Kiliyas, east of the railroad and was advancing northward.

Soon thereafter Colonel von Oppen had to withdraw the entire left group of the Eighth Army from the positions it had held for months, and to take it back to the heights of Kafr Tilt. It was observable that hardly any resistance was being made in the coast sector, hence the right flank of this group was entirely open to the enemy's attack.

When communication between Nazareth and Nablus had been

restored toward noon, the surprising report came that the enemy had quickly pushed forward in all parts of the coast sector, and that what appeared to be parts of the Eighth Army were retreating from Tul Keram in the direction of Anabeta; that much artillery had been lost, and that there was no communication with headquarters of the Seventh Army in Tul Keram.

The headquarters of the Seventh Army reported that in its front the enemy's attacks had, on the whole, been repulsed, but that the Third Army Corps would be withdrawn to positions in rear to gain connection with the troops of Colonel von Oppen. I approved this step and ordered the Seventh Army to set the battalion of the 110th Infantry Regiment at Nablus and any available men at once in march for Anabeta in order to close the valley there.

Anabeta was an important place, because the bald steep heights come up close to the road on both sides, and because this defile could easily be blocked by a small force. As long as Anabeta and the heights on both sides remained in our hands, the left group under Colonel von Oppen, whose further withdrawal was to be expected, could continue its retreat direct to the north through Messudie. No instructions could be given for the divisions of the former coast section, as nothing was known about them.

I informed headquarters of the Fourth Army in Es Salt about the situation, and directed that a cavalry regiment be placed at the disposal of the Third Cavalry Division on the Jordan. The army headquarters informed me that on its Jordan front there were only light engagements; that the 24th Division west of the Jordan was attacked and had given but little ground so far.

Since the enemy cavalry, after breaking through in the coast sector, was continuing northward and might turn northeast, away from the coast and toward the line of retreat of the Eighth Army, I ordered Major Frey, inspector of pioneers of the Army Group, at 12.30 p.m., to occupy at once the defile of

Lejjun. I gave him the still effective parts of Würth von Würthenau's depot regiment, and such gendarmery as I could find in and near Nazareth, in all six companies and twelve machine guns, and ordered him to march at once for Lejjun via Affuleh. The rest of the depot regiment of Würth von Würthenau, about 150 men, and the training personnel of the regiment, were all the troops that remained to me in Nazareth after the departure of Major Frey. The headquarters guard of the Army Group had been sent to the front before this.

In the afternoon headquarters of the Seventh Army reported that the battalion of the 110th Infantry Regiment had been put in march to Anabeta, and that no further troops could be detached, because all the remaining battalions were urgently needed, as its own front was being attacked. It also reported that headquarters of the Eighth Army was said to have reached Anabeta with a small part of the 46th Division; that von Oppen's group was pressed in front and menaced by enemy troops coming from the coast sector against its right flank.

At 3.30 p.m. I telegraphed instructions to headquarters of the Seventh Army, in case a further general retreat should become necessary. The headquarters of the Seventh Army was to repeat these instructions verbatim to the Fourth Army at Es Salt, and furnish a summary of it to the Eighth Army at Anabeta. The instructions assigned the road through Bett Hassan and Beisan to the Seventh Army, and directed von Oppen's groups to withdraw through Messudie toward Jenin, and the Fourth Army to take the direction of the Wadi Zerka. It stated that headquarters of the Army Group would remain in Nazareth for the present. Further the Seventh Army was directed to see to the food and ammunition supply of von Oppen's group.

Toward evening the Seventh Army reported that the Third and Twentieth Army Corps would again have to be withdrawn rearward.

It was hoped that the good road, built in the early summer

from Azzun to Der Scharaf, would remain open for von Oppen's group in spite of flank attacks. At Der Scharaf the valley road of Nablus was joined by the chaussée leading northward to Jenin.

It was only several days later that the Army Group learned that the rout of the Turkish troops of the Eighth Army excepting the 16th Division had been much worse than reported. At Army Group headquarters we were still hoping that the troops from the coast sector had made front against the cavalry farther in rear, and were without communications for the time being. Since early morning we had sensibly felt as a drawback that our fliers were unable to observe and report events on the battle fields and on the lines of retreat.

As a matter of fact the road from Messudie to Jenin was crowded with retreating baggage trains and fugitives of the Eighth Army on the afternoon of September 19th. The latter for the most part belonged to the many Turkish staffs and Turkish etapes, the incredibly large personnel of which we could never get a glimpse of in ordinary times. The road from Tul Keram to Anabeta, and the trails on the hills on either side, were covered by long lines of fugitives. The British fliers, who were relieved every half hour and flying very low, carried on a continuous bombardment and covered the roads with dead men and horses and demolished wagons. The repeated attempts of officers to rally some of the uncurbed troops were in vain, as the men were completely indifferent and thinking only of their own salvation. These were the actual conditions of the right group of the Eighth Army.

There were no German troops in the coast sector. The small German groups distributed among the Turks and attached to wireless stations, telegraphs, telephones, railroads, well drilling commands, hospitals, etc., endeavored for the most part to get through in the direction of Anabeta or direct to Sileh on the road to Jenin, but succeeded only in part.

In the left group (Oppen's) things looked quite different. There the Asia Corps, the 16th Division, and particularly its

Infantry Regiment No. 125, fought bravely in unbroken line from height to height until after dark, in spite of the constantly increasing pressure of the enemy on their right flank.

The rearward movements of the Seventh Army, and of the 24th Division in the valley of the Jordan, were carried out step by step and in good order. With a fairly strong reserve the situation here could have been restored beyond a doubt. Wherever the troops fought, they would, in spite of their small numbers, check the British, and compel them to prepare a new attack.

In rear of the divisions of the Seventh and Eighth Armies in the front line on September 19th—in sectors widely over-extended in comparison with their strength—there was a space more than 200 kilometers deep entirely denuded of combatant troops. In this space were only the remnants of the two Arab depot regiments and numberless etapes with a few German and many inferior Turkish troops from the line of communication, and labor formations, the aviation stations with their personnel, the truck trains, the depots and shops, the numerous overcrowded hospitals and convalescent homes, and the Arab battalions of the coast guard.

On the evening of the 19th the commandant of Haifa reported to Nazareth, that no trace of the enemy was observable at Haifa.

Not a single direct report was received from headquarters of the Eighth Army. It was learned later that headquarters of the Eighth Army had been without wire communication with its divisions in the coast sector since morning, as all wires had been cut or broken by projectiles.

Colonel von Oppen reported in the evening that he had bent his right still farther back, and intended to fall back during the night some distance in the direction of Der Scharaf.

On the evening of September 19th I ordered that outposts be posted for the protection of Nazareth during the night. Until 3 a.m. the outposts were furnished from a company hurriedly made up of the German clerks, orderlies, chauffeurs, telegraphers and postal officials; after 3 a.m. by the remainders of the depot regiment of Würth von Würthenau. The outposts were posted on the roads from Haifa and Affuleh where they begin their steep descent from the plateau to Nazareth.

No message of importance was received during the night.

THE SURPRISE OF NAZARETH

At 5.30 a.m. on September 20th there were shouts and cries of alarm and immediately thereafter rifle and machine gun fire in the southern streets of Nazareth, where the quarters and offices of headquarters of the Army Group were.

The British were in the city to capture the headquarters of the Army Group. How they got in has never been explained, because the outposts of the depot regiment never came back. We assumed that the British had been guided over bridle paths by Arabs.

The British had promptly occupied the Germania hotel some 200 meters from Casanova, Headquarters of the Army Group and captured various officers and officials. A number of chauffeurs, who were working on their cars in the southern part of the city, were likewise captured. On the hills surrounding the city on the south, east and west British machine guns came into action. Soon there was severe street fighting in which the officers took part with the carbine. The riflemen of the company, composed, as above stated, of clerks, orderlies, etc., took position behind walls, fences, etc., others fired from windows or balconies.

After the few men had been somewhat organized and reën-forced by the personnel of the Turkish etape, small parties were sent out to retake the heights on the west of the city. Then remnants of the depot regiment were directed to the same point.

Soon a report came that somehow the exit of the city toward Tiberias had remained free. There the road descended steeply

to the valley in many windings, and passed not far from the
French orphanage.   The enemy could have closed it easily with
a few mounted men and machine guns, blocking the only open
exit from Nazareth.

Soon after the beginning of the attack, while the street

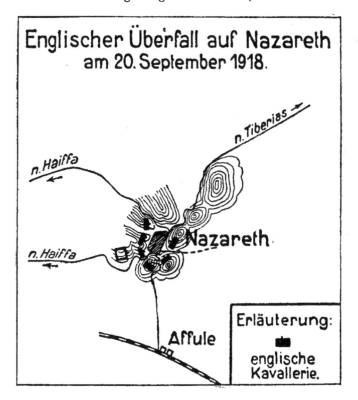

**Englischer Überfall auf Nazareth
am 20. September 1918.**

n. Tiberias

n. Haiffa

n. Haiffa

Nazareth

Affule

Erläuterung:
englische
Kavallerie.

fighting was going on, the hospital and administrative personnel
were put in march by this road to Tiberias, followed by those
parts of headquarters that were not under the direct fire of the
British.

The strength of the enemy could not at first be ascertained.

We estimated them at first as a few squadrons. The numerous machine guns seemed to me to indicate a larger force.

The wireless station east of the French orphanage was blown up by its personnel without orders, after sending an urgent message to Haifa asking for assistance. Telephonic and telegraphic communication between the Army Group and the armies was completely broken from the beginning of the attack, because as we learned later, the central office in Affuleh was in the hands of the British.

The headquarters had to regret the loss of part of its records, which had been burned during the street fighting, in order that they might not fall into the hands of the British, in case Nazareth should be completely surrounded.

It was on the western heights that an advance of the British would result in the closing of the road to Tiberias. When the situation at Casanova was still unchanged at 8.30, I rode up to the French orphanage where I found the remainders of Würth von Würthenau's depot regiment. I ordered him to attack at once with all his men the British detachments which were advancing slowly west of the orphanage, on foot with machine guns, about one kilometer to the west. After the attack had failed twice, I ordered a third attempt no matter at what cost. This attack succeeded and at 10.15 a.m. the British commenced to withdraw from the heights.

The forces of Major Würth von Würthenau must have been greatly overestimated by the enemy, for shortly afterward I saw the lead horses of one squadron galloping toward the assembling riflemen, followed by those of five more squadrons. Toward 10.30 a.m. the brigade with three armored cars withdrew westward, our riflemen following as far as the rim of the plateau. The enemy disappeared behind the next ridge in the direction of Haifa. From the high ground of the orphanage numerous light signals could be observed from the railroad station of Affuleh. It showed that Affuleh was in the hands of the British.

After the departure of the British, I rode down to Casanova

and found the offices of the headquarters almost completely empty. Some of our men were still firing out of windows with machine guns in a southerly direction, though no enemy remained in sight. Such of the records as had not been burned were loaded in autos and sent to Tiberias, as was the last of the personnel.

The bold attempt of the British brigade to capture the headquarters of the Army Group, after a sharp night ride, had failed; we heard later that it had started from the vicinity of Jaffa. We lost forty-three killed in the street fighting. The British removed the prisoners taken on their entry into the city, promptly to Affuleh. Their wounded they took back with them.

I instructed Major Würth von Würthenau to march with the rear guard to Tiberias, and left Nazareth at 1.15 p.m. with General Kiazim, Major Prigge and Captain Hecker. We had to pass an endless column of fugitives, among them many Turkish families on wagons, before we reached Tiberias at 3.30 p.m.

THE RETREAT TO DAMASCUS

In Tiberias I found a number of the officers of my headquarters. I ordered that all fugitives and scattered men arriving by the road from Nazareth should be stopped, collected and organized in fighting units. From Tiberias I made telephonic connection with the Fourth Army at Es Salt, but no connection could be made with Nablus via Beisan. The reports from the Fourth Army stated that Anabeta had to be given up under pressure from superior forces, and that headquarters of the Eighth Army with the accompanying troops had retreated via Messudie; that the Asia Corps and the 16th Division had to turn off eastward to El Funduk under pressure from the west where the enemy was again and again outflanking them. This news was serious and regrettable, because it destroyed our hope of retaining the road to Jenin. The headquarters of the Fourth Army also reported that there was little fighting on the east bank of the Jordan, and that the troops in Maan and on the Hedjas railroad had been instructed to withdraw northward using the railroad.

I instructed the Fourth Army not to delay any longer its retreat to the northeast, and directed that a sufficient force of cavalry be sent to Beisan to guard the crossing there. West of the Jordan, the roads from the south, from Bett Hassan, from Tubas, from Jenin and from Affuleh converged to the plain, which is some fifteen kilometers wide and in which Beisan is situated about six kilometers west of the Jordan. The railroad which from Semakh follows the Jordan here turns in a sharp curve northwestward to Affuleh and Haifa.

I at once proceeded with the chief of staff, General Kiazim, and with Major Prigge and Captain Hecker, by auto to Semakh in order to get from there to Beisan if in any way possible. As we reached the railroad station of Semakh on the southern point of the Lake of Genezareth, a strong attack by British fliers was materializing. It exacted many victims in the station area which was crowded with men and animals. Telephonic connection with Beisan could not be made. Railroad communication between Semakh and Beisan had ceased.

To my great surprise I found Major Frey in Semakh; he reported that he had been unable to occupy the defile of Lejjun in accordance with his orders of yesterday afternoon, because British cavalry had anticipated him; and that his troops had been captured or scattered. I ordered Major Frey to take over the defense of Semakh, which place would have to be held. Some sixty German soldiers and 200 Turks were available for him, and I promised him early reënforcements.

I telephoned Major Ludloff, the senior officer in Tiberias, to occupy that evening the defile of the Jacob's bridge over the upper Jordan, through which the road from Tiberias runs to El Kuneitra and Damascus, and to prepare it for defense. All effective officers and men collected were to be used at that point and for the defense of the town of Tiberias; all disabled fugitives and all wagon transportation were to be passed on to Damascus. Damascus was announced as the seat of headquarters of the Army Group.

In the existing situation there was but one thing to do. The Tiberias section from Lake Hule to Semakh had to be held with all available means, to anticipate the enemy's pursuit; the troops retreating along the Jordan and through the East Jordan section had to hold temporarily the sector of the Yarmuk valley from Semakh to Deraa.

After midnight I rode from Semakh to Deraa. At 7 a.m. on September 21st I made connection with headquarters of the Fourth Army, and learned that since yesterday afternoon it had received scant news of the events on the right bank of the Jordan. Communication with Nablus no longer existed. It was only known that headquarters of the Seventh Army had left Nablus in the direction of Bett Hassan, and that the troops retreating by this road were suffering heavily under repeated air attacks. Nothing could be learned at the time of the left group of the Eighth Army under Colonel von Oppen. We learned several days later that on the forenoon of September 21st its rearguards were engaged at Nablus, whither the enemy was pursuing via Der Scharaf, and from the south via Huwara. Toward noon it continued its retreat northward, crossed Mount Ebel and on the 22d marched toward Beisan in the direction of the Jordan.

The headquarters of the Fourth Army had informed me that the 3d Cavalry Division had been sent to Beisan. I had ordered the Fourth Army on the 19th to send at once a cavalry regiment to the Jordan, to be at the disposal of the Seventh Army; this had not been done. The 3d Cavalry Division failed completely at Beisan. The excellent leader of the division, Colonel Essad Bei, and his efficient representative, the chief of staff, Lieutenant Colonel Machmud Bei, had been furloughed to Constantinople without my knowledge. So it came that an irresolute regimental commander led the two regiments. On receiving fire at Beisan from a very small British cavalry force, he divested himself of his important task and turned in the direction of the East Jordan section.

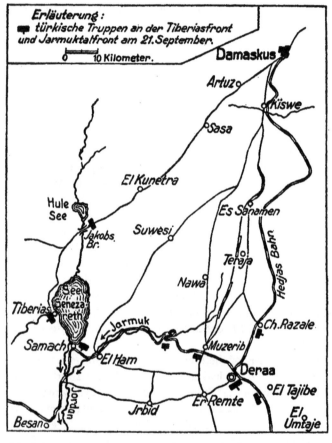

The situation at Deraa had been made fairly safe by the prudent and energetic steps of Major Willmer. He kept down the Arabs in the vicinity, and charged Major Michaelis, a very active officer, with the defense of the Hedjas railroad southeast of Deraa.   There he was fighting against the renewed attacks of the Arabs.

An attempt by Major Willmer of capturing Sherif Faisal at El Umtaje on the morning of September 20th had failed. When the raiding party, sent out by Major Willmer during the night, reached the place, the Sherif had gone, having had timely warning from Arabs.

From Deraa I gave the Fourth Army detailed instructions for the retreat in the East Jordan section, with orders to use every means to get these instructions through to the Seventh Army, and if possible to the Eighth Army.   I assigned to the Fourth Army the line of the Yarmuk valley railroad from Deraa to Irbid as the objective of its retreat, to the Seventh and Eighth Armies—insofar as the latter still existed—the Yarmuk valley from Irbid to Semakh.   The road Irbid-Er Remte south of and parallel to the Yarmuk valley, I ordered to be held as long as possible by the rear guards.   The Fourth Army was instructed not to defer the withdrawal of its troops.

Unfortunately the Fourth Army delayed too long, because it was not pressed and wanted to wait for the arrival of its troops from Maan.

I further directed the commandant of Haifa by wireless, that if his garrison were unable to open a direct way to Tiberias through the British cavalry, it was to march north along the coast and then turn toward the Tiberias front.

Captain von Keyserlingk, headquarters' commandant of the Fourth Army, took command at Semakh.

Major Willmer was placed in temporary charge of the entire Yarmuk valley district from Deraa to Semakh and directed to send reënforcements to Semakh and El Hammi by rail from among the troops retreating through the East Jordan section. Samach was of special importance as the turning point of the Tiberias front and of the Yarmuk valley front.   On the afternoon of the 21st it was learned that an apprehensive officer had blown up the railroad bridge at El Hammi, the next railroad station east of Semakh, without orders from above. Temporary repairs were ordered.

To Damascus I sent instructions that as much subsistence and clothing as possible should be forwarded by rail to Deraa.

On the evening of September 21st several thousand Druse warriors from the Huarun Mountains appeared in Deraa. After riding a fantasia around me with much discharge of guns, their sheiks asked for a conference through the mutessarif of Deraa. The Druses had not yet definitely made up their minds which side to support. In the conference it appeared that they were not disinclined to help us, provided I sent some troops to El Tajibe and Borsa to support them. I had no troops at that moment and promised to comply with their wish as soon as possible. They promised to remain neutral for the present and not to injure our retreating troops. The conference was to be continued next day.

During the night they manifested an extraordinary interest in my person, and every hour a few of them would come into the small house where we four officers were quartered. The house was one of the little colony which had grown up around the comparatively large station of Deraa; the city of Deraa lay two kilometers to the south on a plateau. The population was considered very inimical to the Turks.

In these days of distress and care a telegram from the military mission furnished a refreshing interlude. It showed how little was known in Constantinople of our actual situation, in spite of our uninterrupted reports since the 19th. The telegram inquired whether I was willing to offer a prize for a sack race in a competition in Constantinople on October 8th. Any one will believe me that at the moment I had no interest in a competition, when we ourselves were in such a difficult situation.

On the morning the Fourth Army reported that it was withdrawing from Es Salt in the direction of Irbid, and that Lieutenant Colonel von Hammerstein with the 146th Infantry Regiment had been directed to hold the heights at Es Salt until all troops had retired, and then to retreat himself north-eastward through Jerash.

It became known later that the now ensuing retreat of the Seventh Army, and of the remaining parts of the Eighth Army, to and across the Jordan, was not without great losses. When the troops could no longer retreat on a broad front and had to enter successively the narrow road between the mountains to Bett Hassan and Beisan, they were subjected to incessant attacks by the British flying squadrons which wrought terrible havoc and impaired the morale of the troops. The feeling of defenseless exposure to the enemy fliers had a paralyzing effect on officers and men. The columns of what little remained of the artillery, the autos and other vehicles blocked the road in many places, with their demolished vehicles and dead horses and men.

On the evening of September 22d the commander of the Eighth Army gave a fatal order to von Oppen's group, which at that time had reached the western exit from the mountains west of Beisan. During the night Colonel von Oppen wanted to break through the slight cavalry of the enemy between Beisan and the Jordan in a northerly direction, and to march toward Semakh, presuming correctly that his arrival would be very welcome as a reënforcement to our front at and on both sides of Semakh. At 9 p.m. he had given orders to that effect when he was called to Wadi Shubash for conference with the leader of the Eighth Army. Djevad Pasha disapproved the plan of Colonel von Oppen and directed him to cross to the east bank of the Jordan. How decisive the support of von Oppen's group would have been for Semakh and the Tiberias front is clear today; the safety of the retreat of the Seventh and Eighth Armies depended on the security of that front.

It should be stated, however, that from the 20th to the 22d, none of the orders from the Army Group, forwarded through the Fourth Army, had reached the Eighth Army and that the leader of the Eighth Army therefore did not attach to the Tiberias front the extreme importance for the general situation that the Army Group did.

The failure of all means of communication is unintelligible to German conception, unless the absence of roads in the inhospitable country, the absence of all European means of communication, and the hostility of the inhabitants are properly understood. The inhabitants were armed throughout, and in the habit of attacking orderlies, officers, and patrols. Many were killed and mutilated by the Arabs. Others returned to us after being robbed of all clothing and maltreated, bearing distressing testimony of the disposition of these subjects of the Osmanic empire. Still existing, or newly laid, wires were continually cut by the Arabs. The armies could not take light wireless stations with them, because the draft animals were too weak to pull the heavy wagons over the difficult ground.

On the early morning of September 23d, the Asia Corps effected the crossing of the Jordan without much loss. The staffs of the 16th and 19th Divisions however were captured on the west bank by British cavalry. Turkish soldiers went over to the enemy in crowds as soon as fired upon, or bombarded by British fliers. Most of them had thrown away their arms. It was another consequence of the fatal order of headquarters of the Eighth Army.

After giving all necessary instructions to Major Willmer I left Deraa on September 22d by rail, to join the staff of the Army Group in Damascus and make there the necessary arrangements for the Tiberias front. About ten kilometers north of Deraa our journey was interrupted by a foot march, because a stretch of several kilometers south of Chirbet Razale had been destroyed by the demolition of rails and bridges. Our railway troops were making repairs, when several enemy armored cars appeared about three kilometers east of the railroad; they withdrew as soon as the guard company at Chirbet Razale deployed.

On arrival in Damascus I ordered in the evening the shipment of more subsistence and medical supplies to Deraa. The trains, after being unloaded, were to bring the footsore and the ex-

hausted men to Damascus. We sought in every way to make
troops, and guns from the artillery shops, available for the
Tiberias front. The men were sent to El Kuneitra in trucks.

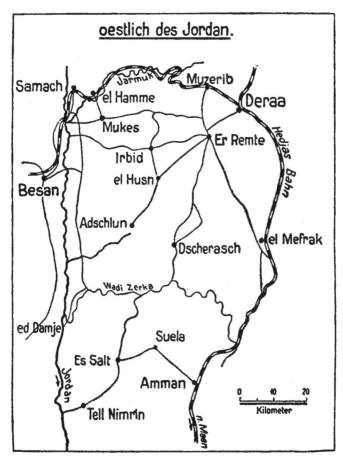

Now that it was too late, the Second Army was placed under
my orders. I requested that it send as many troops as possible
to Damascus. The reply stated that the army had only a few,

mostly Arab, battalions, and would do everything in its power. Nehad Pasha kept his promise, but his means were limited, not through his fault, but through the previously mentioned orders of Enver.

A leader for the Tiberias front was found in the person of Ali Risa Pasha, a general no longer on the active list, and Captain Justi was designated at his chief of staff. The pasha was sent to El Kuneitra with instructions to make the stiffest kind of resistance.

The stone bridge over the Jordan on the road Tiberias-El Kuneitra was prepared for demolition. So far only a few British cavalry patrols showed themselves on the Tiberias front.

On September 23d Major Willmer reported that the leading portions of the troops, retreating in the East Jordan section, had arrived and that he had sent a number of hastily organized units by rail to Mezeirib, El Hammi and Semakh. Mezeirib was the terminus of the old and disused line built by a French company early in the nineties from Damascus to Es Sunamein and Mezeirib for commercial purposes. The place lies on an island of a small lake and is connected with the shore by a dam. The old pilgrim road passed through Mezeirib.

In the meantime the Seventh Army under Mustapha Kemal Pasha had crossed the Jordan and taken the direction of Irbid, since it had received none of the orders transmitted through the Fourth Army. The 24th Division was again attacked on the 20th and 21st and forced back northward; after several hours fighting at Ed Damije on the 22d, it also crossed the Jordan and turned northeastward.

After crossing the Jordan on the 23d, Colonel von Oppen again wanted to take the northerly direction to Semakh. All instructions had been given, when orders came from the Eighth Army to take a southeasterly direction and retire on the Fourth Army. Again the correct decision of Colonel von Oppen was crossed by orders from above. After starting the march in the direction ordered, and which appeared to him the wrong one, this excellent leader soon lost touch with headquarters of the Eighth Army, decided to turn northeastward and took the road to Er Remtheh toward Deraa.

In this way it came that the Seventh Army and the remnants of the Eighth Army were converging toward the line Mezeirib-Deraa, instead of retiring on the broad front Semakh-Irbid as ordered.

Up to noon on September 23d about 3,000 men had arrived at Ammän by rail from Katraneh, and from the stations to the south. They were sent on to Deraa as far as possible. All vehicles and all heavy and bulky equipment had to be left behind.

The transport to Deraa was impeded by the interruption of the railroad some twenty-five kilometers north of Mefrak. About half way between Amman and Deraa a four-arched bridge had been demolished at noon on September 16th by a band of 500 Bedouins accompanied by two British armored cars. A Turkish detachment, posted for the protection of the bridge in a nearby "caracole," remained inactive. Repairs were at once taken in hand by German pioneers, but during the nights to the 20th and 21st of September long stretches of track were destroyed, as well as other bridges north of el Mefrak.

On the evening of September 23rd and on the afternoon of the 24th the last Turkish troop trains left the station at Amman, but were stopped by the demolitions. From there the troops had to make their way through a waterless stony desert to Deraa.

At 10.30 a.m. September 24th the last German personnel under Lieutenant Thalacker left the Amman station. On the morning of September 25th British cavalry arrived there.

On September 24th the British cavalry on the Tiberias front was reënforced. Armored cars and numerous cavalry columns were observed. On the same day large gatherings of Bedouins were now also reported east and southeast of Damascus.

In the evening the sheiks of the Druses, that had been at

Deraa, appeared and wanted to continue the conference. On receiving a considerable sum of gold they promised not to molest our retreating troops. It was now wholly out of the question to furnish them troops. The sheiks kept their word.

On September 24th Captain von Keyserlingk at Semakh came in contact with British cavalry that came from the south. For the defense of the defile and of the town of Semakh, he had in all 120 Germans, eighty Turks, eight machine guns and one gun. At 4 a.m. on the 25th a British cavalry brigade attacked Semakh on the east bank of the Jordan. After a gallant defense of one and one-half hours the detachment of Captain von Kyserlingk was destroyed or captured. Part of his men had taken refuge on a motor boat at the pier, intending to cross the Sea of Galilee and rejoin their own troops. The motor boat received a direct hit from the artillery, went up in flames and the men on it perished. When the British searched the houses of Semakh, they found about 120 Turkish soldiers who had evaded the engagement.

Under the pressure of the enemy, the town of Tiberias had to be relinquished that day, after a stout defense under Major Schmidt-Kolbow, with the loss of all machine guns.

At El Hammi where First Lieutenant Diesinger directed the defense, the enemy was repulsed. At Semakh the enemy received more and more reënforcements.

My plan of holding the Tiberias front and the Yarmuk valley front for some time was frustrated by the fall of Semakh, the consequence of much friction of command and of the fatal orders of the Eighth Army formerly mentioned. It was to be expected now after the passage through Semakh had been opened for the enemy, that the troops of the Tiberias front would be gradually forced back to Damascus.

The Army Group had to be guided by the facts. Hence on the morning of September 26th, I ordered a new front nearer to Damascus, extending from southwest of Rajak to El Kuneitra and Es Sunamein, on the Hedjas railroad, about fifty kilometers south of Damascus. It was to be defended by groups. The right flank, southwest of Rajak, was to be strongly echeloned to check pursuit of strong cavalry forces on the Meissner-Pasha road. It was necessary that the great line of retreat to Baalbek and Homs be kept open.

The headquarters of the Eighth Army, for which, in view of the slight remnants of its troops, there was no further use, was directed to proceed to Constantinople. Djemal Pasha, the leader of the Fourth Army, now the senior general present, was given command of the troops assembling at Deraa-Mezeirib. He was instructed to use every opportunity to send efficient troops by rail from Deraa to Damascus. I intended to push them forward to the new Rajak front.

On the morning of September 26th Colonel von Oppen had reached Deraa with the Asia Corps. After the very difficult and often precarious retreat and its great hardships, these troops still numbered over seventy per cent of their effectives of September 19th. Thanks to the vigorous action of Colonel von Oppen and of his subordinate leaders, the troops were in a good state of order and discipline.

On the same evening the embarkation of the Asia Corps and its transport to Rajak began.

The other considerable German unit, the 146th Infantry Regiment, reached Er Remtheh on the morning of the 26th in good order. All other troops of the armies retreating through the East Jordan section were at that moment passing through Er Remtheh en route to Deraa and Mezeirib. No news of any kind was received by the Army Group of the cavalry brigade of Colonel von Schierstaedt. Various inquiries directed to the Fourth Army brought no result. Colonel von Schierstaedt and Captain von Sydow had been last seen at Amman. We learned later that Colonel von Schierstaedt was captured there and Captain von Sydow killed.

It soon became known among the many disordered bands of Turkish soldiers and stragglers who had left their organizations, that all fugitives were held up at Deraa and Mezeirib, and organized in units. Many attempted to pass by these places at night, and reach Damascus by themselves. Many fell into the hands of the Arabs and were killed.

As my order of the morning of the 26th required resumption of resistance on the new line in rear, I gave orders at 4 p.m. to Djemal Pasha, and direct to Major Willmer, to withdraw the troops and rolling stock from the Yarmuk valley to Deraa, and to destroy completely a part of the many constructions along this railroad. There were seven tunnels and numerous iron bridges, some of them fifty meters long. The order was carried in effect on the morning of the 27th, beginning at El Hammi.

The detachment of Germans and Austrians, retreating northward along the coast, reached Beirut on the 26th after a fatiguing march. There it was ordered to leave a rearguard at Ain Safar (fork of the mountain road to Beirut and Saida) and come to Rajak.

As the gatherings of hostile Arabs to the east and southeast of Damascus became more and more threatening, the first troops arriving from the Second Army were sent on to the railroad station of Kesweh, seventeen kilometers south of Damascus. The station lies close to the village of the same name which is almost exclusively inhabited by Druses.

The Turkish commandant of Damascus was charged with the protection of the deep and narrow Barada valley, celebrated for its scenic beauty, northwest of Damascus, through which chaussée and railroad run to Rajak.

On the evening of the 25th, after the enemy had pierced the line at Semakh, I had ordered the large staff of the Army Group to proceed by rail to Aleppo.

On September 27th the leading parts of the armies which were retreating from Deraa-Mezeirib on three parallel roads, following the direction of the railroad, crossed the heights of El Razale while the rear parts were leaving the line Deraa-Mezeirib. I ordered Djemal Pasha to send a mounted detachment of about 500 men collected at Mezeirib at once to Suweisi via Nawa under command of Major Muther, to reënforce the left of the Tiberias front. It is to be regretted that the order was not carried out, although it had reached headquarters of the Fourth Army correctly.

On September 27th British cavalry with armored cars appeared before Deraa and Mezeirib. It came too late to prevent the retreat. Its artillery fire against the rearguard was without effect.

On the 27th I went by auto to Rajak with the small part of the staff of the Army Group which I had kept with me, to inspect the defenses there, of which I was going to give Colonel von Oppen command. The Asia Corps was expected there at any time.

As the enemy had four strong cavalry divisions, there was good reason to fear that he might anticipate us by sending them in pursuit on the Meissner Pasha road directly from Tiberias to Zahle, at the same time landing troops in Beirut to cut off our retreat completely, while Faisal and British cavalry pursued from Mezeirib-Deraa.

I took quarters with a very small staff in Baalbek in rear of the Rajak front. On the evening of the 27th the Tiberias group reported that the left of the Jordan position was being turned, that the remainder of the Turkish depot regiment had left their position without orders, and had withdrawn in the direction of El Kuneitra, and that Major Schmidt-Kolbow was still there with a rearguard.

From the Jordan crossing it was eighty kilometers to Damascus by way of El Kuneitra. About the same distance separated the rest of the armies at el Razale from Damascus. To make our retreat through Damascus possible, it was necessary that the Tiberias group make a strong step by step defense on the extensive rocky plateau that stretches away toward Damascus.

The situation of the Army Group would not be a simple one,

if the enemy cavalry divisions anticipated us in their pursuit, and if a landing took place at Beirut. Suggestions were made that the retreating armies should turn off into the land of the Druses east of the railroad. I declined because from there no roads led to the north. No railroad would have been there to bring up supplies, and in their present condition the troops would have been delivered up to the mercy of the Arabs led by Scherif Faisal.

The difficulty had to be met the best way we could. On September 28th I personally sent the German rearguard of the Haifa detachment under Major Adelt from Ain Safar in the Lebanon to the Meissner Pasha road, and pushed a detachment of Turkish line of communication troops from Rajak to the south; the Asia Corps arriving at 6 p.m. received the necessary instructions for the occupation of the Rajak front.

A report came from the Tiberias front that the enemy was following from the Sea of Galilee toward El Kuneitra. In lieu of the bridge over the Jordan, which we had blown up, a pontoon bridge had been thrown. Large enemy cavalry camps were observed south of Lake Hule, and between Tiberias and the Jordan bridge. Later reports by German officers stated that it was the Australian and an Indian cavalry division. A large force of artillery and three battalions of infantry had also been observed.

The heads of our retreating armies crossed the ridge of Teraja on the 28th. The enemy followed with cavalry only, apparently two brigades and horse artillery. There were several small rearguard actions.

Our small forces on the Tiberias front halted a short time at El Kuneitra and on the afternoon of the 28th, forced by far superior forces of the enemy, retreated in a northeasterly direction on both sides of the road to Sasa. By evening they had a tolerable position on several small hill tops which they prepared for defense. Its left wing was commanded by Captain Düsel. To show with what small forces we had to fight on the

Tiberias front, I am quoting the exact strength of Captain Düsel's command. He had fifty German infantry, seventy Turks, six machine guns manned by Germans, two field guns and two howitzers. The latter could not be used because the Turks did not understand their service.

On September 29th four British armored cars advanced against the position at Sasa. They were driven back by fire. At 5.30 p.m. four Australian squadrons with four armored cars attacked the troops of Captain Düsel. They were allowed to come close, and were then completely repulsed with heavy loss by machine gun fire. At that moment an enemy infantry brigade was approaching from the Jordan bridge toward El Kuneitra. The growing strength of the enemy western group became more and more noticeable.

The heads of our retreating armies, with which was Mustapha Kemal Pasha, leader of the Seventh Army, reached the neighborhood of Kesweh on the 29th. The Turkish detachment from the Second Army stationed there was now ordered to reënforce the left of the Tiberias group. On account of the low marching power of the extremely exhausted men, it was not practicable to use part of the retreating army to reënforce the Tiberias group, which under other circumstances would have been the proper thing. The permanent rearguard was the 146th Infantry Regiment under Lieutenant Colonel Frhr. von Hammerstein which reached Es Sunamein early on the 29th, and resumed the march toward El Khiyarah at 5 p.m.

The attitude of the people of Damascus at that time had become threatening. Armed bands of Arabs arrived there daily which, though they did nothing but arrange fantasias and fire into the air, formed an ominous element in the city. The population was flooded with British leaflets, which described the bad situation in Bulgaria, and contained exaggerated news of the general German situation.

The troops of Colonel von Oppen occupied the Rajak position as follows: The right group on the Meissner Pasha road south of Kabb Elyas, with a detached post on the mountain road to Beirut; the central group on the road to Damascus in the neighborhood of Mejdel Anjar; the small left group at Ez Zebedani on the Damascus-Rajak railroad.

On the 29th I ordered Mustapha Kemal Pasha to take command of the Rajak front, to which all men of the Seventh and Eighth Armies that might reach Damascus were to be forwarded, and I ordered Djemal Pasha to take command of the Tiberias group in addition to his command of the Fourth Army. It was intended to gain a short rest at Damascus, followed by an ordered retreat.

At 4 a.m. on the 30th the British cavalry with Bedouins resumed its advance on Sasa and pushed our weak force back to Artuz, capturing a part of it. The only possibility that remained was a speedy and uninterrupted passage through Damascus on the part of the armies coming up from the south. I offered Djemal Pasha the choice of the road leading from Damascus to the northeast direct to Homs by way of El Kutefe. He replied that there was no water on that road, and that it was menaced by hostile Arabs. Having been stationed in Damascus a long time, he was a better judge than I was.

A part of the Turkish troops camping at Kesweh started in the night of the 29/30, reached Damascus on the morning of the 30th and continued its march through the Barada valley toward Rajak. In the city many men left the ranks. Others mounted the roofs and steps of the cars in Damascus in order to reach Rajak in that way. In Rajak the removal of the depots to Aleppo by rail and trucks had begun. The rearward parts of the army which did not reach Kesweh until the night of the 30th, or on the next morning, had some engagements with the enemy.

About 11 a.m. on the 30th Lieutenant Colonel von Hammerstein, who with the 146th Infantry Regiment camped in a plantation one kilometer south of Kesweh, observed a hostile cavalry brigade, which was coming from the south and was about to pass to the west of Kesweh. He at once deployed the

146th Infantry Regiment to attack this cavalry which withdrew toward the northwest. The cavalry had more success with the Turks. North of Kesweh it again turned toward the Turkish

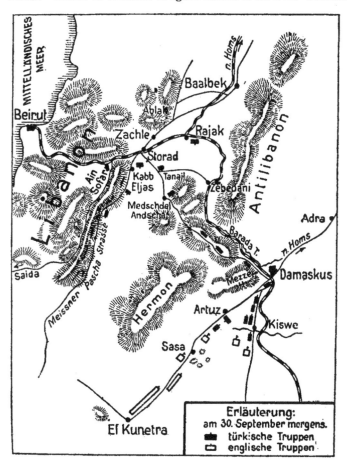

line of retreat, and surprised the 26th and 53d Divisions. They were standing in marching column facing north. Both division staffs had ridden forward in reconnaissance. The cavalry brigade advanced direct from the west to charge the marching columns and after a brief resistance captured a large part of the men, who were demoralized and separated from their leaders.

The 146th Infantry Regiment continued its march unmolested to Damacus where it arrived shortly before 6 p.m.

On the afternoon of the 30th I was with Colonel von Oppen in the agricultural school of Tanail on the Shtora-Mejdel Anjar road in rear of his center group. We saw long columns of disordered Turkish troops which were coming down into the plain by the road to Shtora-Mejdel Anjar. I directed that after passing the outpost they be collected and their ranks restored. The result was poor, as there were hardly any higher officers with the columns, and the reorganized units again and again resumed the march without orders, in order to escape further fighting.

Disturbances and insecurity increased in Damascus. The city was full of Scherif Faisal's agents who incited the population. The four-colored flag of the Scherif was displayed from many houses. Baggage trains were tangled in the streets. More and more Turkish soldiers left the ranks and scattered through the city. Toward evening there were several fires. Thus the railroad station of Kadem, terminus of the Hedjas railroad, and the German depots there were on fire.

At dusk the first British cavalry patrols with two machine guns gained the ridge on the southwest side of the Barada valley, and took the road in the valley under fire. There fugitives and vehicles were wedged together. The fire, though of small effect, increased the disorder and turmoil in the valley.

The 146th Infantry Regiment and the small German units attached to it were to form the rearguard; they were assembling at the burning railroad station of Kadem and were to be the last troops to pass through the town after dark. Kadem street, running northward through the city, was blocked by felled telegraph poles and their wires. Hostile Arabs were firing from all directions from roofs, gates, balconies and from windows.

Some fugitives brought the false report that the Barada valley was blocked by the British. Lieutenant Colonel Frhr. von Hammerstein promptly decided to turn northeast and take the direct road to Homs, in which he succeeded. It was discovered subsequently that Turkish troops, on hearing that the Barada valley was closed by the British, had preceded Hammerstein's column on the direct road to Homs. They were the remnants of the Third Army Corps under Colonel Ismet Bei, of the 24th Division under Lieutenant Colonel Lufti Bei, and of the 3d Cavalry Division, which latter being poorly led, had played no rôle in the retreat.

It turned out that the Barada valley was not seriously threatened. It was mainly Arabs and the few British mounted men mentioned who were firing in the darkness from the heights on the road in the valley.

Toward 9 p.m. on September 30th the last troop train left Damascus and reached Rajak without damage, though frequently fired upon. This is worthy of note because from Damascus the railway and the road in the Barada valley run close together for ten kilometers.

On returning to Baalbek via Rajak late in the evening of the 30th, I received from the 43d Turkish Division of the Second Army a report from the Beirut-Zahle road, that six enemy battalions were advancing on the Meissner Pasha road toward Dchedede and that at noon twelve battalions had been observed marching from El Kuneitra to Damascus. I think the first report was incorrect.

CHAPTER 23

THE MONTH OF OCTOBER 1918

THE RETREAT TO ALEPPO

Disordered Turkish columns of men, horses, pack animals and vehicles from the Barada valley were streaming through the outposts of Colonel von Oppen throughout the 1st of October. It was evening before the stream began to ebb. Attempts to organize units were of small success that day. Even the troops of the 43d Division of the Second Army, which so far had never been under fire, but consisted for the most part of Arabs, were reported as unreliable by the division commander. Two companies of the division deserted in a body with their officers, while on their way to reënforce the outposts of Colonel von Oppen.

On October 1st report came that the British had occupied Beirut. The city declared its adhesion to the Arab government. Other coast towns followed the example. On October 1st Scherif Faisal held his entry into Damascus.

My former plan of a resumption of resistance on the Rajak front became impracticable because of the condition of the Turkish troops and because the direct road from Damascus to El Kutefe and Homs was open to the enemy. On October 1st I called together the generals Djemal Pasha and Mustapha Kemal Pasha in the quarters of Colonel von Oppen in Tanail, and ordered the retreat to be continued to Homs. Djemal Pasha was given the command in Homs; he was to proceed there with his staff ahead of his troops, collect the disordered columns and form new units. Mustapha Kemal Pasha was to command the troops at Rajak, until the last remnants had arrived from the south and southwest, after which this group was to follow to Homs.

On the early morning of October 1st I sent telegraphic orders to Homs and Aleppo to have all available trucks loaded with subsistence to meet the troops retreating on the direct road El Kutefe-Homs, and to take as many men as possible back to Homs on the empty trucks. For their protection the Second Army pushed a mixed detachment to Hasja, twenty kilometers south of Homs. The units retreating by that road, with the 146th Infantry Regiment still forming the rear guard, had an engagement with eight British squadrons and numerous bands of Bedouins. By attacking our troops from the east and west the enemy sought to cut our troops from the defile two kilometers north of Adra, through which the road to El Kutefe enters the mountains. The attack was repulsed by the 146th Infantry.

During the last few days and nights troops of retreating Turkish soldiers were passing through Baalbek, also wagons of all kinds and trucks carrying war supplies from Rajak and other depots. The railroad could not bring away more than a part of supplies. In Baalbek eating stations had been established for all men that passed through.

On the morning of October 2d Colonel von Oppen reported that the road from Damascus to Rajak had been free of fugitives for several hours, that no enemy could be seen in his front, and that the latter appeared not to have followed.

I decided to withdraw at once from Rajak and thus break away from the enemy, and sent orders to that effect to Mustapha Kemal. The withdrawal began that morning. The rear guard under Colonel von Oppen left the line Shtora-Mejdel Anjar at 5 p.m. The withdrawal was not interfered with by the enemy, not even cavalry patrols of the enemy were observed.

Our last train left Rajak toward 6 p.m., after the switches and waterworks of the station had been demolished. The supplies in the clothing, subsistence and ammunition depots not yet issued to the troops, or carried away by the railroad, trucks and wagons, were set on fire.

On October 2d I went from Baalbek to Homs with my officers in autos; in the Bika valley, which separates the parallel ridges of the Lebanon and Anti-Lebanon like a broad ditch, we passed kilometers of retreating troops and of stragglers.   Considerable portions were taking a rest at Ras Baalbek, about midway between Baalbek and Homs.   Few organized units were seen. The small number of Turkish officers present with these columns was conspicuous.   There could be no doubt that these disorganized and enfeebled men would require a long time to become effective for battle.   The crowds that had reached Homs before presented the same appearance.   The first step was to create order at the railroad station of Homs and its vicinity, where thousands of men belonging to every kind of organization had crowded together.   Defensive sectors were formed immediately, extending from the road to Tripoli and across the road Homs-Ras Baalbek to the road Homs-El Kutefe. The most effective troops with a few guns were pushed forward in these sectors.

Djemal Pasha took vigorous action in organizing new troops from the disordered masses.   A line of outposts on all roads leading northward from Homs prevented stragglers from passing by the city and continuing toward Aleppo.   In and near Homs eating stations were everywhere established.   They were the best places for collecting the troops.

The British did not follow up the Rajak group.   So I immediately ordered Mustapha Kemal Pasha to proceed with the staff of the Seventh Army from Baalbek to Aleppo, and to start the reorganization of the Seventh Army in the towns south of Aleppo.   I ordered that the troops of the Seventh Army, then in Homs or expected there, be forwarded by rail, trucks, or foot march to Wudehi and Tuman south of Aleppo.   I also ordered that the troops of Colonel von Oppen, which had reached Baalbek on the morning of October 3rd, be entrained and immediately sent to Aleppo and report to Mustapha Kemal Pasha.   Their departure began on the evening of October 3d.   As the British were not following there was no danger in withdrawing the best troops from the rear guard. Several disquieting reports had come from Aleppo that there and in Hama there was a serious movement on foot to join the Arab government.

The Fourth Army under Djemal Pasha, if it could still be called an army, was to remain at Homs until pushed back by the enemy. It was the only way to gain the time necessary for the formation of usable troops at Aleppo, where the decisive defense of the last part of Syria would have to be made. The group of Djemal Pasha at Homs accomplished its task.

The commandant of the coast sector of Tripoli reported on the 3d that a few war vessels had arrived in Beirut and two armored cruisers at Latakia, which latter city had not yet declared its adhesion to the Arab government.

On October 4th the stream of fugitives on the road from Ras Baalbek to Homs was gradually ebbing. In the afternoon only a few troops arrived. The troops that had retreated by way of El Kutefe were gradually arriving in Homs on the 4th and 5th. They were brought back largely by trucks, among them an Austrian truck company. The British stopped their pursuit at Adra, hence the attacks of the Bedouins also ceased. Equipment and clothing of the troops were renewed as far as possible, as they reached Homs.

For air reconnaissance from Homs we still had three airplanes. Two reconnoitered daily, forenoon and afternoon, toward Damascus, the third observed the coast. Their last reports on the 4th stated that the British were beginning to send large forces from Damascus to the northwest, and that the enemy had reached Zahle, Mejdel Anjar and Ez Zebedani. In front of our outposts south of Homs everything remained quiet.

In order to continue reconnaissance during the night toward Ras Baalbek, German officers with machine guns in automobiles were sent out on the roads toward the enemy, where they remained during the night. What was left of the Turkish cavalry was unfit for extensive patrolling during the night, on account of their enfeebled and exhausted horses.

On October 5th the fliers reported that the enemy troops pushed out to northwest were increasing and closing up for a further advance. Small cavalry detachments had gone forward toward Baalbek.

In Homs General Kiazim Pasha, my excellent chief of staff for years, was taken seriously ill in consequence of the overwork of the last weeks, and had to be sent to Aleppo. Major Prigge acted in his place; he had rendered excellent service during the difficult retreat.

Disquieting reports came in from the hinterland of the rapid spread of the hostile Arab movement. Most of the coast towns, under the pressure of the enemy ships, declared their adherence to the Arab government. Hamah and other places in the interior became more and more untrustworthy. In Aleppo fears of a collapse of the situation grew.

After conference with Djemal Pasha on how to conduct the retreat through Hamah to Aleppo, in case strong British forces advanced against the positions of Homs, I departed with my officers by rail to Aleppo on the afternoon of October 5th. The traffic on the railroad was in very bad shape. In Hamah alone four trains loaded with troops had been standing for hours in the station, because of a lack of locomotives and of water for the locomotives. Further on, as far as Aleppo, there was much disorder. It was absolutely necessary to restore order without delay to enable us to withdraw our last troops from Homs to Aleppo, and to carry away all the rolling stock and supplies.

At 2 a.m. on October 6th we arrived in Aleppo. On the same morning I had conferences with the leaders of the Seventh and Eighth Armies and with the highest civil authorities. Order and quiet must at once be restored in the city and the railroad station of Aleppo put in order.

The progress of the Arab movement on the coast, and the security of the lines of communication of the Army Group required a firm hand. Hence the leader of the Second Army, Nehad Pasha, was directed to move his headquarters from

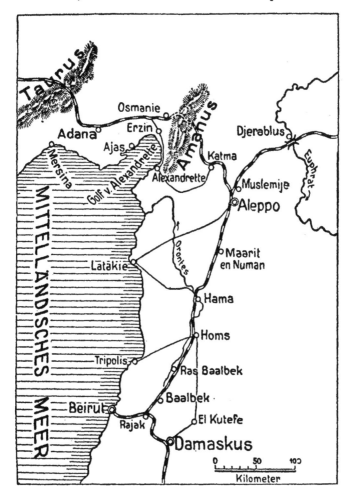

Aleppo to Adana. He was instructed better to organize the defenses against a landing in the Gulf of Alexandretta, or in the

Bay of Ayas, as well as the defense against landings on the coast as far as Mersina.

Turkish headquarters communicated to us their view of the situation to the effect that the enemy would probably land in force in the Gulf of Alexandretta or south of Adana, in order to gain possession of Syria by one blow. I replied that I considered a landing, such as contemplated by headquarters, impossible unless coincident with the advance of strong British forces to Aleppo.

Djemal Pasha in Homs was directed to send the 146th Infantry Regiment to Aleppo by truck.

According to reports from our fliers the British divisions in the vicinity of Zahle and Rajak began to move northward on the morning of October 9th. On the 10th and 11th of October the advance continued to and beyond Baalbek, but the movements were slow and cautious. The direct road Damascus-El Kutefe-Homs was still found free of the enemy. Only Bedouin camps were observed in the vicinity. The reports of the enemy's advance of the 11th are summarized as follows:

Four enemy squadrons are passing Baalbek.

Ten battalions and eight squadrons in four parallel columns about ten kilometers south of Baalbek.

Abreast of them on the road itself a column of artillery four kilometers long.

On the parallel roads from Ablah to Baalbek, west of the Rajak-Baalbek road, twelve battalions and eighteen squadrons.

On the road from Zahle to Ablah a column of artillery with wagons, about five kilometers in length.

At Rajak a British aviation station.

Rumors from Damascus had it that Sherif Faisal had assembled there some 20,000 Arab troops prior to an advance northward.

The greater part of the units formed at Homs were gradually sent to Aleppo by rail, or withdrawn by march via Hamah.

On the evening of October 11th the heads of the British

cavalry, about four squadrons advancing from Ras Baalbek, reached Zera, some thirty kilometers south of Homs. The headquarters of the Fourth Army left Homs that night and reached Hamah on October 12th. The rear guard was en route for the same place. The bridge over the Orontes River and the constructions of the Homs-Hamah railroad were effectively destroyed.

At that time Mustapha Kemal had completed the organization of two divisions, the 1st and 11th. They were posted on the heights between Wudehi and Aleppo. Their artillery was still weak.

The 146th Infantry Regiment left Aleppo by rail, with orders to report to the headquarters of the Second Army at Jenidsche, west of Adana. The Asia Corps was already in that section.

The headquarters of the Fourth Army in Hamah was now ordered dissolved, and the troops retreating toward Aleppo placed under the orders of Mustapha Kemal.

At noon of October 14th hostile cavalry entered Homs and, it was reported, was welcomed with joy. In the whole country south of Aleppo the disposition was about the same everywhere, unfriendly toward the Turks. The Turkish civil authorities left their posts and came to Aleppo the moment they were beyond the protection of Turkish troops.

Torrid heat was brooding over Aleppo in these days of October, and on account of the heavy traffic thick yellow clouds of dust lay over the streets all day. On the heights in the vicinity, especially near railroad stations, large camps had sprung into existence. The transport of the hospitals, and the slightly sick, to Adana and to the Taurus was begun, as well as that of the surplus material of the depots. It encountered many delays from the wholly unsatisfactory conditions obtaining on the stretch from Aleppo to Adana. Vigorous action on the part of Major Mohlsen, just returned from furlough in Germany, soon improved traffic conditions.

In Aleppo the Army Group had uninterrupted telegraphic

communication with the Sixth Army in Mosul.   The superfluous rolling stock of the Bagdad railroad was withdrawn from Jerablus to Muslemije, the junction of the Bagdad railroad and the Syrian railroad a few miles north of Aleppo, so as to be available for our transports.

In these days the movements of enemy ships in the Gulf of Alexandretta became more active.   On the 14th two torpedo boats and a guard ship entered the gulf, and bombarded the harbor batteries of Alexandretta.   Here one of the vessels hoisted a white flag and landed some officers.   They conferred with the local Turkish commandant and returned to their ships, which then left the gulf.   As soon as the Army Group learned of this, such negotiations were strictly prohibited, and headquarters of the 41st Turkish Division, heretofore on the Beilan pass southeast of Alexandretta, was transferred to the latter place.

The formation of the 24th Division was begun at Katama north of Aleppo, where the highroad to Alexandretta leaves the Aleppo-Islahie chaussée.

Meanwhile the enemy had moved up to Homs and pushed part of his troops toward Hamah.   Mustapha Kemal Pasha therefore ordered the evacuation of Hamah on October 17th. The rearguard withdrew to Kumkhaneh, about eleven kilometers north of Hamah.

I now transferred the greater part of the staff of the Army Group to Adana, and of the German staff to Bozanti.   I retained with me only the officers necessary for the conduct of operations, and regulation of the transport.   The work of the chief of staff of the Army Group had to be put back into Turkish hands on account of the large business with the Turkish authorities.   It was turned over by Major Prigge to Colonel Sedat Bei, Mustapha Kemal's chief of staff.   General Kiazim had developed a severe case of pneumonia.   I knew Colonel Sedat from former official association.   He had commanded the 19th Division in Galicia and later in Palestine, with great credit, until called on to take over the office of Major von Falken-hausen in the Seventh Army.

Various reports came from Constantinople that Turkey had entered into negotiations with the Entente powers. The information was not guaranteed, but in view of the general situation, not improbable. Some German officers became restless and wanted to organize transport columns in Ulukishla, with which the German troops were to march through Anatolia to the coast of the Black Sea, and thus secure a safe retreat to southern Russia by ship. I did not listen to the suggestion because I reasoned that, in case Turkey really entered into an armistice, the enemy ships would soon pass through the Dardanelles to the Black Sea, and would blockade the coast long before the projected long and difficult foot march could be completed. I had firm confidence in the Grand Vizir Izzet Pasha, that in case of an armistice he would insist on a free withdrawal of the German troops who had done their duty in a foreign theater of war.

On October 19th a heavy British force entered Hamah where it was said to have met with an enthusiastic reception.

Mustapha Kemal now withdrew the rear guard by rail from Kumkhaneh northward to the railroad station of Hamidije, distant some twenty-five kilometers. A scouting detachment from Idlib proceeded toward the coast of Latakia and found this road free of the enemy.

The Arabs were streaming into Aleppo. Day and night their firing was heard in all parts of the city and its vicinity, however, without causing serious disorders. The withdrawal of the superfluous army stores and other valuable material had been completed, as well as the transport of transportable sick to Adana, Bozanti and beyond.

The new formation of the 43rd Division, north of the railroad station of Muslemije, progressed rapidly, and progress of the 1st and 11th Divisions in fighting efficiency was noted. The 24th Division at Katma was still weak in numbers. · As more and more ships appeared in the Gulf of Alexandretta, a large column of trucks was given the 24th Division at Katma to enable it to send quick reënforcements to Alexandretta.

On the 21st of October our rear guards were abreast of Ma'arrat en Numan, halfway between Hamah and Aleppo. On the following day they were several times attacked by hostile Bedouins and armored cars, and upon orders from Mustapha Kemal they fell back to Ch. es Sebil and the railroad station of Abu ed Duhur.

Our wireless station intercepted and deciphered British wireless messages which reported the embarkation of two divisions on transports in Busra several days previously. It was not impossible that they might be landed on our coast.

On October 23d our outposts at Ch. es Sebil were attacked by numerous Bedouins, armored cars and British cavalry. They had to fall back to the main position south of Aleppo. One portion was surrounded and captured after hand to hand fighting. The outposts at the railroad station of Abu ed Duhur were now also withdrawn to the main position. The enemy chiefly used armored cars in the pursuit. Heavy air attacks were made on the stations of Aleppo.

In the Gulf of Alexandretta, British and French ships were observed. In front of Arsus, southwest of Alexandretta, a ship appeared at dusk on the 23rd, bombarded the coast and attempted to land troops. The attempt was repulsed by the detachments of the 41st Division. The ship returned to the high sea. On October 22d I left Aleppo by auto with the few officers I had kept with me, and on the 23rd met Ali Riza Pasha, commanding the Fifteenth Army Corps with whom I conferred about reënforcing the troops in Erzin and Pajas who were en route to Alexandretta.

On that afternoon we drove to Adana where the Turkish staff of the Army Group had been for four days. After conference with Nehad Pasha, commander of the Second Army, the 41st Division in Alexandretta was transferred to the Seventh Army.

On October 24th the situation in the city of Aleppo became so tense, on account of the arrival of many Bedouins, that we had to declare a state of siege. Enemy armored cars advanced several times through Tuman against our main position at Aleppo, as did enemy cavalry patrols. As soon as fire was opened on them, they withdrew.

On the 22d a British attack took place against the Fetieh position of the Sixth Army south of Mosul. On the night to the 24th the Sixth Army had to fall back. The Euphrates group, formerly of the Second Army, was transferred to the Sixth Army with the understanding that when necessary these troops would defend the crossing of the Euphrates at Jerablus.

On October 25th serious engagements took place south of Aleppo. They were the first since the retreat from Palestine that exceeded the character of rear guard actions. The troops stood well. At the same time the Arabs, in conjunction with the troops of Sherif Faisal, attempted to take possession of Aleppo. The British had brought up a large number of infantry in trucks to reënforce their cavalry. In the early afternoon the Arabs made a frontal attack against the position of the 1st Division which was repulsed. Somewhat later about 1,500 Bedouins entered the city from the east and seized the citadel and the government building. Then they attacked the headquarters of the local commandant, where the headquarters of the Seventh Army was. After gaining a temporary footing there they were thrown out, and pushed out of the city in street fighting. A part of the armed inhabitants took part in the fighting on the side of the Bedouins.

About the same time a heavy infantry attack materialized against our front west of the Tuman-Aleppo road.

In the evening Mustapha Kemal moved his headquarters from the city to a hill about two kilometers north of the Bagdad railroad station, and evacuated the city. The 1st and 11th Divisions, commanded by Ali Fuad Pasha and heavily menaced in rear by Bedouins, were withdrawn northward through the

western part of the city and to one side of it. Part of the
station establishments were blown up. Early on the morning
of the 26th the 1st and 11th Divisions, now the Twentieth Army
Corps, took post at El Husenije and Hujuk, about eight kilometers north of Aleppo. Their right, menaced by British and

Arab cavalry, was bent back to Kefr Basim and Anadan.
Several attacks of Bedouins were repulsed while the withdrawal
was in execution.

About 10.45 a.m. infantry and about four cavalry regiments
supported by armored cars advanced on both sides of the

Aleppo-Katma road and attacked the 1st Division. After an hour's fighting the attack was repulsed. The headquarters of the Seventh Army was transferred to Katma. I ordered the storm battalion and a strong machine gun detachment from the Second Army, to be sent by rail to Katma to report to head-quarters of the Seventh Army.

In the next few days the Seventh Army, often attacked and never beaten, gradually fell back into the positions which they held on October 31st, when news came of the Armistice. The front extended from the slopes of the heights rising there, from Marata to Babulit and Halebli (24th Division), thence crossing railroad and chaussée, from Tennib to Tatmarash and Ain Dakni (Twentieth Army Corps), thence across the Aleppo-Killis road to the southeast of Djibrin (43d Division). Security detachments were pushed from Derel Djmal to Zijaret, which latter place lies exactly twenty-five kilometers northwest of Aleppo.

In the fighting of the last few days the army held high the honor of its arms.

On the evening of October 30th I received a telegraphic re-quest from the Grand Vizier Izzet Pasha to turn my command over to Mustapha Kemal Pasha and return to Constantinople at an early date. At the same time I was instructed to hasten the return of all German officers and troops to Constantinople. The warm and firm intercession of the Grand Vizier, in con-cluding the Armistice, had secured for all German officers and troops free withdrawal from Turkey.

The bulk of the German troops stood ready near Jenidsche for transport. Unfortunately cholera broke out in some towns of the Adana plain and exacted several victims. The dis-tinguished leader of the Asia Corps, Colonel von Oppen, was carried off by the disease; he had ever been a shining example to his troops before the enemy, in good times and in bad. The transport of the German troops began on the morning of November 1st. They carried side arms and ammunition only.

All remaining equipment had to be turned over to Turkish commissions before the departure.

On October 31st I turned the command over to Mustapha Kemal Pasha in Adana.

I bade goodby to the troops under my former command in the following order:

Adana, October 31st 1918.

At the moment when I am placing the command of the Army Group into the hands, proved in many a glorious battle, of H. E. General Mustapha Kemal, I express my heart felt thanks to all officers, officials and men for the services rendered under my command for the weal of the Imperial Osmanic Empire.

The glorious days of Gallipoli, which closely attached to me many officers and soldiers of the Army Group, will ever remain unforgotten in the history of all times, as well as many bold enterprises on the coast of Asia Minor.

In Palestine, besides the uninterrupted tenacious defense of six and one-half months, a chain of victories for us, it was the battles on the Tell Azur, Turmus Aja, El Kafr and the two Jordan battles that gave proofs to the far superior enemy of the devoted bravery of the Osmanic Army, and of the German and Austrian troops fighting in unison with them.

The memory of these deeds gives me the conviction that the Osmanic Empire, trusting in its valorous sons, may confidently face the future.

I trust that God may grant to the Osmanic people and its allies for the future, peace, tranquility and recovery from the wounds inflicted by the long war.

Sgd. LIMAN v. SANDERS.

At noon on the 31st I left Adana with the few German officers of my suite. Mustapha Kemal, with all officers present in Adana, was at the station to bid me goodby. The guard of honor was the last Turkish organization which I greeted in Turkey.

CHAPTER 24

I reached Constantinople on November 4th. The greater part of the German authorities, the Mediterranean Division, the special naval detachment, the German chief of the Turkish general staff with his officers, and the German troops in the vicinity of Constantinople, had already been shipped to Odessa via the Black Sea. They were to get home through the Ukraine. All that could be gathered in Constantinople during the ensuing days were transported by the same route.

The German headquarters had charged me with the command over all German officers and troops still remaining in Turkey and with the arrangements for their shipment. With the officers that had returned with me, I took quarters with the staff of the military mission which was still in Constantinople.

The arrival of officers, troops and detachments from Syria and the distant parts of the empire was slow, because everywhere there were delays in the railroad traffic, and because there was lack of coal. The return of the 1,200 Germans and Austrians from the Sixth Army was bound to be delayed for weeks. Wholly against my wish they had started on the foot march through Samsun to the coast of the Black Sea with automobile columns.

German officers and men arriving in the first half of November were in part quartered in Pera, the greater part, however, in the suburbs on the Asiatic side.

After the opening of the Dardanelles the fleet of the allies appeared at Constantinople in the middle of November, and immediately disembarked British and French troops. At the entry of these heretofore hostile troops in Constantinople, Pera presented more the appearance of a Greek than of a

321

Turkish city. Greek flags were displayed from most of the houses. The Entente troops marching to the sound of their bands were preceded by great crowds of levantine inhabitants who gave vent to their joy by throwing flowers to the officers and men, making a great noise, throwing hats and caps into the air, and embracing each other. None would have credited these demonstrations with any dignity, when considering that all these demonstrations had been tolerated without molestation in the capital of the country throughout the war.

On November 19th General von Lenthe and his present chief of staff, Lieutenant Colonel von Eggeling, with a large part of the military mission, embarked on a Turkish ship to journey homeward by way of Odessa, or Nikolaiev, through the Ukraine; and on the same day myself and officers moved to Moda on the Asiatic side. The Armistice commission, composed of members of the Entente and of Turkish delegates, had decided that all German officers and men were to leave the European side of Constantinople and take quarters on the Asiatic side. The step seemed a timely one, since it was the best way to avoid friction in the future.

The British military authorities in Constantinople made the necessary arrangements for the care of the German troops. On November 13th I had a conference in Pera with General Curry, the British chief of the general staff of the Salonika Army, about the shipment of the German troops, and was well received by him. After his departure General Fuller, the British chief of staff in Constantinople, conducted the further arrangements. In spite of his difficult and thankless task he did everything in his power.

Transportation through Roumania via Constanza was no longer possible on account of the events that had taken place in that country. Shipment via Odessa and Nikolaiev continued for some time, but proved impracticable in December, as there was heavy fighting in the Ukraine and the railroads were often interrupted.

The long return journey through the Ukraine at that time of the year was not advisable in the case of the German troops returning from Syria and Palestine, because these troops were coming from a southern climate and had no winter clothing. The last shipment across the Black Sea had taken weeks to get as far as Kiev. They had to make marches in between railway transportation and in some cases had to fight their way through. For the German troops of Army Group F this route would have caused many losses from disease, because of the inadequacy of their clothing for a Russian climate. How even the change of climate from Syria to Constantinople exercised an unfavorable influence on the health of the men, weakened as they were by hardships, is shown by the fact that within four weeks of their arrival in Constantinople they had eighty deaths, most resulting from colds. The large German etape hospital in Haidar Pasha was much over-crowded with its 1,200 patients. My recommendations for the discontinuance of the Ukraine route, supported by medical certificates, were favorably considered by the British High Commissioner, Admiral Calthorpe. Shipment by boat direct to Germany was now considered. The number of persons to be shipped was in the neighborhood of 10,000.

On December 9th I received a written order in Moda, from the acting Turkish Minister of War, to embark at once on the Ukrainian steamer *Tiger* for Odessa and return to Germany through the Ukraine. I protested to Admiral Calthorpe, because I was charged with the command of the German troops and the arrangements for their departure, and because an order of the Turkish War Minister could by no means relieve me of these duties. The above order was not carried out.

On December 19th I was directed to move to Prinkipo, and instructions were given at the same time that the German officers and troops were to be quartered for the present at that place, and on other Princes Islands. This move was soon made, so that, until their embarkation for home, by far the greater part of the German units were quartered on the Princes Islands. The administrative staff and a small part of the German formations alone remained on the Asiatic side of Constantinople.

In the first days of January 1919 the Germans and Austrians from the Sixth Army in Mesopotamia arrived by boat from Samsun at Haidar Pasha. Due to the hardships of the march through Anatolia and the change of climate a number of men died in Samsun.

On January 24th, 1919, we received instructions to prepare for embarkation on five large ships which were to sail direct for some German port on the North Sea. They were the steamers *Etha Rickmers*, *Lillie Rickmers*, *Patmos*, *Kerkyra* and *Akdenis*, all with German crews. After the ships had been made ready for the long trip, I embarked on January 27th with 120 officers and 1,800 men on the *Etha Rickmers*, the first to sail from Constantinople. It was arranged that the ships were to follow each other at two-day intervals and take on coal at Gibraltar. The departure of the administrative staff of the military mission was to sail on the last ship, the *Akdenis*.

At 4 p.m. January 29th the *Etha Rickmers* left the pier at Haidar Pasha and went to sea. On January 30th, in the forenoon, we passed the Dardanelles amidst a sudden storm with thunder and lightning. The passage through the extensive mine fields was everywhere carefully marked with buoys. The *Etha Rickmers* encountered much high wind and high seas, and reached Malta on the evening of February 3d. Though it had not been provided that we halt at Malta, the ship was ordered by wireless to the port of Marsa Sirokko a few hours before it arrived there. In this port we remained anchored about three weeks. On the morning of February 25th the ship was ordered to the inner harbor of Malta to take on coal, and then continue the journey to Gibraltar. After the unexpectedly long delay and restless worry, the news when published by me was received on the ship with great joy. Every one now hoped to see home again within two weeks.

When we reached the coaling station, I was requested to come ashore alone. As I had submitted to the governor several questions of food and sanitation, I thought it might be an interview with him. After reaching the pier on a motor boat with a British naval officer, I was told, as I set foot on land, that I was a prisoner of war. My adjutants and my servants had remained on the ship which continued its journey to Gibraltar and Germany on the same day.

During our delay in Malta the other ships for the transport of the German troops had been held in Constantinople. Soon thereafter they were permitted to depart for Bremerhaven and Hamburg. The transportable sick had been shipped in hospital ships to an Italian port whence they were transported in hospital trains to Germany.

On August 21st I was permitted to leave Malta on the *Ivy* and returned to Germany via Venice, Verona and Innsbruck.

EPILOGUE

In the foregoing notes I have mostly let the facts speak for themselves.

In consideration of present conditions I have used my records only insofar as necessary to explain certain things.

Other matters can not be discussed until the proper time comes for separating truth from fiction.

Five years of military activity in a high responsible position in Turkey lie behind me. They give me the right to judge of what was aimed at and what was accomplished.

The expectations which Germany entertained before the war of the general development of Turkey, supported in various ways by its direct assistance, were too high, though not entirely without prospect.

The demands which Germany made on the Turkish Ally during the war failed for the most part in the economic field. In the military field the German expectations were excessive and therefore impossible.

Turkey was expected not only to defend the straits and protect her frontiers at immense distances, but conquer Egypt, make Persia independent, prepare the creation of independent states in Trans-Caucasia, threaten India from Afghanistan if possible, and in addition furnish active assistance in European theaters.

Turkey and her leaders must be held to account for not making their aims conform to the available means.

Germany is to be blamed for the lack of calm and clear judgment of what was within the powers of Turkey.

It seems that thoughts of the tales of *The Thousand and One Nights*, or the *fata morgana* of the Arabian desert dimmed judgment at home.

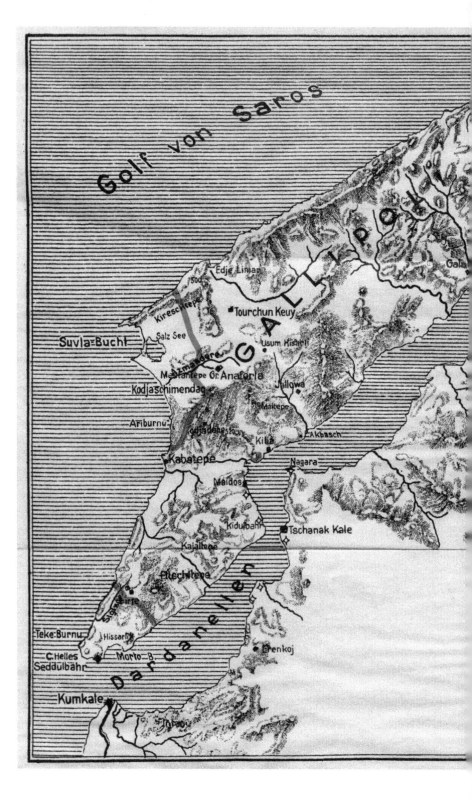

Skizze
des Schauplatzes des
Dardanellen Feldzuges.

Liman von Sanders
General der Kavallerie.

0 1 2 3 4 5 6 7 8 9 10   15   20   25   30

Kilometer

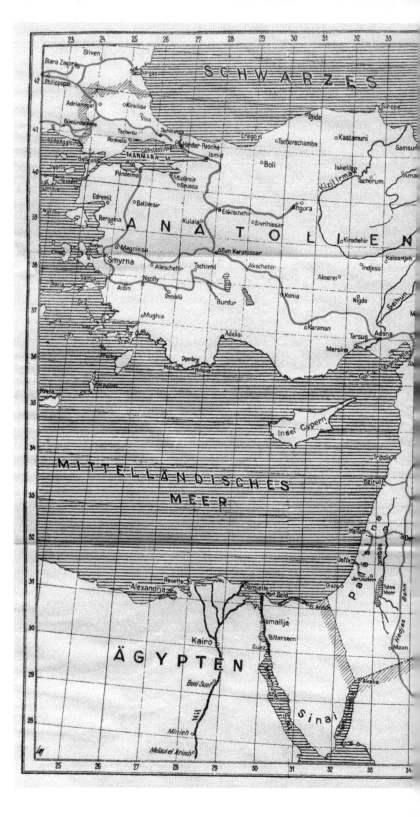

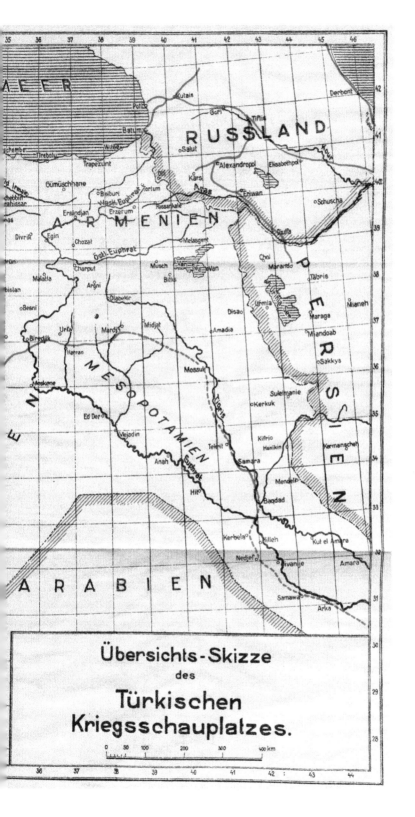

Übersichts-Skizze

des

Türkischen

Kriegsschauplatzes.

0 50 100   200   300   400 km

Die
Orientbahnen.

0 50 100   200   300
Kilometer